THE
URBAN WEST

Edited
by
Gerald D. Nash

ISBN 0-89745-004-3

Sunflower University Press®

BOX 1009   •   MANHATTAN, KANSAS 66502, USA

THE URBAN WEST

Introduction

Gerald D. Nash

Only during the last decade have historians begun to recognize that the history of the American West in the twentieth century is a field worthy of serious study. In fact, it could readily be argued that the development of the West in the century after 1880 constituted one of the most significant epochs in the long and fascinating history of the region. But a fuller understanding of the nature of that growth still awaits many detailed studies by scholars with diverse interests. They are needed to unravel many of the obscure threads of what came to be an increasingly complex technological society, caught up in the whirlwinds of change that characterized twentieth-century America. The analysis of the Western American experience in the last hundred years is one of the major challenges confronting students of the region in this generation.

Among those who are making an auspicious beginning in confronting this challenge is a group of young historians who have focused on the urban dimension in Western growth. If the urban experience of the twentieth-century West did not encompass the lives of all Westerners, it will profoundly affect a large majority of people in the area. Hence, a comprehension of city growth in the West is essential to a deeper understanding of the broader contours of the region's development.

The essays presented here deal primarily with selected phases of the process of urbanization in the West since the later nineteenth century. They represent reports on work in progress which will result in book-length studies within a decade. They constitute what in my opinion will be a significant corpus of literature bearing on twentieth-century Western history. I believe that these essays are an exciting prelude to future work in the field and will whet the desire of readers for more by these authors in future years.

Although the papers vary greatly in context, they touch directly on concepts as well as data relating to Western urban history. Carl Abbott explores the idea of the Sunbelt as it has been discussed during the last decade and raises cogent questions about conceptual approaches to the study and understanding of major portions of the trans-Mississippi region. As he demonstrates, simplistic theories will not suffice to explain recent Western growth. Historians must utilize a whole range of social science concepts and tools to delineate meaningful trends in Western development.

If the Sunbelt concept provides one fresh perspective for viewing the West, then Roger Lotchin introduces another approach by suggesting that the emergence of a metropolitan-military complex constituted a significant dimension of twentieth-century Western expansion. An awareness of the existence of such a complex, Lotchin argues, will be a useful tool not only for historians of the West but also for students of urban America. The West, more than any other region, for more than one hundred years, has been the recipient of federal largesse. As an underdeveloped area, its growth has been shaped in many ways by military and industrial policies emanating from the nation's capital. California's major cities provide striking evidence to substantiate Lotchin's fruitful hypothesis.

The influences forming the twentieth-century West were manifold, and among them transportation was as important in the years after 1880 as it had been in earlier periods. Mark Foster's essay explores this important factor by tracing the impact of urban transit on the configuration of three Western cities in the years between 1880 and 1940. As he clearly demonstrates, the conscious choices made by Westerners determined the directions of urban growth for the twentieth century. In some respects, they borrowed from the experience of Eastern cities; in other particulars, they blazed new and unique paths. His article opens up a hitherto obscure but crucial dimension of the Western experience.

Other essays allow readers a glimpse of the rich diversity of life in Western cities, a dimension that still needs to be uncovered. Bradford Luckingham touches on the historical development of important cities of the Southwest, including Phoenix, Tucson, El Paso, and Albuquerque, cities which spearheaded the phenomenal growth of the region. Harold Platt, making skillful use of concepts borrowed from geographers, fills a void in his account of one phase of Houston's emergence as a major metropolitan center. Moreover, he reveals that even in the highly technological world of the twentieth century the impact of natural disaster was by no means insignificant. Galveston's great tidal wave in 1900 seriously retarded that city's growth. Howard Rabinowitz focuses on the history of Albuquerque and relates its growth patterns to those of other cities in the region. He illustrates how city-planning policies, and their absence, shaped its physical contours during intensive periods of expansion. Lyle Dorsett emphasizes how important it is for students of the West to consider the values held by the founders of Western cities such as Denver. Their conceptions of right and wrong, and their visions of the future, determined in part the type of

4

settler they hoped to attract. They could wield their influence, as he demonstrates, by granting or withholding the necessary capital funds that newcomers needed to develop untapped resources.

Collectively, these essays break new ground and immeasurably enrich the developing field of twentieth-century Western American history. This is not to say that they do not also have implications for national history. But one of the contributions of this collection is to suggest exciting new concepts and approaches to Western history as well as to call attention to innumerable unexplored topics awaiting further inquiry. The essays testify to the vitality of urban history and demonstrate its usefulness as one of the most fruitful avenues towards a better understanding of the American West in the twentieth century.

Professor Gerald D. Nash has been professor of history at the University of New Mexico at Albuquerque since 1961. A graduate of New York University, he received his Ph.D. from the University of California. He is the author of *The American West in the Twentieth Century: a survey of the region*.

Museum of Albuquerque

Downtown Albuquerque circa 1941 looking east on Central Avenue. Central was the heart of downtown which in turn was the center of shopping, banking, government, and entertainment for the metropolitan region. As part of Route 66, it brought tourists as well as residents into the city's core.

The American Sunbelt:
Idea and Region

Carl Abbott

The extraordinary growth of Atlanta in the 1960s and 1970s has helped to call attention to the increasing economic independence of the Sunbelt.

Houston is the symbol of the new America. Writers in the 1830s and 1840s sought the essence of their coming age in the gritty streets and sooty factories of Manchester. Social critics and novelists at the turn of the century found the future of an industrial nation prefigured in Chicago's strange amalgam of teeming misery and bustling opportunity. So now contemporary journalists travel to the Gulf coast to discover the character of the American Sunbelt. At the start of the seventies, when space-age corporations discovered Houston's possibilities as a headquarters city, *Business Week* and *Fortune* gave star billing to its management boom. Since mid-decade, Houston has been "the place that scholars flock to for the purpose of seeing what modern civilization has wrought." Its free-form growth unimpeded by zoning, its single-function downtown, its political conservatism, its business spinoffs from the NASA space center, and its purring air conditioners in the steamy night all seem to epitomize the booming metropolitan areas that have transformed life in the American South and West.[1]

If Houston as a symbol has become a commonplace, the phenomenon which it represents has become a cliché. Coined in the late 1960s, the term "Sunbelt" has entered the everyday vocabulary of public affairs. Business writers, political journalists, academic experts, and politicians find it a convenient catchword, a shorthand description of present and future growth patterns and a quick referent for a major national policy debate. The same vividness which has contributed to the term's popularity, however, has also helped to perpetuate a lack of precision in its meaning and use. The idea of a Sunbelt is so elastic that there is not even agreement on a geographical definition. The most common suggestion is to set the region's boundary at the enticingly continuous line of state borders which

During the last decade, Houston has replaced Los Angeles as the symbol of explosive metropolitan growth in the Sunbelt.

run along the northern edges of North Carolina, Tennessee, Arkansas, Oklahoma, New Mexico, and Arizona.[2] A poll of national political journalists taken in the fall of 1977, however, showed considerable disagreement with the idea of a thirteen-state region. Commentators variously specified the addition of Virginia, southern California, Nevada, northern California, the mountain West, or the upper South. Several other writers, in contrast, suggested a much more limited region with a focus on the Gulf of Mexico. One excluded the entire Southwest from the Sunbelt and another excluded the entire Southeast.[3]

If the discovery of the Sunbelt has become ''a media event fogged by an uncommon number of misconceptions,'' historical analysis can help to widen the focus from current policy debates and assist in developing

areas of agreement.[4] The present study briefly examines the career of the sunbelt idea itself and takes a more detailed look at the changing patterns of economic development and population distribution which underlie the recognition of a new region. Such analysis clearly shows that the evolution of a sunbelt region can be traced to the impact of World War II on southern and western cities and followed through the entire postwar era. It is equally important that the Sunbelt is an urban region. By creating similar economic and social environments in historically dissimilar sections of the United States, the explosive metropolitan growth of the last four decades has allowed Americans to identify a single region stretching around the southern and western rim of the nation.

Houston Chamber of Commerce

Houston's high-rise skyline indicated the importance of white collar employment in the sunbelt economy.

The publication of Kevin Phillip's *The Emerging Republican Majority* in 1969 marks the introduction of "sunbelt" into the analysis of national politics. In his discussion of the South and West, Phillips used "Sun Belt" and "Sun Country" interchangeably to describe a region of conservative voting habits where Republicans might expect to solidify their status as a majority party. The following year, Samuel Lubell in *The Hidden Crisis in American Politics* made a single use of the term in treating the Nixon coalition, but preferred to organize his analysis of trends in voting around the traditional regions of South, Mountain states, and West.[5] During the early 1970s, the new term remained in limited circulation, failing to make a strong impression on practicing journalists or scholars.[6]

The rapid expansion of attention to the idea of a developing economic and political region across the southern tier of the United States can be specifically dated to the second half of the seventies. Kirkpatrick Sale's *Power Shift* in 1975 described the development of the nation's "Southern Rim" from the viewpoint of a liberal New York journalist. Sale found that the South and West since 1945 had developed as a "rival nexus . . . a truly competitive power base" whose conservative citizens stood in political, cultural and economic opposition to the liberal North. Early in 1976 the *New York Times* gave respectability and publicity to the "sunbelt" concept with a five-part series analyzing the region's economic and demographic patterns, its urban growth and environmental problems, and its political tendencies. Here again the underlying concern was to explain the economic and financial problems of New York City and the Northeast in terms of a broad national transformation which far exceeded the reactive capacity of local governments and politicians.[7]

The *Times* series and subsequent articles in *Business Week*, the *National Journal*, and the *Saturday Review* have worked to narrow the initial concern over a fundamental transformation of the American landscape to a specific question of national policy. The *Times* pointed out that the balance of federal taxes and federal expenditures left the sunbelt states with an annual surplus measured in the billions. The newspaper also noted that the increasing representation of southern and western states in Congress promised to maintain the pattern. Likewise writing at a time when the Northeast still felt the effects of the 1974-75 recession, the *National Journal* in July 1976 argued that "federal tax and spending policies are causing a massive flow of wealth from the Northeast and Midwest to the fast-growing Southern and Western regions." Its state by state comparison of federal tax revenues with federal spending on public works, defense contracts, salaries, grants-in-aid, and retirement programs found a net surplus in fiscal 1975 of $11.5 billion for the South and $10.6 billion for the Mountain and Pacific states. Although the article agreed that the inequities were largely "accidental," it also argued that the "economic underpinnings of the Northeast quadrant" were in danger from the massive transfers of federal funds into more prosperous states. The month before, *Business Week* had described the "flood tide" of population and industrial migration which threatened a "second war between the states" and had suggested that the nation now required a more even-handed distribution of federal subsidies and spending in place of policies set in a previous era.[8]

As presented in the national press, the contrast of structural decline in the old industrial belt and self-sustaining economic growth in the Sunbelt required redistribution of federal expenditures to aid declining urban centers of the eastern and Great Lakes states. Indeed, the last three years have seen an explosion of debate in Congress and the media over the issues of balanced national growth. Both in and out of Congress, the identification of specific policy issue triggered the organization of "anti-sunbelt" coalitions among elected officials. The summer and fall of 1976 saw the organization of a Northeast-Midwest Economic Advancement Coalition among House members led by Michael Harrington of Massachusetts, a less formal Senate coalition chaired by Howard Metzenbaum of Ohio, and regional sub-coalitions of Senators led by Daniel Moynihan of New York, John Culver of Iowa, and William Proxmire of Wisconsin. The Council for Northeast Economic Action in Boston and the Academy for Contemporary Problems in Columbus have also concentrated on the analysis of economic problems in the old industrial states. On the other side of the argument, the Southern Growth Policies Board

was conscripted to serve as professional staff to defend the interests of the Sunbelt.[9]

Although the conflict between the Sunbelt and the Frostbelt or Snowbelt involves a range of regional growth issues, policy debate has centered even more narrowly on the competition for federal funds among older and newer cities. The most important Congressional victory for the Northeast has been a 1977 revision of the formula for distributing Community Development Block Grants to favor cities with older housing. In turn, urban officials in the South and West have charged that northern cities have raised a false issue of federal discrimination in order to mask their own inability to stem population declines and industrial obsolescence. The opposing interests of the northern and the sunbelt cities during 1977 and 1978 have threatened to split both the National Conference of Mayors and the National League of Cities. Typical of the sunbelt response was a resolution passed unanimously by 3000 delegates to the Texas Municipal League convention in October, 1977 which called for developing accurate information on federal spending patterns, soliciting political action from sunbelt leaders, and establishing an effort in Congress to represent the cities of the South and West.[10]

The attention which policy-makers give to the fortunes of sunbelt cities reflects the region's predominantly urban character. Most descriptions of the Sunbelt give prominent place to the movement of population into new and fast-growing metropolitan areas. Where Sale described an "incredible urban explosion," Phillips referred repeatedly to "booming cities," to "urban boom counties," or to the "new urban complexes of Texas and Florida" which represent a "new urban America."[11] The public image of the Sunbelt similarly centers on the rise of a new set of metropolises with aspirations to national leadership. Economic diversification has involved the acquisition of high-technology manufacturing, booms in recreation and education, the emergence of regional market centers linked by air travel, and the expansion of federal employment. All of these factors along with the growth of metropolitan markets have played major roles in the prosperity of southern and western cities. On top of this economic base, newer cities like Miami, Atlanta, Dallas, Denver, Houston, Phoenix, and Seattle as well as the established centers of Los Angeles and San Francisco are reproducing the headquarters/business service/communications complex of Manhattan in a more detailed format.[12]

The national importance of metropolitan growth in the South and West is confirmed by aggregate regional data. After ranging between 20 percent and 40 percent for several decades, the share of national metropolitan growth attributable jointly to the two regions jumped to 60 percent in the 1930s and held between 57 percent and

61 percent for the 1940s, 1950s, and 1960s. The gain in percentage share during the thirties is explained by the fact that the numerical increment in metropolitan population fell more sharply in the North and Middle West than in the South and West. Since 1940, however, the latter regions have held their high percentage share because of enormous absolute increments in their metropolitan populations. The dominance of southern and western cities was even more spectacular between 1970 and 1974, when the regions accounted for 93 percent of the nation's metropolitan growth.[13] In total, the metropolitan population increase in the South and West between 1940 and 1974 was 52,000,000 compared to 35,000,000 for the remainder of the United States.[14]

It was American rearmament in 1940 and 1941 and full mobilization in 1942 that triggered this extraordinary metropolitan growth. Even in the year before Pearl Harbor, growth of at least 10 percent was re-

corded in Seattle, Long Beach, San Diego, Wichita, Wichita Falls, Corpus Christi, Norfolk and Newport News. The regional impact continued to be unequal in 1942 and 1943, as military bases were concentrated in the warmer states and as roughly three quarters of all defense contracts went to sixty corporations. In response, 70 percent of wartime federal defense housing was built in the South and the West. There were a few boom cities like Hartford and Philadelphia in the Northeast and a few more like Detroit and St. Louis in the Middle West. Most of the war towns, however, were strung along the nation's warmer coasts— Richmond, Charleston, Savannah, Jacksonville, Mobile, New Orleans, Baton Rouge, Houston, Los Angeles, San Francisco, and Portland in addition to towns already mentioned. In the interior of the Southwest were other burgeoning cities around air bases and aircraft plants—Dallas, Fort Worth, Tulsa, San An-

National Aeronautics and Space Administration

The Lyndon B. Johnson Space Center of NASA has been a key factor in the emergence of Houston as one of the boom cities in the high technology Sunbelt economy.

Dallas/Fort Worth Airport

Air travel and the aerospace industry have enormously benefitted the development of the sunbelt economy. The Dallas/Fort Worth Airport is designed as the gateway between the Sunbelt-Southwest and the Sunbelt-West.

tonio, Albuquerque, Denver, Phoenix, Tucson. In aggregate for 1940-43, metropolitan counties in the Mountain and Pacific states gained 920,000 civilian residents, those in the South Atlantic states gained 791,000, and those in the South Central region gained 603,000. By contrast, the metropolitan counties of the North Central states gained only 331,000 civilians and those of the Northeast lost 1,023,000. [15]

Despite worries about economic reconversion, the prosperity of World War II in the South and West was a prelude to an extraordinary regional boom which has lasted for more than three decades. Sunshine cities such as Denver, Tucson, Phoenix and Albuquerque enjoyed unexpected growth as servicemen returned to settle in cities they had first visited on weekend passes. Continued defense spending and the onset of the Cold War helped to maintain the population of military cities like Norfolk, Mobile, San Antonio, and El Paso. At the

same time, new manufacturing and services filled the demands of expanded metropolitan markets in other growing cities. The number of new or expanded manufacturing plants in Los Angeles, for example, was 50 percent higher for 1945-48 than for the war years of 1942-44. The Pacific states, Mountain states, and South all received a disproportionate share of new investment in manufacturing facilities as measured against prewar industrial capacity. Texas, Oklahoma and the Pacific coast in particular telescoped a generation of industrial maturity into a decade. [16]

The first general analysis of the emerging sunbelt economy was offered by Edward Ullman in 1954. Under the title "Amenities as a Factor in Regional Growth," he described the physical attractions of the southwestern and Gulf states as key factors in their rapid growth. Physical amenities accounted for the concentration of recreation, aircraft manufacturing, military training, and retirement communities. Good weather and recreational opportunities also helped to draw footloose manufacturing (the assembly of fabricated components and other manufacturing with low transportation costs and dependence on skilled labor), administrative headquarters, quarternary or information-processing industries, and other functions dependent on their ability to recruit and hold qualified personnel. In turn, the expanding demands for services and for capital investment in social overhead from the growing population helped to sustain the regional boom.[17]

Subsequent interpretations of American economic growth have elaborated on the same ideas. Between 1939 and 1954, according to Harvey Perloff, California accounted for 30.5 percent of the nation's net upward shift in trade, service and government employment, Texas for 15.9 percent, and seven other western states for 14.2 percent more. The South Atlantic states from Maryland to Florida accounted for an additional 23.4 percent. The results of economic change since mid-century can be judged from information on State Economic Areas (SEAs). As defined by the Department of Commerce, the United States is divided into 173 SEAs, each of which consists of a metropolitan area or smaller trade center and the surrounding counties with close economic ties. For the South and West in 1973, either government or services was the dominant industry in 48 of 99 SEAs, a figure half again as high as that for 1950. By comparison, only 7 of the 67 SEAs in the Northeast and Middle West depended primarily on government or service jobs. In the early seventies, Brian Berry summarized the forces which had transformed the economy of the former hinterland region around the "outer rim" of the United States:

> The changes have been cumulative, for regional growth within the context of the national pattern of heartland and hinterland has brought these regions to threshold sizes for internal production of a wide variety of goods and services at the very time that changes in the definition of urban resources made their rapid advance . . . possible. Hence the explosive metropolitan growth of the south, southwest, and west, led by the tertiary and quarternary sectors.[18]

Although it is convenient to describe the broad patterns of economic change in terms of traditional regions, the Sunbelt as an historical phenomenon is not simply a new name for "South" and "West." Analysts of the "New South" during the postwar decades have been very much aware that the pace of modernization has been faster on its coastal fringes than in the southern interior.[19] It has also been commonly acknowledged that California's extraordinary attractiveness tilted the far western states toward Los Angeles from the forties through the sixties.[20] Because only *parts* of the West

and *parts* of the South have in fact experienced rapid growth and urbanization over the past several decades, more detailed examination of the extent and nature of the new region requires attention to states and metropolitan areas. In particular, the regional divisions of the Bureau of the Census conceal the growth of the Sunbelt by cutting across the north-south divide between faster and slower growing areas. The Mountain division includes both Arizona and Montana, the South Central division both Texas and Kentucky, the South Atlantic division both Florida and West Virginia. Attempts to determine whether the Sunbelt is myth or reality by analyzing data for such census regions build in a bias against the concept by merging historically stagnant states with those more likely to show postwar booms.[21]

More precise analysis of the Sunbelt can therefore start with state-level growth data. Economists and demographers in the 1950s and 1960s, who were able to draw on information from one or two decades after Pearl Harbor, noted the outstanding economic performance of California, Texas, and Florida, but saw their booms as special cases within the broad historic patterns of western regional development and southern poverty. The classic study of *Regions, Resources and Economic Growth* argued that the bases of growth in Florida and California were fundamentally different and asserted that Texas offered "further contrast to the two cases already examined." The impressive prosperity and growth of the eastern Great Lakes states and northeastern suburban states also helped to conceal the emergence of a special growth region across the southern United States.[22]

The availability of data for the 1960s and for 1970-75 makes the long-term trends more evident. The western states of California, Nevada, Utah, Colorado, Arizona and Texas, and the southeastern states of Florida, Virginia and Delaware had population growth rates which exceeded the national average in all four of the periods 1940-50, 1950-60, 1960-70, and 1970-75. Seven other states exceeded the national average in three of the four periods: Oregon in all but the 1950s; New Mexico in all but the 1960s; Washington, Maryland, New Jersey, Connecticut and Michigan in all but the 1970s. Taken together, these states cover a Texas-Pacific triangle angled toward the southwest, the northern and southern ends of the South Atlantic coast in Florida and Maryland-Virginia-Delaware, and scattered parts of the Northeast. Ohio and Indiana, which surpassed the national growth rate from 1940 to 1960, have since decelerated, while Georgia, Vermont and New Hampshire have grown more rapidly than the nation since 1960.

A similar regional pattern emerges from the examination of growth rates for metropolitan population by states. In order to minimize the impact of the definition of new SMSAs on the percentage increases, the figures used are the 1940-50 population increase within 1950

Table 1
Metropolitan Growth Rates,
1940-1970
(SMSAs 300,000+ in 1970)

	West	South-east	Mid-South	Mid-West	North-east
2.16 ratio of higher, 1970/1940	25	16	1	8	2
Ratio 1.94 to 2.15	2	1	3	2	1
Ratio under 1.94			5	13	21
Total SMSAs	27	17	9	23	24

SMSA boundaries, the 1950-60 increase within 1960 boundaries, and the 1960-70 increase within 1970 boundaries. Two sets of states surpassed the national rate of metropolitan growth in all three decades or in the 1940s and 1960s: Washington, Oregon, California, Utah, Colorado, Arizona, New Mexico, Texas and Oklahoma in the Pacific-Southwest triangle and Delaware, Maryland, Virginia, North Carolina, South Carolina, Georgia and Florida along the South Atlantic coast. These two regions of above-average metropolitan growth fill in more solidly the two sunbelt regions suggested by total state growth data. In particular, they add the sunbelt states of Oklahoma and the Carolinas in which massive metropolitan growth was counterbalanced in aggregate population data by rural depopulation.

An alternative method to describe the geographic concentration of rapid urban growth areas is to examine the relative prosperity of the 100 SMSA which had populations of 300,000 or more in 1970. Tables 1 and 2

Table 2: Metropolitan Growth Rates, 1940-1979

WEST	SOUTHEAST	MID-SOUTH	MID-WEST	NORTHEAST
Anaheim 10.83				
San Bernardino .7.10				
San Jose 6.09				
Oxnard 5.37				
Phoenix 5.20				
Tucson 4.84				
Sacramento 4.73				
San Diego 4.70				
Albuquerque 4.62				
Dallas 3.90	Fort Lauderdale ..15.50			
Houston 3.75	Orlando 6.11			
Fort Worth 3.39	Miami 4.73			
Denver.........3.01	West Palm Beach .4.36			
Seattle 2.84	Tampa...........3.72			
El Paso 2.74	Columbia 3.08			
Salt Lake City ..2.63	Washington 2.96			
Oklahoma City .2.63	Charlotte 2.69			
San Antonio ...2.56	Atlanta 2.68		Lansing 2.88	
Los Angeles ...2.52	Norfolk 2.63		Wichita 2.68	
Tulsa 2.47	Jacksonville 2.52		Dayton 2.57	
Honolulu.......2.44	Charleston 2.51		Indianapolis ...2.41	
Bakersfield.....2.44	Baltimore 2.42		Columbus 2.41	
Fresno.........2.31	Wilmington 2.24		Grand Rapids .2.19	
Tacoma........2.26	Greenville 2.19		Flint 2.18	Hartford 2.24
Beaumont 2.18	Greensboro 2.16	Mobile 2.65	Gary 2.16	Syracuse 2.16
		Memphis ...2.15		
SF-Oakland 2.13		Nashville 2.11	Toledo 2.01	
Portland 2.01	Richmond 1.95	Little Rock ..2.07	Akron 2.00	Rochester 2.02
		New Orleans .1.89	Minn-St. Paul ..1.93	Paterson 1.89
		Louisville 1.83	Milwaukee 1.83	York 1.85
		Knoxville 1.62	Kansas City ..1.83	Binghampton ..1.82
		Birmingham .1.61	Davenport 1.83	Bridgeport 1.78
		Chattanooga .1.44	Detroit 1.77	Harrisburg 1.63
			Cincinnati 1.76	Trenton 1.54
			Omaha 1.66	Albany 1.54
			St. Louis 1.65	Phildelphia 1.51
			Cleveland 1.63	New Haven 1.48
			Peoria 1.61	Springfield 1.45
			Canton 1.58	Buffalo 1.41
			Chicago 1.54	Allentown 1.37
			Youngstown ...1.13	Worcester 1.36
				Providence 1.35
				New York 1.32
				Utica 1.29
				Boston 1.26
				Newark 1.17
				Pittsburgh 1.15
				Jersey City 93

Median, 100 large SMSAs

Average, all SMSAs

confirm the distinction between high growth zones in the ten-state West-Southwest region and in a Southeast consisting of seven states and the District of Columbia and an area of slower growth in the six states of the Middle South (Alabama, Mississippi, Tennessee, Kentucky, Arkansas, Louisiana). For all 100 SMSAs, the median ratio of 1970 to 1940 population is 2.16 (the ratio uses 1970 population in 1970 SMSA boundaries and 1940 population in 1950 metropolitan area boundaries, since metropolitan areas were not defined in 1940). For the same period, the ratio for total metropolitan population in the United States is 1.94. The West and Southeast contain 40 of the 49 SMSAs with growth ratios above the median figure and 44 of the 61 SMSAs above the aggregate national ratio. In contrast, 56 percent of the large SMSAs in the Middle South and the Middle West fell below the United States ratio and 88 percent in the Northeast. The difference is even sharper if Mobile is placed in the Southeast rather than the Middle South and if Wichita is placed in the West rather than the Middle West (see Tables 1 and 2).

The same pattern of metropolitan growth continued in the first years of the 1970s. Between 1970 and 1974, *all* of the metropolitan areas which attracted a net migration of a least 25,000 were located along the southeastern coast, in the Southwest, or in the West. Similarly, the urban areas with the highest growth rates in the early seventies were smaller sunbelt SMSAs which have the size to offer a diverse and skilled labor pool and to support a full range of services but which retain the attractiveness of smaller communities. All of the SMSAs which grew by more than 20 percent between 1970 and 1974 were located in Florida, Texas, Colorado and Arizona.[23]

Economic profiles of metropolitan areas can help to distinguish the Sunbelt from the remainder of the United States. Data on the sources of personal income in 1975 can be used to derive location quotients for economic activities. The location quotient for each activity is computed by dividing the proportion of total metropolitan income which it generates by the proportion of total national income attributable to the same activity. A figure greater than 1.00 indicated that the metropolitan area had more than its proportionate share of that particular activity. As Table 3 indicates, 43 of the 52 large southern and western SMSAs showed one of three economic patterns in 1975: a specialization in government services, a specialization in trade and private services, or a dual concentration in tertiary activities in both the public and private sectors. Trade and service cities are found throughout the South and West, with Portland, Dallas, New Orleans, Atlanta, and Charlotte as typical examples. Government cities such as Norfolk, San Antonio, Sacramento and Tacoma are of major importance only in the core sunbelt regions of Southeast and West.[24]

A definition of the Sunbelt based on patterns and sources of state and metropolitan population growth since 1940 results in the delineation of two distinct regions. In terms of state boundaries, a Sunbelt-Southeast runs from Delaware to Florida along the Atlantic coast and a Sunbelt-West includes Texas, Oklahoma, Colorado, New Mexico, Utah, Nevada, California, Oregon, and Washington. This definition does not follow the transcontinental line along the 36th parallel commonly used by journalists. Instead it extends northward to include the environs of Chesapeake Bay, the Columbia Valley, and Puget Sound, all of which are major centers for outdoor recreation. It omits the lower Mississippi and Tennessee valleys, the northern Great Plains, and the northern Rockies, all of which remained dependent through the 1950s and 1960s on agriculture or traditional manufacturing.[25]

Such a definition places more importance on the census than on sunshine. If "Sunbelt" is anything more than a striking metaphor, the region has to be described in uniform and objective terms. It is not enough to point

---

Table 3
Economic Base of Large
Sunbelt SMSAs, 1975

	West	Southeast	Mid-South
Commerce/ Services	7	5	4
Government/ Commerce/ Services	5	5	2
Government	11	4	. . .
Government/ Manufacturing	. . .	. . .	2
Manufacturing	2	3	1

Source: Bureau of Economic Research, United States Department of Commerce, location quotients based on sources of personal income.

Note: The Location quotient data are provided in the standard industrial categories: farm, manufacturing, contract construction, wholesale/retail trade, finance/insurance/real estate, transportation/communications/utilities, services, all government, federal civilian, military, state and local government. Cities were allocated to the several groups in Table 2 according to the following criteria:

(1) commerce/services—LQ > 1.00 in at least three of the four categories of trade, finance, transport, and services and LQ < 1.20 for each government category.

(2) government/commerce/services—LQ > 1.00 in at least three of the categories of private trade and services and LQ > 1.20 for at least one category of government employment.

(3) government—LQ > 1.40 for all government employment and no more than category of private trade and services with LQ > 1.20.

(4) government/manufacturing—LQ in manufacturing > 1.20 and LQ in at least one government category > 1.20.

(5) manufacturing—LQ in manufacturing > 1.20 and higher than LQ for any other category.

Portland's high-rise business district encircled by an inner freeway loop is typical of postwar growth patterns in southern and western cities.

to Phoenix and Houston and to assert that the larger region includes those areas which resemble the extreme cases. Nor is it valid to take the alternative frequent among contemporary politicians and assume that "Sunbelt" is simply a new name for the familiar and comfortable political regions of South and West. Since the recognition of the Sunbelt in the 1970s has resulted from the passage of critical thresholds in city size and economic independence, it is necessary to examine objective data on state and metropolitan population growth and economic base. In such historical perspective, the Sunbelt can be viewed as a pair of regions oriented toward the southeastern and southwestern corners of the United States which have shared similarities of economic and demographic change since the 1940s.

Analysis of the development of the Sunbelt also suggests that the United States has entered a new era in regional development. From the later nineteenth century through the middle of the twentieth century, Americans viewed both the South and the West as exceptions to the national norm represented by the cluster of industrial cities reaching from Boston to St. Louis. The South was a consumption colony which furnished cheap labor and a captive market for northern industry, while the West was a resource colony which offered abundant land and raw materials for the indust-

rial East. Writers and historians consistently thought of the South as a culturally and economically limited backwater and focused on rural poverty as its essential problem. Both visitors and residents in the West worried about the immaturity of its "frontier" society and recognized that the development of natural resources was the most pressing regional concern.

Shifts of population and productive capacity among the United States in recent decades have reduced both the objective and the perceived uniqueness of the South and West. As scholars explore the character of the evolving Sunbelt, they will find it most useful to ask new questions which move beyond the standard topics of regional social science. One concern which relates to the experience of the entire Sunbelt rather than specifically to the development of the South or West is the region's dependence on the federal government for defense spending, civilian employment, urban aid, and environmental modification. A related question is the extent to which metropolitan growth in the Sunbelt has altered the national locus of economic power and decision-making and reversed the historic American division between heartland and hinterland regions. A third subject is the effect on sunbelt politics and society of the massive suburban sprawl characteristic of cities whose growth has come in the automobile era. It will require research both by historians and by other social

The American Sunbelt: 1940 - 1975

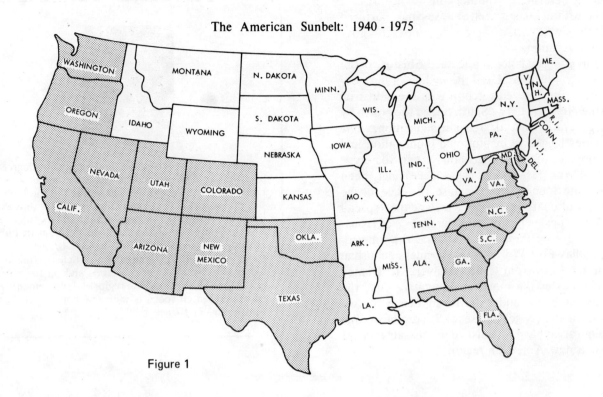

Figure 1

Fast Growing Metropolitan Areas: 1940 - 1970

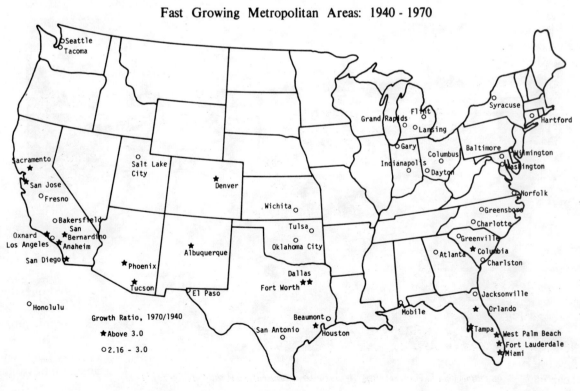

Figure 2

scientists to determine whether the reshuffling of population within instant metropolises has nurtured ideological conservatism or an openness to governmental innovation.

As the foregoing questions indicate, the history of the Sunbelt is urban history. Until the middle of our century, sunbelt cities played catchup with the industrial giants of the Northeast. The South trailed the North by roughly a generation in its degree of urbanization, while western cities lagged in institutional innnovation and the development of a heterogeneous urban society.[26] Since World War II, however, it has increasingly been the cities of the Sunbelt which have set the pace for the nation. The "ultimate" metropolis may be the "spread city" of Los Angeles or the "nowhere city" of Houston. It may also be Phoenix or Atlanta, the "metroplex" of Dallas-Fort Worth or the formless suburban mass that stretches from Cape Canaveral to Disney World.[27] Whatever the most representative city, the internal development and external influence of two dozen major metropolises and several score of smaller metropolitan areas have established the character of the Sunbelt as a new American region.

Carl Abbott received his undergraduate degree at Swarthmore College and his graduate degrees at the University of Chicago. He has worked at the University of Denver, Old Dominion University, and Portland State University, where he has most recently been associate director of the graduate program in Public History. He has published *Colorado: A History of the Centennial State* and a number of articles on the internal geography of American cities and on the role of urban growth in American regional development. His current research focus is metropolitan growth in the American West since 1940.

Oregon Historical Society

Vanport was an empty field in August, 1942. A year later it housed more than 40,000 residents.

NOTES

1. "Houston is Where They're Moving," *Fortune*, 83 (February, 1971), 83-91; "The New No. 1 City in the Southwest," *Business Week*, June 12, 1971, pp. 82-86; Larry King, "Bright Lights, Big Cities," *Atlantic*, 235 (March, 1975), 84; Thomas Muller, *Growing and Declining Urban Areas* (Washington: The Urban Institute, 1975); Ada Louise Huxtable, "Deep in the Heart of Nowhere," *New York Times*, February 15, 1976, Sec. D, pp. 1, 34; Lynn Ashby, "The Supercities: Houston," *Saturday Review*, 3 (September 4, 1976), 16; Susan Bischoff, "Houston: Booming Even by Sunbelt Standards," *New York Times*, January 9, 1977, Sec. 3, p. 41.

2. Kirkpatrick Sale, *Power Shift: The Rise of the Southern Rim and Its Challenge to the Eastern Establishment* (New York: Random House, 1975); *New York Times*, February 8, 1976, pp. 1, 41; Gurney Breckenfeld, "Business Loves the Sunbelt (and Vice Versa)," *Fortune*, 95 (June, 1977), 134-35.

3. Seventy nationally syndicated political journalists were surveyed by letter and telephone during August-September, 1977. Replies were obtained from eighteen.

4. Breckenfeld, "Business Loves the Sunbelt," 133.

5. Kevin Phillips, *The Emerging Republican Majority* (New Rochelle, New York: Arlington House, 1969); Samuel Lubell, *The Hidden Crisis in American Politics* (New York: W. W. Norton and Co., 1970), 269.

6. Only six of the political journalists who replied to the questionnaire traced their first awareness of the term to Phillips, with equal proportions unable to recall their first encounter or dating it to 1976.

7. Sale, *Power Shift*, 270; *New York Times*, February 8-12, 1976.

8. *New York Times*, February 9, 1976, p. 1; "Federal Spending: The North's Loss Is the Sunbelt's Gain," *National Journal*, June 26, 1976, pp. 878-890; Horace Sutton, "Sunbelt vs. Frostbelt: A Second Civil War?" *Saturday Review*, 5 (April 15, 1978), 28-37.

9. "A Year Later, the Frostbelt Strikes Back," *National Journal*, July 2, 1977, p. 1031; Sutton, "Sunbelt vs. Frostbelt," 28-37.

10. Daniel P. Moynihan, "The Politics and Economics of Regional Growth," *The Public Interest*, No. 51 (Spring, 1978), 3-21; Robert Scott and David Boren, speaking at symposium on "Alternatives to Confrontation: A National Policy Toward Regional Change," Austin, Texas, September, 1977.

11. Sale, *Power Shift*, 18; Phillips, *Republican Majority*, 273-274, 438.

12. Leonard Reissman, "Urbanization in the South," in John C. McKinney and Edgar T. Thompson (eds.), *The South in Continuity and Change* (Durham: Duke University Press, 1965), 84-86; James Clotfelter and Thomas H. Naylor, *Strategies for Change in the South* (Chapel Hill: University of North Carolina Press, 1975), 237-239; Southern Growth Policies Board, *Growth Management Policies for the South* (1974), 9-10, 27; W. Eugene Hollon, *The Southwest: Old and New* (New York: Alfred A. Knopf, 1961), 438-64; Beverly Duncan and Stanley Lieberson, *Metropolis and Region in Transition* (Beverly Hills, California: Sage Publications, 1970), 135-216.

13. Brian J. L. Berry and John Kasarda, *Contemporary Urban Ecology* (New York: The Macmillan Co., 1977), 167; George Sternlieb and James Hughes, *Current Population Trends in the United States* (New Brunswick, New Jersey: The Center for Urban Policy Research, 1978), 72.

14. The figures used are 1974 metropolitan population within 1974 SMSA boundaries and 1940 population within 1950 SMSA boundaries, since SMSAs were not defined for 1940.

15. Robert K. Lamb, "Mobilization of Human Resources," *American Journal of Sociology*, 48 (November, 1942), 323-30; Catherine Bauer, "Cities in Flux," *American Scholar*, 13 (Winter, 1943-44), 73-75; Louis Wirth, "The Urban Community," in W. F. Ogburn (ed.), *American Society in Wartime* (Chicago: University of Chicago Press, 1943), 67; United States, Bureau of the Census, *Statistical Abstract of the United States: 1946* (Washington: Government Printng Office, 1946), 780.

16. Earl Pomeroy, *The Pacific Slope* (New York: Alfred A. Knopf, 1965), 300-302; Morris Garnsey, *America's New Frontier: The Mountain West* (New York: Alfred A. Knopf, 1950), 119; Mel Scott, *Metropolitan Los Angeles* (Los Angeles: The Haynes Foundation, 1949), 40; Wendell Berge, *Economic Freedom for the West* (Lincoln: University of Nebraska Press, 1946), 7-14, 74; Calvin B. Hoover and B. U. Ratchford, *Economic Resources and Policies of the South* (New York: The Macmillian Co., 1951), 130-32; William H. Nichols, "The South as a Developing Area," in Avery Leiserson (ed.), *The American South in the 1960s* (New York: Praeger Publishers, 1964), 25-27.

17. Edward Ullman, "Amenities as a Factor in Regional Growth," *Geographical Review*, 44 (January, 1954), 119-32.

18. Harvey Perloff, *et al.*, *Regions, Resources and Economic Growth* (Baltimore: The Johns Hopkins Press, 1960), 464-66; "The BEA Economic Areas: Structural Changes and Growth, 1950-73," *Survey of Current Business*, 55 (November, 1975), 14-21; Brian J. L. Berry, *Growth Centers in the American Urban System* (Cambridge, Massachusetts: Ballinger Publishing Co., 1973), 5.

19. Joseph Spengler, "Demographic and Economic Change in the South, 1940-1960," in Allan P. Sindler (ed.), *Change in the Contemporary South* (Durham: Duke University Press, 1963), 49-52; Leonard Reissman, "Urbanization in the South," and Richard L. Simpson and David B. Nosworthy, "The Changing Occupational Structure of the South," both in McKinney and Thompson, *South in Continuity and Change*, 87-88, 92-97, 204-205; Clotfelter and Naylor, *Strategies for Change in the South*, 222-224.

20. Carey McWilliams, *California: The Great Exception* (Westport, Connecticut: Greenwood Press, 1971), 10, 363; Neil Morgan, *Westward Tilt: The American West Today* (New York: Random House, 1963), 3-12. Between 1940 and 1970, California accounted for 60 percent of the total population growth and 78 percent of the net migration in the mountain and Pacific states.

21. Carol Jusenius and Larry C. Ledebur, *A Myth in the Making: The Southern Economic Challenge and Northern Economic Decline* (Washington: Department of Commerce, Economic Development Administration, 1976).

22. Perloff, *Regions*, 34-35, 39, 47, 475-477, 484. Also see Henry S. Shryock, Jr., *Population and Mobility within the United States* (Chicago: University of Chicago Community and Family Study Center, 1964), 404.

23. Peter Morrison and Judith Wheeler, "Rural Renaissance in America?" *Population Bulletin*, 31 (October, 1976), 2; United States, Bureau of the Census, *Current Population Reports*, Series P-25, No. 618, "Estimates of the Population of Metropolitan Areas, 1973 and 1974" (Washington: Government Printing Office, 1976).

24. Data supplied by the Bureau of Economic Analysis, Department of Commerce. The manufacturing centers in the West are the chemical and oil town of Beaumont and the space-age city of San Jose. The manufacturing centers in the South are Wilmington, Greensboro, Greenville, and Louisville. The TVA towns of Knoxville and Chattanooga are the cities which combine government and manufacturing. The data used for the analysis combine Dallas and Fort Worth as a single metropolitan economy. Fresno does not appear in the table because its only concentrations of activity were in farm employment and "other industries."

25. Recent data indicate that it may be necessary to add parts of the Middle South and northern Rockies to the definition of the Sunbelt as a current rather than an historical phenomenon. For the period 1970-74, increases in metropolitan population greater than the rate for the United States as a whole were shown by the six southeastern states from Maryland to Florida and by the nine southwestern-western states from Texas to Oregon. Above average rates were also recorded in Idaho, Montana, Tennessee, Arkansas, Mississippi, and Louisiana. In the central South, however, rapid metropolitan growth continued to coexist with a sluggish nonmetropolitan sector. The 5.9 percent growth of total population in the six states of the Middle South for 1970-75 was greater than the national figure of 4.8 percent but lagged behind rates of 6.3 percent for the Pacific states, 8.7 percent for Texas-Oklahoma, 9.9 percent for the South Atlantic region, and 16.3 percent for the Mountain states. See United States, Bureau of the Census, *Current Population Reports*, Series P-25, No. 640, "Estimates of the Population of States with Components of Change, 1970-75" (Washington: Government Printing Office, 1976).

26. For the South, see Blaine Brownell, "The Urban South Comes of Age, 1900-1940," in Blaine Brownell and David Goldfield (eds.), *The City in Southern History* (Port Washington, New York: Kennikat Press, 1977), 123-34; Joel Fleishman, "The Southern City: Northern Mistakes in Southern Settings," in H. Brandt Ayers and Thomas

H. Naylor (eds.), *You Can't Eat Magnolias* (New York: McGraw-Hill Book Co., 1972), 170-185; T. Lynn Smith, "The Emergence of Cities," in Rupert Vance and Nicholas Demerath (eds.), *The Urban South* (Chapel Hill: University of North Carolina Press, 1954), 24-37. For the West, see Lawrence Larsen, *The Urban West at the End of the Frontier* (Lawrence: The Regents Press of Kansas, 1978); Pomeroy, *Pacific Slope*, 215-52.

27. The descriptive phrases are from Christopher Rand, *Los Angeles: The Ultimate City* (New York: Oxford University Press, 1967); Victor Gruen, *The Heart of Our Cities: The Urban Crisis, Diagnosis and Cure* (New York: Simon and Schuster, 1964), 69-70; Huxtable, "Deep in the Heart of Nowhere."

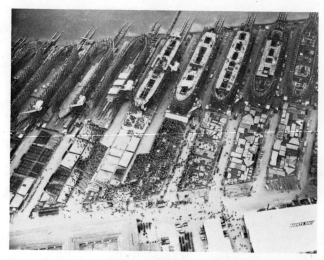

Oregon Historical Society

The massive assembly yard for merchant shipping in Portland during World War II typifies the defense production boom which triggered a generation of rapid growth in a score of sunbelt cities.

Oregon Historical Society

Defense housing projects during World War II provided practice for the suburban sprawl of the 1950s and 1960s. Vanport, Oregon was the second largest city in the state in 1944.

Oregon Historical Society

Portland shipyards employed 120,000 workers at their peak in 1943.

Ships of the USN anchored off San Diego about 1922.

The Metropolitan-Military Complex In Comparative Perspective:
San Francisco, Los Angeles, and San Diego, 1919-1941

Roger W. Lotchin

Today San Diego boasts a total capital investment of $28,000,000 in naval establishments, with an annual naval payroll of $30,000,000 [out of an 'annual naval appropriation' of $300,000,000]. We should protect this great investment and keep this vital payroll . . .

San Diego Union
November 6, 1934

The kind of prosperity which comes from warship building is like the wild dance of some savage before casting himself into the flames. It is the prelude to a catastrophe.

Los Angeles Times
December 24, 1937

The President's announcement of plans for immediate upbuilding of the Navy must be approved by thinking Americans.

Los Angeles Times
December 30, 1937

For most of the inter-war period, urban California upheld the claims of peace while pursuing the instruments of war. The explanation for this seeming inconsistency lies less in the fear of external aggression than in the efforts of city builders and Navy men to mate two monumental forces in modern America: militarization and urbanization. By analyzing their convergence in California, where both urbanization and militarization have appeared in an extreme form, this essay seeks to explore their relationship and to assess its significance for American and urban history. Due to its West Coast pre-eminence, the Navy provides an excellent test case with which to begin.

Although historians of earlier eras and other countries have noted the frequent convergence of the city and the sword, historians of twentieth-century American cities have neglected the topic. Given the enhanced importance of both militarization and urbanization, it would seem appropriate to bring the connection between urban and military history back into focus. In the

United States Naval Institute Photographic Collections

*Rotten Row, Mare Island, 1920-1925. The cage-mast battleships are the **Vermont, Georgia, Nebraska** and **Rhode Island** with the tanker **Tippecanoe**, with nearest in the foreground the old cruiser **New Orleans**. The size of the fleet on the West Coast at this period was indicative that the only likely enemy, especially in the minds of Californians, was Japan.*

process, this essay will consider the importance of this connection to a number of subtopics: the rise and timing of the military-industrial complex; federal urban policy affecting cities, or the "New Federalism;" metropolitanism; the influence of cities upon national defense policy; some little-noticed outcomes of city politics; the integration of the military with civilian society; and the rise of the alliance between Sunbelt cities and the military establishment.

The story goes back at least to 1919, to metropolitanism among California cities, to the decline of the "Cool Grey Lady," [San Francisco] and to what might be called the "second coming" of the Great White Fleet. The second decade of the century found the main components of urban California unsure of their status and competing furiously for pre-eminence. In 1920 the census would show that Los Angeles had forged ahead in population, but that city remained relatively unindustrialized compared to similar or even smaller Eastern cities.[1] San Francisco and San Diego had grown impressively between 1910 and 1920, but both had lost ground to the explosive Southland metropolis of Los Angeles. Thus, despite their vigor, each of these Sunbelt cities had to cope with its own version of relative decline — or status anxiety.

The transfer of the fleet to the Pacific in 1919 seemed at least a partial answer to these problems. Although strategic factors have not generally been considered important to the process of urbanization, they were crucial to the development of urban California — and long before World War II.[2] The sinking of the German fleet after World War I, the increase of the Navy during that conflict, the United States' rivalry with Japan, and the scrapping of Admiral Mahan's One-Fleet Theory all allowed the relocation of the major portion of the American fleet to Pacific waters between 1919 and 1921. Even before the ships had cleared the locks at

Panama and steamed north, every city on the West Coast scrambled to get a share of the naval booty.[3]

Although the competing cities always deferred publicly to the opinions of the Navy's experts and the imperatives of "national defense," other considerations were paramount in civilian minds. It is well known that international insecurity and Depression-born unemployment provided a powerful stimulus to martial expenditure in the 1930s, but military spending had an earlier, more diverse, and more specifically urban rationale in metropolitan California. San Francisco saw this military money as a general economic multiplier which would restore its predominance; and that city as well as San Diego and Los Angeles hoped that militarily stimulated manufacturing would help overcome the Sunbelt's industrial lag.[4] San Diego wanted economic stabilization from its military payrolls, and, in addition, saw defense dollars as the means to redress its chronic balance of payments deficit.[5] Finally, all three regarded Navy dollars and development as a means to commercial aggrandizement.

The Navy's imperatives were different, being military instead of economic; but until well into the Roosevelt Administration, its dilemma was similar. Its decline was both relative and absolute. Congressional economizers assaulted the Navy's budget from 1919 on; air-power advocates questioned its role; the Washington Naval Limitation Treaty froze its strength; and government neglect and hostile public opinion kept this service below treaty strength for years thereafter.[6] Thus, the Navy needed civilian allies to protect itself from further slippage just as urban California needed military resources to realize its schemes of development and defense. This mutual problem brought the civilian and military sectors into a close association that lasted for twenty years.

Even before the Navy steamed to the West, that service had worked out plans for the allocation of its resources on the Pacific Coast. Secretary of the Navy Josephus Daniels announced in 1919 that the Mahan One-Fleet Theory was dead and that, after a decent burial, half of the Navy would be stationed in Pacific waters.[7] To accommodate the fleet, the Navy had planned a series of shore installations. These were distributed both strategically and politically. The Navy had learned in World War I that an emergency would require many shore facilities not always needed in time of peace, and they made sure that these would be placed in or, in the case of Portland, near the major West Coast metropolitan areas. The two most desirable plums were to be given to Puget Sound and San Francisco Bay respectively, and the Bay Area was to have the main West Coast operating base of the fleet.[8] This facility would cost $60,000,000 to $100,000,000, would bring with it as many as 45,000 naval personnel, and was grandiosely referred to in Northern California as the "American Singapore."[9]

These allocations had been made by the naval experts, and the various urban spokesmen never tired of commending an arrangement so obviously in the interest of national defense. Such an argument appealed to a generation of businessmen and politicians undergoing Taylorization in the economic world and experiencing the more specifically urban version of this idea in the realm of government — the "Goo Goo doctrine of expertise" frequently employed in American cities on behalf of charter and structural reform. In fact, the Goo Goo doctrine of expertise formed the basis of the political strategies worked out by coast cities to get and hold the fleet and to distribute naval resources among the Pacific cities. For instance, all the cities united in demanding the fleet for Pacific waters, citing the naval experts and their various strategic theories to back up this claim. Once the sailors had been secured, the cities again publicly deferred to the experts' judgment in placing their facilities around the coast and even within specific parts of the various metropolitan areas. In the San Francisco Bay Area, for example, the two leading contenders for the operating base site, Alameda and Hunter's Point in San Francisco, each fought vigorously for that prize but agreed to let the naval experts decide ultimately.[10]

This logical formula should have contained the political in-fighting for naval personnel and material, but in practice various influences undermined the doctrine of expertise. For one thing, the successive fleet commanders had considerable discretion as to where they would station the Pacific Navy; and each time they moved it around, they whetted local appetites for permanent possession. At the same time, technological development rendered obsolete the decisions of earlier experts. The dawning importance of air power called into ques-

tion the choice of San Francisco Bay as a main base, and the use of carriers and larger battleships made certain Bay Area sites, such as Mare Island, obsolete or at least obsolescent. Simultaneously, the multiplying urban advantages of the Southland increased that area's ability to handle the entire fleet, and military improvements to the installations there strengthened southern claims even more. Moreover, the naval experts frequently disagreed. The future role of the Mare Island Navy Yard, the location of the main operating base, the site of the West Coast dirigible base, the strategic defense perimeter of the fleet, and even the supposedly dead issue of the One-Fleet Theory aroused enormous controversy within the Navy itself.[11] These discords, in turn, sabotaged the Navy's claim to expertise and encouraged the civilian defense boosters to take sides based on metropolitan interests rather than on national defense grounds. This recrudescence of met-

North Carolina Collection of the Wilson Library, The University of N. Carolina at Chapel Hill
Photograph of Secretary of the Navy Josephus Daniels and Mrs. Daniels, 1915.

ropolitanism further undermined the doctrine of expertise and encouraged the Navy in self-defense to play off one city against another.[12]

These problems surfaced very quickly and just as quickly centered on the issue of the main West Coast operating base. Some of the Navy's placements were readily accepted, and shore installations grew up from them. Between 1920 and 1923, for example, Congress confirmed San Diego's possession of its marine base and naval field, moved the Bay Area's naval training station at Treasure Island to San Diego, and approved the creation of an operating base, a new naval district, a supply depot, a destroyer base, and a major naval hospital at that southern city.[13] Its Southland neighbor, Los Angeles, got a submarine base; the two shared the fleet anchorage; and Southern California remained the fleet training ground.[14] San Francisco Bay representatives agreed to most of these decisions, thinking their own share was forthcoming soon. And according to naval plans, it should have been.

In 1920, Secretary of the Navy Josephus Daniels had accorded the Bay Area operating base at Alameda a high priority, but metropolitan politics revised the Navy's shopping list.[15] This political opposition was led by Vallejo, located at the northern end of San Pablo Bay. That city depended upon the adjacent Mare Island Navy Yard to an extraordinary degree, and Vallejo feared that a main West Coast operating base at either Alameda or Hunter's Point would mean the dismantling of its own Navy facility, since the new base supposedly had to be centralized. In addition, Vallejo wanted the new base for itself. From 1920 to 1925, Congress listened to the representatives of Vallejo rather than to the Navy and San Francisco and annually refused the appropriations to initiate the American Singapore.[16]

Despite allegations that the Washington arms limitation agreements and Republican budget cutting caused these rejections, these matters were not important. The Navy did not have shore installations to accommodate

Sailors from Admirals Evans "Great White Fleet" landing at the San Diego Wharf in 1908. Normal practice was for the steam pinnaces in the background to tow the whalers close ashore so that sailors going on liberty would not soil their blues with a long row. Whether ashore for duty or pleasure, and this appears to be a funeral parry armed with rifles, sailors meant business for port cities.

even the tonnage allowed under the limitations treaty, and the amount needed to initiate the San Francisco base was a trifling amount of the naval appropriations, much less of the national budget. Instead, the extremely decentralized patterns of urbanization in metropolitan San Francisco proved decisive. Geography and history had left the Bay Area even more fragmented than Los Angeles. In particular, San Francisco and Vallejo lacked the physical contiguity and the obvious identity of interests of Long Beach and Los Angeles in the south. As a result, Vallejo's Congressman Charles Curry, possibly with outside help from the south, masterminded San Francisco's defeat.[17]

Downtown San Diego in 1913 with Coronado to the left and LaJolla in the center background.

This failure left the Navy with its battle fleet stationed on the Pacific Coast without a main operating base. The construction of the main base at San Francisco Bay, considered indispensable by the Navy, was stalled, while the minor installations went on building. The fleet was stationed in the south, but the main West Coast supply depot remained in Vallejo; and Mare Island and Bremerton, Washington, held onto their dry docks. This forced the sailors to steam hundreds of miles for supplies or repairs.[18] Although the Navy designated San Francisco an operating base in 1923, for the entire 1920s the strategic disposition of naval resources on the West Coast continued to reflect this pattern of Bay Area and West Coast urbanization rather than the designs of the Navy's strategic operations planners.

In the meantime, with the base issue stalemated, each of the cities forged ahead in lesser ways, improving their physical facilities and building a close interface with the military. As these ties matured, the militarization of urban California insinuated itself into many other phases of urbanization, urbanism, and local history: city planning, metropolitan decentralization, the search for community, police-community relations, the media, city politics, government, society, urban renewal, metropolitan cooperation, and the development of urban welfarism. Perhaps city politics reflected the growing entente between the city and the sword most clearly. In each of the major California cities, new political alliances grew up to attract major military investment, Army as well as Navy, to protect naval investment in the Pacific, and to back the Navy on key matters of national military policy.

Since large urban areas, or metropolitan "families," as the *San Francisco Examiner* put it, supplied the bases for these alliances, the term "metropolitan-military complex" would seem more appropriate than "military-industrial complex."[19] Industries singly or in groups provided only one element in these local coalitions, and not necessarily the most important one. In fact, as was noted earlier, the militarization of urban California was a means to overcome the industrial lag of

the area. Probably the most important leadership element in each coalition was the city government, particularly the mayors. James Rolph and Angelo Rossi of San Francisco and the appropriately named John Forward of San Diego stand out among these executive leaders of urban navalism, but many others played similar roles.[20] Besides government, the metropolitan-military coalitions included Down Town clubs, chambers of commerce, labor councils, the media, local Congressmen, shipping groups, veterans' organizations, Propeller clubs, harbor commissions, diverse businesses, and dozens of other organizations.[21] In addition, Hollywood, of course, provided other bona fide defense experts to the Los Angeles grouping. Although the literature on metropolitan cooperation has focused on the consolidation of governments, military metropolitanism was also crucial to the growth of area-wide cooperation in urban California.

Everywhere these political ties were institutionalized. In the Bay Area, the San Francisco and other urban-military pressure groups came under the umbrella of the Bay Cities Naval Affairs Committee, which was part of the Bay Area Industrial Development Committee. Los Angeles had both a military affairs committee of the Board of Alderman and a mayor's committee on naval base development. San Diego had an Army and Navy committee of the Chamber of Commerce, and other organizations featured the same kind of institutional relationships.[22] The Navy, perhaps unwittingly, facilitated this institutionalization in 1920 by a reorganization which added local districts to the bureau system already in existence. This geographic decentralization produced naval districts at San Diego, San Francisco, and Seattle, with the same population bases and many of the same empire-building interests as their urban navalist counterparts.

These ties were supplemented by others to the federal government in Washington. Each of the cities tried to secure representation on the U.S. Shipping Board, to get a member on the House Naval Affairs or Rivers and Harbors committees, and to woo the U.S. Army Corps of Engineers. Each cultivated members of the naval officer corps politically, and each secured valuable service allies, both within the Eleventh and Twelfth Naval Districts at San Diego and San Francisco and within the central offices of the Navy as well.[23] The service members of the metropolitan-military complexes were less stable due to their frequent moves. However, ex-servicemen, especially in San Diego where many retired, were more stable and often played a significant role, holding important civilian posts after their military careers had ended.[24] These local alliances constituted relatively long-term political coalitions of government,

service, and business personnel, comparable to what today is called the military-industrial complex.

All these groups represented the elites of urban California, but they accurately expressed the wishes of the mass of city dwellers as well. Every major California metropolitan area donated large and immensely valuable tracts of land to the Navy, and the voters usually ratified these gifts at special referenda, frequently by stunning majorities.[25] Whether we ultimately judge the growing partnership of the city and the sword as an encouragement to militarism or as a prudent development of national defense in a dangerous world, it is clear that the elite and the electorate agreed upon it.

Other more subtle, yet nonetheless political, links supplemented these overt ones. Just as the ties of the metropolitan-military complexes stretched upward to Washington, they also descended into everyday urban

United States Navy Destroyer Repair Base, San Diego, in 1927. The destroyers seen here are the famous four-stackers who became famous in West Coast history for one of the largest known multiple shipwrecks in world history and as part of the Destroyers-for-Bases deal made by Franklin Roosevelt in World War II. Repair facilities meant many crews with time on their hands and liberty to spend.

United States Naval Shipyard, San Francisco, drydocks, a picture taken by the U.S. Army Corps in September 1939, according to the stamping on its back, but appearing to have been taken in 1923 according to the negative key.

politics. City politicians found themselves constantly faced with the necessity of raising a new subsidy, providing another piece of land, finding a new anchorage, winning yet another referendum, or supplying some new benefit. This, in turn, led the civilian-military partners into considerable city planning efforts. From 1920 on, the Navy participated in Bay Area harbor and transportation planning that eventuated in the bridging of San Francisco Bay. Los Angeles shared this experience, and San Diego improved upon it. San Diego was known to the Navy as the city that tried harder. Unlike San Francisco, San Diego vetoed its own bridge scheme at the behest of the Navy. Moreover, that city also planned well in advance of naval demands to improve its harbor in order to secure ever greater military patronage. It set up a harbor trust fund, reminiscent of the contemporary highway trust fund, to finance port development — administered by the harbor commission and insulated from the ordinary pressure of "politics." This arrangement guaranteed the Navy a continuing commitment to its interests.[26] The Los Angeles Harbor Commission claimed $30,000,000 worth of improvements devoted to the same end. Even before the New Deal, federal funds aided these efforts. Although such long-range, comprehensive planning was unusual for its time, it reinforced rather than altered the decentralizing dynamics of urban spatial development. De-

spite the fact that urban historians have almost completely ignored the military origins of city planning, these were certainly important in the California military cities.

Throughout the 1920s and 1930s, the civilian-military interface grew steadily closer in other spheres. The Navy continually courted the media, and the press repaid the compliment with interest. The newspapers publicized military activities fully, opened their columns to service spokesmen advocating defense measures, and frequently denounced those opposing them, particularly pacifists, whose activities the Navy and Army feared.[28] Rotary, veteran, commercial, and other clubs supplemented the media communications pipeline by frequent invitations to Navy speakers to present service views. Social events added to the growing entente. The Southland Navy Ball held in Los Angeles annually was *the* event of the early Southland "society" calendar.[29] Harbor Day in San Francisco went even farther, working both the classes and the masses into the social interface. This was a massive civic-military festival which featured a "society" Navy Ball as well as one for the sailors and something for almost everyone else — sham battles, inspection tours, concerts, water shows, aerial shows, and so forth.[30] The Navy took these exercises seriously. On Memorial Day, the ships would be spread out from one end of the

Another view of the USN Destroyer Repair Base at San Diego in 1927.

Coast to the other to participate in commemorative services; while at other times all or part of the Pacific squadron would appear at such "national defense" events as the Portland Rose Festival, the San Diego Exposition, and the Golden Gate Bridge Fiesta. The latter two claimed the entire fleet in 1935 and 1937.[31] Urban California used these occasions to encourage a sense of community, both because many thought that the process of urbanization had fragmented it and because these celebrations were a way to mobilize the entire populace behind further demands for naval largesse.[32] The Navy linked itself to this sense of community wherever possible — naming a cruiser for San Francisco and a dirigible for Los Angeles and fulsomely praising pliant San Diego.

These efforts paid off for both sides. The naval investment grew steadily over the years, and, in turn, urban California moved progressively toward a kind of military welfarism. Reversing the contemporary practice that allocates extra federal funds for areas impacted by the military, urban California subsidized the Navy instead. Besides dredging its harbors, either through local, rivers and harbors, or its PWA and RFC funds, urban California gave away massive portions of its enormously valuable waterfront. By 1929, San Diego had already alienated one-third of its waterfront to the Navy and by 1955, had donated nearly 3,000 acres. Alameda twice gave 5,340 acres; and Los Angeles, San Mateo County, Oakland, Vallejo, and others followed suit.[33] Special piers, docks, and other facilities added to the sailors' convenience. In San Francisco, special public works relief programs, municipal civil service exemptions, city employment preference, paid vacations for civilian military trainees, free use of the Civic Auditorium, a war memorial building built on urban renewal land, and free rides for thousands of sailors on the Municipal Railway benefited veterans and servicemen. San Diego rented dancehalls, established special servicemen's relief committees upon the advent of the

Depression, supplied cut-rate water to its bases, leased municipal airport land, and constructed spur tracks, seaplane landings, made land, and many recreation facilities for the sailors. As usual, San Diego went all out. In 1933, when a storm literally washed the fleet out of its poorly protected anchorage at San Pedro, one cruiser division was relocated at San Diego. Its commander called the Harbor Commission about additional recreation facilities for the new arrivals, and the next day the bulldozers began building ball fields and tennis courts on made land that the city had created in 1928 — just in case.[34] The Navy pushed especially hard to get the harbor improvements and land donations, almost ritually threatening to decamp if it were turned down. San Diego in particular was bombarded with these threats, although it is difficult to see how that city could have been more cooperative short of electing an admiral to the mayoralty.[35]

The city and the sword were drawn together by a host of other mutual interests that were both local and strategic in nature and which, in turn, produced valuable support for the Navy's position on national defense. A prosperous American merchant marine ("the second line of defense") in the Pacific, a thriving aircraft industry, a revival of West Coast shipbuilding, drydocks to repair both merchant and military vessels, airport construction, pilot training, and, especially after 1929, rearmament would benefit both parties.[36] The regional character of such issues often overcame metropolitan jealousies and produced regional political coalitions that helped realize these goals. These positions were not without their delicious ironies. Until well into the 1930s, civilian defense boosters rated the menace of

The fine flying weather made San Diego an ideal base for aircraft carriers. Here in 1939 the original converted collier, the U.S.S. Langley, once a full flight-deck carrier, is seen going alongside after rebuilding as a seaplane tender, in which guise she was sunk off Indonesia in World War II. The basing of carriers with their high proportion of officers in San Diego increased the demands for housing, schools and other facilities, whether on or off base.

their Japanese trading partners below that of Hitler and Mussolini. Simultaneously, they supported the placement of most of the fleet ("the first line of defense") in Pacific waters and the creation of a vast urban-military infrastructure to accommodate it. [37]

As these institutional relationships matured in the 1920s and early 1930s, the urban installations of the Navy continued to grow. What Robert Caro called "stake driving" in his biography of Robert Moses holds true of urban-military affairs as well. Once a stake had been driven or a project started, it would grow to completion and sometimes beyond. Unfortunately, the main operating base at Alameda had not yet received its first stake by 1920 and remained stalled the rest of the decade. That jeopardized the naval interest in the entire

San Francisco region. Both the political infighting of the Bay Area and the growing importance of the southern metropolitan areas led the Navy to cast longing glances southward. As the harbors in the Southland improved, as its metropolitan infrastructure supplied more of what the Navy needed, and as its cooperation increased, the Navy wavered in its commitment to San Francisco Bay. [38]

While Los Angeles drove stakes and San Diego burrowed ever deeper into its harbor floor, San Francisco and its Bay allies waited for the base to appear. Then in 1929 the House Naval Affairs Committee's investigation of a West Coast dirigible base site revealed that the Navy was split several ways over the operating base question as well as over that of the dirigible station. An

United States Naval Institute Photographic Collection

Navy yards have commonly built naval vessels since the founding of the Republic and it has nearly always been a good business. Mare Island was established in the nineteenth century, but is seen here on 9 March 1933 as the heavy cruiser **San Francisco** *left the ways.*

This view of San Diego was taken in 1959 somewhat further to the east than that in 1913 shown earlier and somewhat closer to the docks. Some of the same buildings are recognizable and the distant skyline is still the same.

almost comic parade of expert military witnesses, backed by their metropolitan-civilian allies and armed with strategic theories tailor-made for each city, marched before the committee, asserting the superiority of their own West Coast localities. Carl Vinson joined in the spirit of things and asserted the claims of the historic South; and Congressman McClintic of Oklahoma even put forward the name of Oklahoma City as a compromise dirigible station site, though he did have the self-restraint not to ask for a naval base.[39]

Sunnyvale in the Bay Area finally got the nod, but not before the Bay Area metropolitan-military complex had been badly shaken. After 1929 it organized for sustained action.[40] Sunnyvale also initiated the reconciliation with Vallejo, since that city eventually came to support the claims of the south-bay dirigible site and joined the Bay Area base coalition. And although it amounted to only a $5,000,000 commitment, the establishment of a base at Sunnyvale broke the long dry spell for the San Francisco Bay Area. As many from the Southland recognized, that minor airship station was really the entering wedge for the operating base, since dirigibles were supposed to operate with the fleet.[41]

By 1933, an ever more threatening world situation, plus the elevation of a President and Congress more anxious to end unemployment and rebuild the Navy, brought fresh naval resources into the West Coast contest. However, money had never really been the problem. Politics had; and, fortunately for the Bay Area, its own stalemate broke in these same years. Congressman Curry died in 1930, and in 1933 the metropolitan-military complex at Los Angeles moved openly to secure the coveted main West Coast operating base. Admiral Thomas J. Senn, commandant of the Eleventh Naval District, backed this move, and the Navy Department allowed him to investigate the idea.[42] A main operating base would have duplicated the dry-dock and supply facilities of Mare Island, and this threat solidified the adherence of Vallejo to the San Francisco coalition while galvanizing that group into redoubling its efforts.

By this time, however, the Navy had already lurched back into San Francisco's camp. In fact, Admiral C.C. Cole, commandant of the Twelfth Naval District at San Francisco, had by 1930 conceived the strategy that, together with the ominous threats from the south, would finally break the deadlock amongst Bay Area cities. Cole noted that the Navy could no longer hope for a centralized base at Alameda because the process of urbanization had claimed much of the land and threatened other potential Bay Area base sites as well.[43] To salvage the situation, the Navy hit upon a base strategy that matched military decentralization to the urban decentralization and the urban rivalry of the Bay Area.

The Navy conceived a secret plan for the new operating base. It would be decentralized around the bay; it would be built up one step at a time instead of in one dramatic burst; and it would contain something for each of the cities competing for naval riches.[44] This plan was finished by 1932, and the Navy then devised an ingenious maneuver to implement it. To quiet the suspicions of Los Angeles and San Diego, the Navy played down the immediate need for new shore facilities and asked Congress to concentrate its spending on the "floating Navy" and the existing installations instead.[45] Congress did, and then the Navy began pointing to the overtaxed shore facilities which needed more money to handle the expanded fleet. This strategy of

A more impressive view of the growth of the city is to be seen in this aerial view which encompasses many of the elements which make up the Western urban environment — sunny skies, water, sprawling business and home areas, growing vertical downtown area and mountains in the distance together with pleasure boats and airplanes.

overload worked to the distinct advantage of San Francisco; it had been denied so much for so long that its overloading was more dramatic when the ships and planes finally came.[46] In the meantime, Twelfth Naval District Commandant G. W. Laws brought the warring Bay Area factions together to negotiate a peace treaty, which coincided with a media blitz, reinvigorated pressure group activity, and renewed Congressional activity by civilian Bay-Area service boosters.[47] The Navy went farther. What the newspapers called the ''most significant'' war games in naval history — an attack on coastal cities to test their air defenses — occurred just before the advent of the Roosevelt Administration in 1933. The new administration, from which the Navy expected great things, came to power just as the West Coast newspapers broadcasted the news that the mock attack had proven the coastal cities defenseless.[48]

From that point onward, Bay Area fortunes brightened. A new supply depot, a major naval air station, a new shipyard, a training station, improvements to Mare Island, an aeronautical research laboratory, and, in 1938, shipbuilding subsidies rapidly overcame the Bay Area naval lag.[49] San Francisco missed out on a West Coast naval academy, and, fortunately, the Navy and other bay cities rejected ''the City's'' clamatious suggestion to obliterate a large portion of San Pablo and San Francisco bays with a massive military-industrial landfill.[50] However, by 1941 the Bay Area had finally gained the position that the Navy had assigned it over twenty years earlier. It had secured the main operating base and a total naval investment of one billion dollars.[51] Interestingly enough, Los Angeles, which still claimed the main fleet anchorage, apparently did not learn of the secret base build up in the Bay Area until mid-1937.[52]

The Southland metropolitan-military complexes likewise claimed further resources during these years, but they were usually additions to existing installations rather than new ones. San Diego, for example, added the Army half of North Island to its naval air station, gained a minor dry dock in 1935, and extensively dredged its harbor in 1931 and 1936.[53] Los Angeles likewise crept ahead, acquiring Reeves Field, expanding its artificial harbor, and claiming a growing proportion of the burgeoning fleet until war claimed the sailors.

This brief consideration of the comparative dimension of the city and the sword suggests several conclusions. Western civilian-service ties that have been called the military-industrial complex obviously came before, rather than during or after, World War II, as has been generally supposed.[54] In this part of the Sunbelt, these ties had an urban rather than an industrial base.[55] They were also significant to both national defense policy and Western economic development. Quite possibly, they were as, or more, important than those

San Diego Convention and Visitors Bureau

This is a favorite activity year-round in San Diego. Weekend races are held in San Diego Bay, Mission Bay Aquatic Park and in ocean waters 12 months a year. And the Navy, which helped take California, is still much in evidence over a century later, and still liked by civilians.

civilian-military ties since discovered at the national level in this period.[56] Most certainly, the metropolitan-military complexes provide us with new insights into the topic of twentieth-century metropolitanism, city politics in general, and city planning in particular. Also, urban navalism allows us to reopen the discussion of the historic relationship between the city and the sword and to do it in such a way as to speak to national history as well as to urban. Not only do the metropolitan-military complexes reveal something about national defense and economic development, they also tell something about federal policy affecting cities that we have long overlooked in favor of things like housing, FHA, relief, and public works, which may not have been any more important.[57] And finally, the study of the city and the sword casts new light on the historic role of urbanism and urbanization as an integrative force — not, in this case, for Blacks, women, or immigrants — but for the military. The comparative view of urban California certainly would not support the conclusions of Samuel P. Huntington that the military in the 1920s returned to their pre-war isolation from society, that they were harassed by ''business pacifism,'' or that civilians did not try to take advantage of them.[58] Although the experience of urban California would not support the speculation of Lewis Mumford that cities *generate* the forces of war, urban California certainly stood ready to use these forces for *civilian* purposes. If they were not ''Merchants of Death,'' the urban navalists surely qualified as ''Merchants of Defense.''

Roger W. Lotchin received his Ph.D. from the University of Chicago. He is now Professor of History at the University of North Carolina at Chapel Hill. His special interests are American urban history, comparative urban history, and city politics. He has authored *San Francisco, 1846-1856: From Hamlet to City* (Oxford, 1974) and articles in the *Journal of American History* and the *Pacific Historical Review*. His reviews have appeared in the *New York Times Book Review*, the *Journal of American History*, the *Pacific Historical Review*, the *Journal of Southern History*, and the *Western Historical Quarterly*.

FOOTNOTES

1. Robert M. Fogelson, *The Fragmented Metropolis: Los Angeles, 1850-1930* (Cambridge, Massachusetts, 1967), 132.
2. For the impact of military matters on urban affairs after World War II, see Gerald Nash, *The American West in the Twentieth Century: A Short History of an Urban Oasis* (Englewood Cliffs, N.J., 1973).
3. See Committee on Naval Affairs, *Hearings Before the Committee on Naval Affairs: Appropriation Bill Subjects, 1919*, U.S. Congress, House of Representatives, 66th Cong., 1st sess., 1919, pt. 2 (Washington, D.C., 1919).
4. *San Francisco Journal of Commerce,* April 7, 1920, p. 1. Cited hereafter as *Journal of Commerce. Los Angeles Examiner,* October 4, 1933, p. 16, ed.
5. *San Diego Union,* Feb. 26, 1933, I, 1; Jan. 29, 1933, I, 12.
6. Donald W. Mitchell, *History of the Modern American Navy* (New York, 1946), p. 250ff; Vincent Davis, *The Admirals' Lobby* (Chapel Hill, N.C., 1967), pp. 3-157.
7. *Hearings . . . on Naval Affairs . . . 1919, op. cit.,* pp. 60-61.
8. *Ibid.* Naval allocations of West Coast resources appear throughout this hearing.
9. U.S. Congress, *Congressional Record,* 66th Cong., 3rd. sess., 1921, LX, p. 4126-140.
10. Naval Affairs Committee, *Hearings . . . on Estimates Submitted by the Secretary of the Navy, 1920,* U.S. Congress, 66th Cong., 2nd sess., pp. 1096-1103 (Washington, D.C., 1920).
11. Committee on Naval Affairs, *Hearings on Sundry Legislation Affecting the Naval Establishment, 1929-30,* U.S. Congress, 71st sess., 1930, throughout (Washington, D.C., 1930).
12. "In unmistakable terms, naval officials assert San Diego must meet this competition [of rival Pacific Coast ports] by accentuating its own harbor program." *San Diego Union,* Jan. 15, 1933, II, 1.
13. Edward J. P. Davis, *The United States Navy and U.S. Marine Corps at San Diego* (San Diego, 1955), pp. 29-73.
14. *Hearings . . . on Estimates . . . 1920, op. cit.,* pp. 2334-335.
15. *Ibid.,* p. 2227.
16. Lt. Commander Arnold S. Lott, *A Long Line of Ships: Mare Island's Century of Naval Activity in California* (Annapolis, Md., 1954), pp. 183-206.
17. Robert G. Albion, "The Naval Affairs Committees, 1816-1947," *United States Naval Institute Proceedings,* 78 (Nov. 1952), 1234; U.S. Congress, *Congressional Record,* 71st Cong., 3rd sess., 1931, LXXIV, pt. 5:5408-410.
18. Adm. Wm. D. Leahy, Chief of Naval Operations, to Congressman Byron N. Scott, Dec. 29, 1937, General Correspondence, 1926-1940, General Records of the Department of the Navy, RG 80 (National Archives).
19. *San Francisco Examiner,* July 1, 1922, I, 16, ed.
20. *San Diego Union,* Feb. 26, 1933, I, 1.
21. San Francisco Board of Supervisors, *Journal of the Proceedings,* Vol. 36, No. 1 (April 7, 1941), p. 607. Cited hereafter as *Journal.*
22. *San Diego Union,* April 12, 1933, II, 8.
23. *San Francisco Examiner,* April 4, 1933, p. 19.
24. *San Diego Union,* Feb. 17, 1935, I, 5.
25. *San Francisco Daily Commercial News,* Jan. 26, 1921, p. 1. Cited hereafter as *Daily Commercial News.*
26. *San Diego Union,* June 25, 1933, I, 1, 10, and II, 1 give the historical background of the San Diego interlock.
27. *Los Angeles Times,* May 15, 1937, II 4, ed.; Jan. 8, 1938, I, 9.
28. *Ibid.,* Jan. 24, 1937, II, 4; *Daily Commercial News,* March, 1935, p. 8.
29. *Los Angeles Times,* Jan. 3, 1937, IV, 1.
30. *San Francisco Examiner,* August 1, 1933, p. 5.
31. San Francisco Board of Supervisors, *Journal . . . ,* Vol. 32, No. 1 (March 29, 1937), pp. 499-500; *San Diego Union,* August 8, 1935, I, 2.
32. *San Diego Union,* June 18, 1933, II, 1; *San Francisco Call and Post,* Jan. 3, 1925, p. 7.
33. Davis, p. 72; *Daily Commercial News,* Jan. 26, 1921, p. 1.
34. *San Diego Union,* Feb. 23, 1933, II, 5.
35. *Ibid.,* Jan. 15, 1933, II, 1; Oct. 18, 1935, I, 4.
36. *Los Angeles Times,* March 27, 1933, II, 4; *San Francisco Examiner,* July 8, 1922, I, 22, ed; Jan. 2, 1923, I, 26; Jan. 31, 1933, ed. pg.; *Down Town* (San Francisco), Jan. 25, 1939, p.1; *Daily Commercial News,* April 10, 1940, p. 8; U.S. Congress, *Congressional Record,* 69th Cong., 2nd sess., 1927, LXVIII, pt. 2: 990-97, 1735-736.
37. *Los Angeles Times,* March 27, 1933, II, 4, ed.; *San Diego Union,* March 10, 1935, I, 6; U.S. Congress, *Congressional Record,* 75th Cong., 3rd sess., 1938, LXXXIII, pt. 4:3767.
38. Memo from Director of Material Division to Chief of Naval Operations, June 3, 1928, General Correspondence, 1926-1940, RG 80 (National Archives).
39. *Hearings on Sundry Legislation . . . 1929-30, op. cit.,* pp. 2633, 2696, 2774, 2826, 2700-701, 2713.
40. *San Francisco Chronicle,* May 14, 1929, ed. pg.; May 22, 1929, ed. pg.; June 15, 1929, ed. pg.
41. Memo from Director of Material Division to Chief of Naval Operations, *op. cit.*
42. *Biographical Directory of the American Congress, 1774-1971* (Washington, D.C., 1971), p. 813; *San Diego Union,* Jan. 30, 1933, I, 1; *Los Angeles Examiner,* Sept. 30, 1933, I, 5.
43. W. C. Cole to Chief of Naval Operations, Nov. 14, 1930, Confidential Correspondence, 1927-1939, General Records of the Department of the Navy, RG 80 (National Archives).
44. *Ibid.*
45. Statements by Secretary of the Navy Claude Swanson in *San Francisco Examiner,* Sept. 25, 1933, p. 17 and Oct. 21, 1933, p. 5.
46. Subcommittee of the Committee on Appropriations, House of Representatives, *Hearings on the Navy Department Appropriations Bill for 1939* (Washington, D.C., 1938), pp. 820-25.
47. *Daily Commercial News,* Sept. 12, 1933, p. 4; Sept. 14, 1933, p. 4.
48. *San Diego Union,* Jan. 23, 1933, I, 1; Feb. 18, 1933, I, 5.
49. *San Francisco Chronicle,* June 25, 1938, p. 11; E.P. Hartman, *Adventures in Research: A History of Ames Research Center, 1940-1965* (Washington, D.C., 1970), pp. 1-42.
50. San Francisco Board of Supervisors, *Journal . . . ,* Vol. 36, No. 2 (Nov. 13, 1941), pp. 2161-163, 2167.
51. *San Francisco Downtowner,* May 29, 1941, pp. 1-2.
52. *Los Angeles Times,* May 9, 1937, I, 11.
53. Davis, pp. 29-73; *San Diego Union,* June 27, 1934, I, 4; Jan. 6, 1935, I, 17; *Los Angeles Times,* Jan. 2, 1937, Annual Midwinter Number, p. 11.
54. The usual interpretation of the military-industrial complex stresses the importance of World War II or the Cold War. See, for example, Richard Polenberg, *War and Society: The United States, 1941-1945* (Philadelphia, 1972).
55. Benjamin F. Cooling, ed., *War, Business, and American Society: Historical Perspectives on the Military-Industrial Complex* (Port Washington, New York, 1977) and Paul Koistinen, "The 'Industrial-Military Complex' in Historical Perspective: The Interwar Years," *Journal of American History,* 56 (March, 1970), 819-39 stress the importance of industrial ties to the military, but correctly emphasize the importance of earlier periods in civil-military relations.
56. For these latter, see the works of Cooling and Koistinen.
57. For a recent historical work on federal urban policy, see Mark I. Gelfand, *A Nation of Cities: The Federal Government and Urban America, 1933-1965* (New York, 1975).
58. Samuel P. Huntington, *The Soldier and the State: The Theory and Politics of Civil-Military Relations* (Cambridge, Mass., 1964), pp. 282, 312.

Colorado State Historical Society
Turn of the century street scene in Denver when the trolley was still king.

The Western Response To Urban Transportation: A Tale of Three Cities, 1900-1945

Mark S. Foster

The vast majority of cities in the American West were founded in the nineteenth century, or even earlier; yet most developed their essential metropolitan characters in the twentieth century. While the post-World War II urban sprawl of metropolitan regions such as Houston, Dallas, Ft. Worth, Phoenix, and Los Angeles is obvious to the most casual observer, the period between 1900 and the war brought the primary commitment to what local decision-makers labeled a "unique" pattern of development in at least three major cities. Denver, Seattle, and Los Angeles are distinctive not only in their geographical separation and topographical settings, but in their economic, ethnic, and social variations. Nevertheless, during the forty-five years between the turn of the century and V. J. Day, each assumed a largely horizontal pattern of physical development.

The most important factor contributing to urban decentralization was widespread adoption of the automobile as the primary mode of urban transportation. In 1900, Western cities' response to urban transportation largely imitated those of Eastern cities. By the early twentieth century, Western planners perceived an opportunity to assume a leadership role in the application of rapidly developing transportation technology.[1] They matched, or even exceeded their Eastern counterparts in their enthusiasm for the automobile, by

which they hoped to promote beautiful, functional cities where they would take advantage of their "unique" Western environments. In relying almost exclusively upon individualized mass transit, decision-makers not only allowed existing street railways to decline, but they consciously and consistently rejected concrete proposals for significantly updated rapid transit systems. As a result, by World War II these Wesxtern cities were even more firmly committed to the automobile than the majority of their Eastern rivals. It was a rare urban planner or traffic expert who did not view that "achievement" with a mixture of relief and pride.

The development of Denver and Seattle commenced in the mid-nineteenth century, and the founding of Los Angeles dates back to the late eighteenth century; nevertheless, all three cities experienced their most important urban growth in this century. Of the three cities, Denver had the largest population in 1900, with 134,000 souls; Los Angeles contained 103,000, and despite the largest population gains between 1880 and 1900, Seattle boasted but 80,000 permanent residents. Eighty years later each of these cities is the center of a huge metropolitan region, Los Angeles' population in excess of eleven million, and Denver and Seattle each with roughly one and one-half million. Through the first four decades of the twentieth century, Los Angeles'

William G. Evans, dynamic and aggressive street-railways promoter in Denver at the turn of the century.

population gain was undeniably the most spectacular. By 1940 its population had reached 1,504,000, compared to 368,000 for Seattle and 322,000 in Denver.[2] Perhaps even more significant in its effect upon the ultimate shaping of these cities was the timing of population surges in each. Seattle experienced its major pre-World War II growth between 1880 and 1910; in those three decades it grew from 3,500 to 237,000. Denver's growth was considerably more gradual, from 134,000 in 1900 to 213,000 in 1910, and 256,000 a decade later. Los Angeles experienced enormous population gains, both numerically and proportionately in each decade before the Depression. From its 1900 base of just over 100,000, its population tripled by 1910; in the following decade it nearly doubled to 576,000, and during the 1920's it more than doubled yet again, to 1,238,000.[3]

Significantly, despite their varying growth rates, leaders perceived the most desirable patterns of future physical development in very similar terms. Even when the population of each city was considerably under one quarter of a million, decision-makers consciously promoted projects that would help their regions avoid the

density, squalor, and ugliness of many older, Eastern cities. Nobody expressed the prevailing view more convincingly than Dana Bartlett of Los Angeles, who believed that a spread-out city would be more healthful and morally uplifting. As he put it in 1907, "Here the tendency is to open and not crowded quarters; on morality, for those who cultivate taste for natural pleasures are not tempted to the grosser sins. Here even the pauper lives in surroundings fit for a king." He concluded that "the laying out of new subdivisions far out beyond the city limits makes cheap and desirable homes available for a multitude of working men."[4] Planners in Seattle and Denver shared Bartlett's vision. In 1927 Seattle's City Engineer William H. Tiedeman stated that his city was "fortunate to be in the plastic state at the time when the automobile imposes its special requirements upon cities." A year later, the Seattle planning commission's annual report stated that "Modern methods of transportation have so largely annihilated time and space that there is now no shortage of land for all our needs, leaving neither necessity nor excuse for crowding, since crowding is not in the interest of economy or of efficiency."[5] In 1930 Denver planner Saco R. DeBoer similarly endorsed that view: "The expansion of the whole city has made it possible for people to have more light and air in their homes." And horizontal development also had beneficial side-effects, according to DeBoer: "The decentralization has meant that a considerable portion of the traffic congestion downtown has been eliminated."[6]

To a far greater degree than Seattle, Denver and Los Angeles capitalized upon their immediate physical environments through promotion of tourism and health care. "Exploitation" of Denver's mountains and scenery and Los Angeles' beaches and temperate climate encouraged horizontal development in those cities. As early as the 1870's town boosters in Denver proclaimed the Mile-High city's unsurpassed pure, fresh air; later the region achieved a reputation as a good place in which to recover from tuberculosis.[7] Southern California in general, and Los Angeles in particular, became noted "retirement meccas" for thousands of former Midwestern dwellers. Although this phenomenon really achieved national recognition only after World War II, the trail to the sunny haven of southern California has been nearly continuous for the last century. Prior to the unparalleled post-war growth of Los Angeles, the area experienced major land-booms in the 1880's and 1920's.[8]

The availability of large amounts of vacant land, combined with their relatively late development, provided Western cities an opportunity to stretch outward rather than upward. Compared to their Eastern counterparts, most Western cities had extremely low population densities. For example, in 1910 Boston and New York contained in excess of 16,000 persons per square mile; that figure was in sharp contrast to density figures for Denver, Los Angeles, and Seattle, which ranged from 3,200 to 4,200.[9] Perhaps the simplest explanation is that residents in these Western cities were never *forced* to live close to one another by technological limitations or other factors. Although urban cores in Eastern cities began losing population during the 1930's, and even more noticeably after World War II, those cities which were densely settled at the turn of the century remained very crowded in the 1970's. Western cities, experiencing their most important urban growth in the twentieth century, spread outward from the very beginning.[10]

The timing of major surges in population may have largely accounted for differences in visual appearance and population density even in Western cities. Although Seattle was but one-fourth the size of Los Angeles on the eve of World War II, its population density of 5,377 persons per square mile was nearly doubled that of the City of the Angels.[11] An important reason was that Seattle experienced its greatest pre-World War II population surge between 1880 and 1910; during the next thirty years it witnessed only a fifty percent increase in population. Hence, the automobile, the single most critical technological advance affecting horizontal growth made relatively little impact upon Seattle until it experienced a second great surge in population after World War II.

In contrast, Los Angeles' population increased five-fold between 1910 and 1940. Los Angeles "came of age" during a period in which the automobile was permitting an unprecedented degree of decentralization.[12] Just as important, Los Angeles attracted a class of newcomers who preferred a spread-out city, A variety of observers noticed that vast numbers of Los Angeles' new residents were transplanted Midwesterners, who developed communities within Los Angeles which physically resembled those they had recently left.[13] As popular writer Carey McWilliams noted,

> In the process of settlement, they reverted to former practices and built not a city, but a series of connected villages. They wanted homes, not tenements, and homes meant villages. The grouping of houses and the use of land was not determined by industrial considerations, for there was little industry. The ex-villagers gave Los Angeles its squat appearance, its flattened out form.[14]

A handful of critics scored decentralization not only in Los Angeles, but in Denver and Seattle as well. Yet the vast majority of planners and other urban observers in Western cities noted with satisfaction that by the late 1920's Eastern cities were struggling mightily to overcome excessively dense patterns of settlement. They flattered themselves in assuming that Eastern planners of the post-World War I period were attempting to copy the more spread out patterns of development in Western cities. Speaking before the National Conference of Planners in 1924, Gordon Whitnall of Los Angeles claimed that

> We know, too, the mistakes that were made in the east and to a degree the things that contributed to these mistakes. We still have our chance, if we live up to our opportunities, of showing the right way of doing things. It will not be the west looking back to the east to learn how to do it, but the east looking to the west to see how it should be done.[15]

Regional chauvinism aside, Whitnall's perspective was shared by planners in other Western cities.

From the time fixed rail transit systems were first introduced in American cities in the 1830's, promoters praised their ability to spread out urban development. By greatly speeding up the movement of patrons, the street-railway car would permit the wider distribution of the masses of urban dwellers.[16] However, by the time the electric trolley appeared on city streets in the 1880's, many Eastern cities were already densely settled industrial and commercial giants. In contrast, Western cities, including Los Angeles, Denver, and Seattle, were still villages in the 1880's. Without densely settled, long-established urban cores, decision-makers could use the trolley almost at their will as a tool in shaping their cities.

This is not to suggest that Western civic leaders did not copy their Eastern counterparts in significant respects. In fact, all three Western cities developed significant numbers of tall buildings within distinct urban cores. But the key point is that Western urban transit developers used the trolley to initiate a decentralized pattern of development long before there was massive physical crowding at their cities' cores. To be sure, they were motivated by the same forces that spurred their Eastern counterparts; profits and power. Nevertheless, John P. Evans in Denver, L. H. Griffith of Seattle, and Henry E. Huntington of Los Angeles extended their trolley lines out into the countryside from the very beginning. No land developer was more aggressive than Huntington, who used his inter-urban trolley system to develop real estate holdings located many miles from downtown Los Angeles. In Denver, John P. Evans subdivided land near the present location of the University of Denver. Trolleys connecting Evans' development with the downtown area traversed several miles of largely undeveloped land.

Whatever the reasons for the foundings of street railways, all three cities had well developed systems as the twentieth century opened. Street railway maps in each city reveals that the ubiquitous trolley cars blanketed developed areas. The companies themselves variously claimed that between ninety and ninety-seven percent of all residents in the cities lived no more than one quarter of a mile from the lines. During the early years of the twentieth century, all evidence suggests that they provided a brand of service that the general public found more than acceptable. Although there were frequent public outcries in all three cities against the "rapacious" nickel fare, most residents unhesitatingly relied upon the trolley not only for business, but also for pleasure travel. Generally speaking, the trolley companies extended service to lightly developed areas very quickly. Only in Seattle, about the time of World War I, did the public mount criticism of the street railway company for failing to extend lines to rapidly developing areas.[18] Despite generally praiseworthy service, Western urbanites frequently joined their Eastern counterparts in maintaining that the streetcar companies earned unconscionable profits.

As the pictures on this page by Jacob Riis from the New York Public Library show, in the 1890s, the Eastern slums were squalid. Western city planners hoped to avoid this sort of development by encouraging the use of transportation so that western cities could be spread out and airy.

Unfortunately from the standpoint of fixed-rail transit's future in the American city, the trolley industry suffered a series of reversals during and immediately after World War I which to a large degree sealed its ultimate doom. Several factors were beyong control by the industry itself. A doubling of the cost of living between 1914 and 1920 meant that those trolley systems which were locked into long-term franchise arrangements with fixed rates of $.05 were forced to provide service for a greatly depreciated fare. As automobiles crowded city streets and helped spread out urban development, trolley service appeared increasingly inconvenient and slow. As a result, patronage dwindled from the mid-1920's until World War II. With shrinking revenues and aging equipment, street railways across the country were increasingly incapable of competing with individualized mass transit.

Had the street railway companies preserved a favorable public image, they might have survived in larger numbers. Unfortunately, by the turn of the century, they had generally exhausted the public's patience and good will. At the pinnacle of their power in the 1890's and early 1900's, local transit companies had all too frequently arranged corrupt alliances with urban governments and exacted what at the time appeared to be unconscionable fares from a public which had no recourse to alternative modes of travel. Local "reform" groups, goaded into action by muckraking newspapers and fiction writers, made transit companies primary targets of their righteous wrath.[19] Although the most celebrated conflicts between street railways and the public occurred in older, Eastern cities, transit companies jarred the sensibilities of local patrons in the West as well.

Unfortunately, transit companies in Western cities experienced some of their most disastrous public-relations failures just when they most needed local support: at the end of World War I. In Seattle, public discontent over high fares, combined with the private company's inability or unwillingness to extend service to rapidly developing areas during World War I, induced the electorate to approve municipal ownership of all lines in 1919.[20] Unfortunately, hasty negotiations resulted in a $15 million price tag, which was later judged to be roughly twice the actual value of the lines. As a result, transit managers were unable to do more than meet the interest rates on the crushing capital debt, let alone make inroads against the principal.[21] Within a year of public takeover, even its friends labeled municipal ownership a "monumental failure."[22] Denver residents did not flirt seriously with municipal ownership, yet they felt little sympathy with the Denver Tramway Company, particularly regarding its treatment of employees. A strike against the company in August 1920 turned into a three-day riot when the Tramway Company imported hired thugs to break the strike. The *Denver Post's* office was sacked, and during the riot several innocent bystanders lost their lives. An independent commission investigating the incident assigned the majority of the blame to the transit company, because of its refusal to bargain in good faith with striking motormen.[23] The negative publicity surrounding these developments augured ill for street railway companies' efforts to rally public support for more "realistic" fares and expensive proposals for improvement of local transit.

During the 1920's and 1930's, urban transit experts in many American cities proposed dramatic changes in fixed-rail systems, including sparkling new, "comprehensive" rapid transit lines. Time and again, such proposals were subjected to close scrutiny by responsible city officials, including planners, only to be rejected. Such was the fate of a series of rapid transit plans for Seattle and Los Angeles. Nationally renowned transit expert Bion J. Arnold had proposed a comprehensive subway system for Los Angeles as early as 1911, but little came of it.[24] As increased numbers of trolleys, buses, and automobiles competed for space on the city's crowded streets in the early 1920's, the City Council commissioned the mass-transit plan.[25] Although the plan won endorsements from downtown merchants and a handful of real estate developers, it was opposed by a vast majority of powerful local interests, as well as the city's most influential urban planners.[26] While some debated whether rapid transit should consist of subways or elevateds, the City Club Report of 1926 epitomized the thinking of a majority of the city's planners and public officials.

> Considering the results obtained in cities like New York, Boston, and Philadelphia, we may well ask whether L. A. is justified in beginning an endless chain program of expenditures in subway and elevated structures which inevitably have tended to increase the congestion in those centers

of population.[27]

The report specifically noted that cheap power, the automobile, and universal use of the telephone had all developed after rapid transit systems were constructed in large, Eastern cities. These new developments presented Los Angeles with a golden opportunity to develop in a pattern wholly different from Eastern cities.

In a similar vein, decision-makers in Seattle considered — and rejected — plans for comprehensive rail rapid transit lines as just about the same time. They shared the "conservative" view of their counterparts in Los Angeles that fixed-rail rapid transit could never be self-supporting from patrons' fares. Perhaps in part as a reaction to the civic black-eye caused by Seattle's nightmare experience with the publicly owned trolley, the Municipal League of Seattle stood against any rapid transit proposal for the city. In 1929 that body's official newsletter editorialized against even a $15 million "starter" experiment in subways:

> It has seemed to us that the plan for subways, etc., as proposed, is premature for a city the size of Seattle, that there is no traffic congestion such as to warrant an expenditure of this amount of money for the acquisition and building of subways at the present time, which estimate may of course prove far below the actual cost when completed.[29]

Reginald H. Thomas, Chief Engineer for Seattle, and one of the most respected public utilities experts on the West Coast, also demurred. Citing cost, Seattle's relatively low population density, lack of real congestion, and adequate parking facilities, Thomas was "hesitant to recommend the beginning of construction at this time." He also pointed out that

> Persons have urged me to use my influence to construct rapid transit in Seattle, saying that the advertising we would receive because of undertaking such construction would amply repay our apparent loss occasioned by reason of unsuccessful operation. My feeling is that such advertisements were better not made.[30]

In contrast to unsuccessful efforts by friends of public transportation to bring rapid transit systems to Los Angeles and Seattle, their conterparts in Denver never mounted a serious bid to build new fixed-rail systems.

Many transit experts realized that fixed rail systems could not carry as large a share of total public transit in spread out cities as in older, more densely settled areas. Once cities began to spread out, distances between radial transit lines naturally grew larger. In outlying areas, there were frequently gaps of several miles between fixed rail lines. Prospective patrons found them inconvenient even for trips to the central districts, for using them meant at least one transfer and one or more waiting periods. Short journeys of three or four miles between outlying areas often brought even greater frustration, as partrons frequently had to ride ten or fifteen miles into a central district, then transfer to another line to reach a given destination. It is hardly

Before and after shots of the Bronx River in 1907 and after the Parkway was built in 1922. In certain respects Western planners followed the lead of their Eastern brethren in using parkways for city beautification.

This 1924 photograph shows the elevated railway of Chicago's "Loop," which represented the kind of visual pollution Western city planners hoped to avoid by promoting automobile thoroughfares rather than expensive rapid transit systems.

As this 1910 photograph of a Chicago street scene shows, urban congestion antedated the widespread use of the automobile. Western city planners wished to avoid such "eastern" congestion by promoting decentralization.

Even in western cities, as this Denver street scene in the early 20th century shows, installation of trolley lines frequently created inconvenience.

surprising that by the 1920s urbanites generally preferred to ride automobiles directly from points of origin to destinations, unrestricted by schedules and delayed by no waiting periods.

At the same time planners in Western cities consciously rejected rapid transit proposals, they enthusiastically supported plans for the more expeditious movement of automobiles. Planners in a variety of Western cities perceived the good fortune that their relatively late development had brought. As Walden E. Sweet, Executive Secretary of the Denver Planning Commission put it in 1930,

The Denver Plan had been developed from a western viewpoint with almost unlimited space in which the city can expand and develop, and with a city of peculiarly open character — the density of population is extremely low, 6.7 persons to the acre — the ideal of spaciousness has been pursued. To avoid the evils of congestion and overcrowding attendant upon excessive use of land, Denver has aspired to spread widely rather than reach high.[31]

Similarly, planners for Los Angeles, including such influential traffic experts as Clarence A. Dykstra, Gordon Whitnall, and L. Deming Tilton had urged a spread out pattern of development for many years.[32]

The "defeat" of the rapid transit proposal in L.A. in the 1920's presaged a massive commitment to the automobile as the preferred means of moving the masses throughout the region. Ironically, when Bion Arnold presented his rapid transit proposal back in 1911, he foresaw that "In fact, the enterprise appeals strongly on account of its automobile possibilities, for L.A. needs an automobile speedway with all crossings eliminated, and this proposed highway between city and the sea is most fortunately located for both pleasure and business."[33] Arnold's vision, minus his center-strip reservation for a rapid transit line, would not be built until the development of the Harbor Freeway to San Pedro following World War II. Nevertheless, as early as the 1920's, planners in Los Angeles were laying the groundwork for the freeway system which would emerge, beginning in the late 1930's.[34]

According to freeway enthusiasts, advanced concepts in highway design would not only permit the continued "opening up" of the American city, but would positively contribute to a more harmonious environment. In his dedication speech at the opening of the Pasadena Freeway in 1940, California's Director of Public Works, Frank W. Clark, stated that old fashioned highways had created an ugly urban environment of "string towns" and "ribbon cities" almost overnight

Service stations, nightclubs, fruit stands, junk yards, and other commercial establishments were thrown up with utter disregard for aesthetics of or

the purpose for which the road was built. As a result, the modernized highway facility, which the motorist had paid for out of gas tax funds, often became little more than ugly city street serving a few local interests. For the sake of safety these roads had to be zoned for restricted speeds. In many cases, the final result was a facility little better than the one which the new improvement had been built to replace.[35]

In Clark's view, however, the new freeways, by carefully controlling both access and commercial development in the immediate vicinity, would not violate even the sylvan beauty of the Arroyo Seco Canyon. Designers of Denver's Valley highway projected a similar vision of that improvement's impact upon the local environment.

Many communities have given full recognition to this [esthetic] element of freeway planning. The magnificent parkways that have been built in various metropolitan centers — New York, Detroit, St. Louis, Chicago, Los Angeles and others — are evidence of such endeavor, and their effect testifies to the human values inherent in such proper esthetic planning of urban traffic arteries. The Denver Project thoroughfare is no less subject to the requirements that it shall enhance rather than detract from the value and attractiveness of the city.[36]

Finally, in Seattle, traffic consultant Maxwell Halsey, of Yale University's Bureau of Traffic Research, concluded that the city could "look forward to the ultimate development of a full limited way system such as has been started in cities like New York, which has its west side highways and parkways; Chicago, with its Outer Drive; St. Louis with its depressed highways; and Los Angeles with its Arroyo Seco."[37]

By the late 1930's there were a few planners and urban critics peering into the future of the automobile-dominated city who feared that prospect. Even in Los Angeles, the quintessentially automobile-oriented city, former disciples of decentralization began to have second thoughts as World War II loomed. Gordon Whitnall feared that an overly rapid rate of decentralization destroyed property values; in 1941 he pointed out that those values in Los Angeles had declined forty percent during the Depression decade.[38] Denver Mayor Ben Stapleton and several members of that city's planning commission voiced similar concerns at an Urban Land Institute Conference the same year. Pointing out that some suburban areas were outgrowing Denver at a ratio of five to one, the Denver planners concluded that, "Denver, while not in so acute a stage of disintergration as many of our larger cities, has its own blighted areas which are spreading, and already there are startling evidences of the flight of Denver residents across corporate boundaries."[39]

Surprisingly, even some observers with a vested interest in the future of the automobile suggested its potential to do damage as well as encourage a healthy urban environment. In 1941 the Chief Engineer of the Southern California Auto Club admitted that during the heyday of the street railway, there was adequate land-use control, and sensible urban development:

> But the popularity of the automobile broke the power of the railway system to control land uses without providing any other method of control. The result is the present day American city, sprawling, nonconformist, ugly, and inefficient. The fluid state of most growing American cities cannot be controlled or stabilized without an effective transportation system. Los Angeles is perhaps the best example among such uncontrolled American cities.[40]

Finally, another urban critic from Los Angeles complained that the automobile had simply gone of control.

> Frankenstein is thundering across the map of America today, spouting exhaust smoke and reeking burnt gasoline fumes . . . The automobile, designed to be the emancipator of man, to give man freedom . . . is defeating its own purpose. Man is being enslaved again by the servant he created. The emancipation is a mockery and a memory.[41]

Significantly, however, even these prescient critics believed that it would merely be a matter of time before the "Frankenstein" would indeed be domesticated and put to the best possible use. However strong their aversion to the automobile's *past* urban impact, they envisioned the modern freeways as the ultimate means of effective control.

It seems clear that urban development in the West during the twentieth century was not wholly unique. As historian Gerald Nash has recently observed, until well into the twentieth century, Western America, including its cities, largely looked to the East for much of its direction; at times, its reliance appeared almost slavish.[42] Yet close examination also reveals that Western "importation" of Eastern ideas was highly selective. Significantly, in the realm of urban transportation, Western cities "copied" Eastern cities' freeway designs, adding — at least in the case of Los Angeles — a few new wrinkles of their own. Yet Western cities consciously rejected proposals to build "Eastern type" subway and fixed-rail rapid transit systems. There were several reasons for such an outcome.[43] In the eyes of many twentieth-century planners, fixed-rail systems of *any* type were symbols of an outdated transportation technology. Not only did transportation planners take the conservative position that public transit must be self-supporting, but also they perceived that, given low population densities in the Western cities, such an eventuality was highly unlikely. Perhaps most important, they generally perceived the Western city's potential for horizontal growth as a virtue rather than a defect. The massive scale of urban sprawl in many Western cities in the post-World War II period has demonstrated the inherent drawbacks in that philosophy. Nevertheless, the commitment to horizontal growth was conscious, not accidental, and the roots of that decision were laid in the early twentieth-century American city.

Mark S. Foster received his Ph.D. from the University of Southern California in 1971. Before joining the department of history at the University of Colorado at Denver, he taught at the University of Missouri, St. Louis. He is the author of articles in the *Pacific Historical Review*, the *Journal of Urban History*, and other journals.

NOTES

1. For an absorbing and far wider ranging analysis of the impact upon American culture of Western economic and social leadership groups, see Gerald D. Nash, *The American West in the Twentieth Century; A Short History of an Urban Oasis* (Englewood Cliffs, New Jersey: 1973).

2. U.S. Census, *Sixteenth Census of the U.S., 1940 Population, Volume II, part 1* (Washington, D.C.: 1941): 580.

3. U.S. Census, *Fifteenth Census of the U.S., 1930 Population, II* (Washington, D.C.: 1931): 18-19.

4. Dana Bartlett, *The Better City: A Sociological Study of a Modern City* (Los Angeles: 1907): 20; 39; 72.

5. Seattle, Department of Public Works, *An Investigation of Street Widths, etc., in American and Foreign Cities, Report by W. H. Tiedman* (Seattle: January 11, 1927): 29; Seattle City Planning Commission, *Annual Report, 1928* (Seattle: January 8, 1929): 2.

6. DeBoer, "Denver Downtown Traffic" (undated M.S. ca. 1930) in DeBoer Papers, Western History Room, Denver Public Library, Box 2a.

7. Lyle W. Dorsett, *The Queen City: A History of Denver* (Boulder, Colorado: 1977): 31-32.

8. See Glen S. Dumke, *The Boom of the Eighties in Southern California* (San Marino, Claifornia: 1944); and Mark S. Foster, "The Model-T, the 'Hard Sell,' and Los Angeles' Urban Growth: the Decentralization of Los Angeles During the 1920's" *Pacific Historical Review* 44:4 (November, 1975): 459-484.

9. U.S. Bureau of the Census, *Population: The Growth of Metropolitan Districts in the U.S., 1900-1940* (Washington, D.C.: 1947): 27-32.

10. The most notable exception is, of course, San Francisco. In 1910 its density of 8,966 persons per square mile gave it a visual appearance more reminiscent of Boston or New York than Denver or Los Angeles. For a fascinating analysis of the factors contributing to that city's uniqueness, see Gunther Barth, *Instant Cities: Urbanization and the Rise of San Fransisco and Denver* (New York: 1975).

11. *The Growth of Metropolitan Districts,* 27-32.

12. See Sam Bass Warner, Jr., *The Urban Wilderness: A History of Urban America* (New York: 1972): 113-149; Robert M. Fogelson, *The Fragmented Metropolis: Los Angeles, 1850-1930* (Cambridge, Massachusetts: 1967); and Foster, "The Decentralization of Los Angeles During the 1920's."

13. Jack Lilly, "Metropolis of the West," *North American Review* 232 (September, 1931): 241; Carey McWilliams, *Southern California Country* (New York: 1946): 161.

14. *Southern California Country,* 158-159.

15. Whitnall, untitled, mimeographed MS, Whitnall Scrapbook dated April 7, 1924, City Planning Commission Library, City Hall, Los Angeles.

16. Perhaps the best single treatment of this phenomenon is Sam Bass Warner, Jr., *Streetcar Suburbs: The Process of Growth in Boston, 1870-1900* (Cambridge: 1962).

17. See Spencer Crump, *Ride the Big Red Cars: How the Trolley Helped Build Southern California* (Los Angeles: 1962); Leslie Blanchard, *The Street Railway Era in Seattle: A Chronicle of Six Decades* (Forty Fort, Pennsylvania: 1968); no history of the Denver Tramway Company exists, but Kenton Forest and Robert C. Jones, *Mile High Trolleys* (Boulder, Colo.: 1974) provides good photographic coverage.

18. Blanchard, *Street Railway Era in Seattle,* 100-102.

19. One of the more colorful portrayals of a street railway mogul in a generally unfavorable light is Theodore Dreiser's trilogy, *The Financier, The Titan,* and *The Stoic,* published between 1912 and 1946.

20. Blanchard, *Street Railway Era in Seattle,* 81, 101; Mansel G. Blackford, "Sources of Support for Reform Candidates and Issues in Seattle Politics 1902-1916" (M.A. thesis, University of Washington, 1967):4.

21. Seattle Transit System, *Annual Report, 1940* (Seattle: 1941): exhibit VII.

22. "Municipal Street Cars Fail in Seattle," *Public Service* 29:4 (October, 1920):121.

23. Edward T. Devine, et al., *Report on Denver Tramway Strike of 1920, Under the Auspices of the Denver Commission of Religious Forces* (Denver,1921).

24. Arnold, "The Transportation Problem of L.A.," *Supplement to the California Outlook* 11:9 (November 4, 1911): 3.

25. Kelker, de Leuw and Co., *Report and Recommendations on a Rapid Transit Plan for the City and County of Los Angeles* (L.A.: 1924).

26. See Foster, "The Decentralization of Los Angeles During the 1920's."

27. S. A. Jubbe, et al., to the Board of Directors of the Los Angeles City Club, *Supplement City Club Bulletin: Report on Rapid Transit, January 30, 1926,* p. 9.

28. Seattle City Planning Commission, Rapid Transit Committee, *Report on Rapid Transit,* by William P. Trimble, et al., (Seattle: 1926). Seattle, like Los Angeles, had also considered a subway and elevated system in 1911. See Virgil C. Bogue, *Plan of Seattle: Report of the Municipal Plans Division* (Seattle: 1911):132.

29. *Seattle Municipal News* 19:15 (April 13, 1929):1.

30. Thomas to Rapid Transit Committee of Seattle, November 18, 1925, Thomas Papers, Suzzallo Library, University of Washington, box 13.

31. Sweet, "The Denver City Plan," *Western City* 6:5 (May, 1930):16.

32. A number of words have probed the uniqueness of Los Angeles' pattern of urban development. See in particular Fogelson, *The Fragmented Metropolis,* Sam B. Warner, *The Urban Wilderness,* 113-149, and Foster, "The Decentralization of L.A. During the 1920's."

33. Arnold, "The Transportation Problem of Los Angeles," 3.

34. See, for example Frederick L. Olmsted, Harland Bartholomew, and Charles H. Cheney, *A Major Traffic Street Plan for L.A.* (Los Angeles: 1924); L.A. County RPC, *A Comprehensive Report on the Regional Plan of Highways, Section 2-E, San Gabriel Valley* (LA:1929). Opponents of freeway building argued that they were far less efficient than rail lines for moving masses of people. Freeway advocates did not effectively counter this argument, but suggested that if but five percent of vehicles using freeways were buses, their movement capacity would be doubled (see Hugo H. Winter, "Solutions Which Have Been Offered for the Los Angeles Area's Transportation Problem," Paper Presented at the University of Southern California, June 11, 1941):27.

35. Clark, "Speech at Dedication of Arroyo Seco Parkway, December, 1940," mimeographed, City Planning Commission Library, City Hall, Los Angeles.

36. Crocker and Ryan Engineering Co., *Preliminary Report on a North-South Limited Access Highway Through Denver* (Denver: December 9, 1944): 5.

37. Halsey, *Defense Traffic Plan for Seattle, Prepared for the Mayor and Council of Seattle* (Seattle: November 17, 1941): 45.

38. "The Problem of Decentralization and Disintegration in Cities," as Discussed in the Conference Held in Boston, Massachusetts at the MIT, Under the Auspices of the ULI, October 15-17, 1941, *The Denver Plan, vol. 7* (Denver, 1941): 9.

39. *Ibid.,* 5, 6.

40. E.E. East, "Streets, the Circulatory System," in George W. Robbins and L. Deming Tilton, (eds.), *L.A.: Preface to a Master Plan* (Los Angeles: 1941): 92.

41. Ed Ainsworth, "Out of the Noose" (a series of seven articles in the *Los Angeles Times,* reprinted in pamphlet form), (Los Angeles:1938): n. p.p.

42. Nash, *The American West in the 20th Century.*

43. For a more extensive analysis of the evolution of this thought process, see my own "City Planners and the Evolution of Urban Transportation in the United States, 1900-1940," *Journal of Urban History* (forthcoming, February or May, 1979).

The Southwestern Urban Frontier, 1880-1930

Bradford Luckingham

Any student of urbanization in the Southwest is presented with the problem of definition. This study follows the view put forth by the geographer, D. W. Meinig, in his fine work *Southwest*. As he defined it, the region contains Arizona, New Mexico and the western promontory of Texas. Within this area, the major centers of urbanization have been El Paso, Albuquerque, Tucson and Phoenix.[1]

Small communities until the arrival of the railroads in the 1880's, El Paso, Albuquerque, Tucson and Phoenix nevertheless served the region as important outposts of civilization; along with a few other towns in New Mexico and Arizona, they worked as generators of progress and prosperity. Reflecting the influence of a variety of cultures, Spanish, Mexican and American, the towns played a dominant role in the military, economic, social and cultural life of the early Southwest. With the coming of the "iron horse" in the 1880's, El Paso, Albuquerque, Tucson and Phoenix entered into a period of emergence which assured their future as the principal cities of the Southwest.

Table A

	1880	1890	1900	1910	1920	1930
El Paso	736	10,338	15,906	39,279	77,560	102,421
Albuquerque	2,315	3,785	6,238	11,020	15,157	26,570
Tucson	7,007	5,150	7,531	13,193	20,292	32,506
Phoenix	1,708	3,152	5,544	11,134	29,053	48,118

Paso del Norte, founded in 1659 as a Spanish missionary and military outpost, became in time an agricultural town and the business center of the rich, Rio Grande irrigated El Paso Valley. Located on the *Camino Real*, or the Royal Highway, it also became an important link between Santa Fe to the north and Chihuahua and Mexico City to the south. When Mexico won its independence from Spain in 1921, the economic activity in Paso del Norte and other towns along the Santa Fe-Chihuahua trade route accelerated as Mexican officials, for a number of years, encouraged business with the United States.[2]

War broke out between Mexico and the United States in 1846, and following the conflict Americans founded settlements on the north side of the Rio Grande across from Paso del Norte. As service centers, these villages on the American side of the river profited from the local population, the presence of the military, and from California-bound travelers who stopped over for rest and supplies. One settlement, Franklin, led the others in growth and development, and it became El Paso in 1859.[3]

The Civil War caused dissension and retarded progress in the town and valley, and following the conflict recovery was slow, but in the late 1870's not just one but four railroads, attracted by the town's strategic location at the Pass of the North, constructed tracks toward El Paso. In May of 1881 the first train, the Southern Pacific, entered the bordertown.[4] The coming of the "iron horse" transformed the little adobe oasis into a boom place, and a new era opened for El Paso. Soon the Santa Fe and other railroads entered the growing town, and by 1884 it was a significant railroad hub with main line connections to San Francisco, New Orleans, St. Louis and Mexico City. As each new railroad link was formed, the boom in El Paso accelerated, and the population of the crossroads town jumped from 736 in 1880 to 10,338 in 1890. As the seat of El Paso County, and the principal city in a vast territory extending hundreds of miles into west Texas, northern Mexico, southern New Mexico and southeastern Arizona, the border community commanded attention. In and beyond the El Paso Valley, farming, ranching and mining interests, many of them recently established, recognized the busy railroad hub as the best service center in the area. During the 1880's El Paso became the largest and most important urban oasis in the Southwest.[5]

Urban services and amenities kept pace with the mounting population which reached 15,906 by 1900. The town offered the services of bankers, doctors, lawyers and other professionals, and town merchants carried large stocks of goods. Mining, farming and ranching increased in the hinterland and smelters, mills and factories contributed to regional resource development. By 1900 also, El Paso's "matchless climate" was recognized as a marketable resource and the desert oasis emerged as a health center. Nearby Fort

Fort Bliss U.S. Army post contributed to the well-being and growth of El Paso. Photo taken in the 1890s.

Bliss, first established in 1854, served as a major military center in the Southwest. As El Paso matured, the "vice and violence" inherent in the frontier population boom declined, and those who had once been inspired to such epithets as "Hell Paso" now proudly referred to the budding metropolis as the "Queen City of the Southwest."[6]

In 1910 a reporter for the *Overland Monthly* stated that no place in the country could offer "better railroad service rates to all parts of the compass." He noted that in the past year the railroad had handled millions of tons of freight, including "tremendous stocks of merchandise which are first brought to El Paso and then distributed throughout its thousand square miles of trade territory." The city, moreover, served as the chief border point of entry to Mexico, and the total dollar value of imports and exports passing through El Paso increased from 1.4 million dollars in 1885 to 11.4 million dollars in 1910.[7]

Conditions in the interior of Mexico encouraged the ongoing migration across the border and in 1910 people of Mexican origin made up half the population of El Paso, while the power, prestige and prosperity belonged to the Anglos. The majority of the Mexicans employed in El Paso held cheap labor jobs and the Mexican neighborhoods of south El Paso were marked by poverty. The Mexican Revolution of the next decade caused a massive migration and while the refugees represented all classes, most of them were poor, and they contributed to the severe economic and social problems that existed in "Chihuahua" or Little Chihuahua, the Mexican section of south El Paso.[8]

During and after the Mexican Revolution and World War I, Fort Bliss expanded its facilities. Additions included the construction of William Beaumont Army Hospital and Biggs Field in the early 1920's. El Paso also expanded its cultural and educational facilities. Liberty Hall, a municipal auditorium that compared with the best in the country, opened in 1918, and the following year it became the home of the El Paso Symphony Orchestra. In 1914 the Texas State School of Mines and Metallurgy was established. Enrollment in-

The El Paso smelter in the 1920s—copper provided one of the basic ingredients of the success of the metropolitan area.

Downtown El Paso in the 1930s showing the railroad's influence and facilities, a prime ingredient in the rise of the city.

creased from twenty-four in 1914 to ninety-three in 1921 to 510 in 1927 when a College of Liberal Arts was added to the curriculum.[9]

El Paso acquired a reputation as a convention town in the prohibition era because of its proximity to the liquor establishments and other "excitements" of Juárez (Paso del Norte until 1888). At the same time the four "C's"—climate, cattle, cotton and copper—continued to enrich the border city. One writer noted that it enjoyed a "climate that cannot be bought, but may be sold," and "El Paso sells it." The city's hinterland contained over two million dollars worth of beefstock by 1929, and El Paso offered excellent stockyard, market and shipping facilities. The completion of Elephant Butte Dam, 125 miles north of the city in 1916 brought an agricultural boom to the valley, encouraging the large scale production of cotton, and by 1920 that crop was king in the area. County cotton production alone rose to 48,483 acres by 1929, encouraging the appearance of more cotton gins and cotton mills. The copper business also boomed, causing the El Paso smelter, established in 1887 and the largest of its kind in the world, to increase its capacity, and inspiring the Nichols Copper Company, a subsidiary of Phelps Dodge, to complete in 1929 a 3.5 million dollar refining plant capable of processing per year over one hundred thousand tons of copper. The El Paso area produced forty-five percent of the copper mined in the United States and twenty-percent of the world's supply. Oil fields, including the largest one in the state, discovered in west Texas during the 1920's, also contributed to the city's prosperity; by 1929 three oil refineries operated in El Paso and they distributed their products in west Texas, New Mexico and Arizona.[10]

In 1928 a survey showed that El Paso contained 225 manufacturing concerns; they issued an annual payroll of fifteen million dollars and produced a variety of goods valued at forty-five million dollars. Many of El Paso's products entered the border community's vast trade area, a region declared "greater in extent than the New England states and New York combined." Wholesale trade, overall, brought into the city in 1930 fifty-seven million dollars worth of business, up from twenty-one in 1919. Along with 149 wholesale establishments, 1,280 retail outlets existed in El Paso and they generated sales worth fifty million dollars in 1930; part of this amount came from Juárez residents who as early as 1926 were reported to have spent fifteen million dollars a year in the city. In addition, as the "Gateway to Mexico," El Paso continued to benefit from a sizeable annual export-import trade.[11]

During the 1920's El Paso became an automobile supply and service center, and a rest haven for tourists driving over eleven highways leading to the city. Automobile ownership and bus service in the city increased, reducing streetcar use and giving impetus to urban sprawl. By 1930 eighteen truck lines operated out of the city and they delivered 120 tons of freight daily in the community's trade territory. The municipal Airport opened in 1928 and by 1930 many regional, national and international connections were available. El Paso not only retained but advanced its position as "the great traffic center of the Southwest." The city, moreover, had experienced steady growth since the turn of the century, increasing to an impressive 102,421 in 1930; in that year El Paso remained "the metropolis of the Southwest."[12]

Albuquerque, located 250 miles north of El Paso along the Rio Grande River, was founded in 1706 by families recruited from the province of New Mexico. The presence of a detachment of troops made Albuquerque a military outpost, but essentially it was a farming and livestock raising community, made productive by the development of an irrigation system fed by the Rio Grande. Cattle, sheep, corn, wheat and fruit thrived in the valley; wine was a specialty and of fine quality. The settlers traded with friendly Indians and with the occasional wagon trains that traveled the *Camino Real* between Santa Fe and Chihuahua. By the turn of the century the population had reached 1250, agriculture flourished and the oasis town had become an important trade and transportation stop.[13]

In 1821 when Mexico won its independence from Spain, Mexican officials, for a time, encouraged business with the United States, and as the volume and value of trade over the Santa Fe-Chihuahua route increased, Albuquerque became a vital "middle station" on the most important highway in the Southwest. In 1846 war broke out between the United States and Mexico, and soon United States troops occupied Albuquerque, made it an importaant army quartermaster center, and during and after the war sent supplies over old and new roads to military outposts in other parts of the territory.[14]

In the years following the Mexican War, Albuquerque began to attract a few Anglo settlers, mostly merchants, who prospered as they joined in serving not only the military and the valley, but also the many wagon trains of California-bound emigrants. The Civil War, for a time, disrupted the peaceful existence of Albuquerque and retarded progress, but following that conflict more people moved in, and by 1870 the population reached 1307, including 54 Anglos.[15]

In the late 1870's it became known that the Santa Fe railroad was going to bypass the mountain town of Santa Fe and come to Albuquerque. Railroad officials decided to locate the depot two miles east of the Albuquerque plaza, thus encouraging the development of a new town, and in April of 1880 the first Santa Fe passenger train arrived. After reaching Albuquerque, the Santa Fe continued to lay track into El Paso, Mexico, Arizona and California, making the New Mexico town an important railroad hub.[16]

The arrival of the "iron horse" brought a boom to Albuquerque, and New Albuquerque, or New Town, the "end of track" community near the depot, quickly became a rip-roaring railroad division point. Old Albuquerque was often ignored by the newcomers, who despite its raucous nature, preferred the more "American" New Town. New Albuquerque, as a result, was predominantly Anglo from the beginning, and it soon overtook Old Albuquerque in population and significance. In the 1880's it became a shipping and supply center for a vast hinterland covering much of New Mexico and northern Arizona. Business activity became so intense that merchants from Santa Fe and Las Vegas moved to New Albuquerque to take part in the activity, and outside investment was evident.[17]

The town served as the seat of Bernalillo County and during the decade most Anglos had dropped the appurtenance New and simply referred to the town as Albuquerque. The population rose from 2,315 in 1880 to 3,785 in 1890, and in the 1880's Albuquerque residents pressed the legislature to move the capital from Santa Fe to Albuquerque, but in 1898 the Congress of the United States declared Santa Fe to be the permanent capital of the Territory of New Mexico.[18]

Table B

Population	1880	1890	1900	1910	1920	1930
Albuquerque	2,315	3,785	6,238	11,020	15,157	26,570
Santa Fe	6,635	6,185	5,603	5,072	7,236	11,176

By 1910 the population reached 11,020, and nearly two thousand residents worked in some capacity for the Santa Fe, which meant a payroll often exceeding one-hundred thousand dollars per month. Albuquerque was the chief terminal point between Topeka and Los Angeles, and the Santa Fe owned millions of dollars worth of property in the city, operated fifty miles of tracks in its yards, handled at least a dozen passenger trains a day, and millions of dollars worth of freight traffic annually. The Santa Fe also put forth a tremendous amount of regional and national advertising, detailing the many attractions of Albuquerque and New Mexico.[19]

The railroads, along with Albuquerque's central location and facilities, brought people and business to the oasis from all directions. In February 1812 the *Morning Journal* noted:

Albuquerque's location is strategic: midway of the great valley of the Rio Grande which stretches through the state from north to south; midway between the great mining and timber districts of north and south, east and west; midway between the great farming districts of the eastern half and the limitless grazing lands of the west; radii drawn out from this city terminate in countless smaller centers of growth and development, and these radii are rapidly materializing year by year into lines of steel over which the products of the soil and forests and mines come into Albuquerque.[20]

Albuquerque Museum Photoarchives

The Santa Fe RR Station and Alvarado Hotel, Albuquerque, NM, the heart of "New Town" and symbolic of the largest industry in the city until the arrival of Sandia Laboratories and the decline of the railroad.

Kirtland Air Force Base Historical Office, USAF

The original Albuquerque Airport buildings about 1930, still in use in 1979. The coming of air transport made cities of the Southwest accessible for vacation and business as they had never been before.

Albuquerque increased its standing as the dominant city in the territory year by year, and when New Mexico became a state in 1912, its status as the "Queen City of the Rio Grande" was enhanced. Some writers, however, directing their comments from points east, could not understand how much a small city could be the leading urban center in the new state. The *Morning Journal* tried to explain:

In an eastern state a town the size of Albuquerque would be relatively unimportant; in the southwest it is a metropolis with all the features of and importance of a city of 100,000 in the east. You will strike no other city as large as this nearer than El Paso, 250 miles south, Colorado an equal distance north, Phoenix, Arizona, 500 miles southwest, or a city well into the interior of Texas on the east. In other words Albuquerque has the leading place as to size and importance in a territory fully 500 miles square.[21]

In the Rio Grande Valley running thirty miles north and thirty miles south of Albuquerque water was applied to the land by an irrigation system utilizing the most modern methods, and local promoters boasted that the valley offered the "heaviest returns on scientific farming to be secured anywhere in the country." They also advised prospective newcomers of the coal, copper, zinc, lead and gold mines located in the vicinity, and noted that most mining companies in New Mexico headquartered in Albuquerque. In addition the city developed as a manufacturing center with wool and lumber concerns leading the way. The city also gained from its reputation as a health center. Local boosters conducted a nationwide campaign to attract more health seekers, and by the end of the 1920's the health industry was second only to the Santa Fe railroad as a source of income in the city.[22]

In 1889 the legislators chose Albuquerque as the site of the Territorial University of New Mexico. The school opened in 1892, and Albuquerque became the educational center of the state. From the primary to the university level the city offered the best facilities and programs in New Mexico, and when statehood arrived in 1912 the University of New Mexico received over three hundred thousand dollars worth of grants from the federal government. From that year on progress was steady as the campus expanded to over three hundred acres, several impressive buildings were erected, and the enrollment rose from 99 in 1912 to 348 in 1919 to 1,001 in 1930.[23]

Camp Funston was constructed and opened in 1917 to train soldiers for service in World War I, and in that same year the federal government established a branch office in Albuquerque to represent a number of its departments. Both developments boosted the city's population and economy, and strengthened the relationship between Albuquerque and the national government, pointing the way to the future. At the same time the commission-manager form of local government, adopted by Albuquerque in 1917, brought improvements to the city, expanding services and achieving more efficiency.[24]

As a transportation hub with many regional and national highways leading into and out of it, Albuquerque became a supply and service center for motorists. In the city auto ownership and bus service increased rapidly during the 1920's, eliminating the streetcar system and contributing to urban sprawl. In addition the oasis became the distribution center of the new trucking industry in the state; trucks not only gave overnight delivery anywhere in New Mexico, but they also penetrated areas not served by the railroad. The city became an aviation crossroads with the opening of Albuquerque Airport in 1928. Because of its climate and geography, the place was considered an ideal site for a major stop on a transcontinental air route from New York to Los Angeles and that service was in operation by the end of 1929. The urban center, moreover, had experienced a steady growth in population during the decade, increasing from 15,157 in 1920 to 26,570 in 1930.[25]

In 1776 by the Santa Cruz River in the Santa Cruz Valley on the northern frontier of New Spain, Spanish troops established the military post of Tucson. The presence of the soldier fostered local settlement, and in time the presidio became a walled village surrounded by fields of crops and herds of livestock. The troops, civilians and friendly Pima Indians supported peace in the 1780's, the Tucson community began to enjoy an era of growth and prosperity that lasted until the 1820's.[26]

But then, following Mexico's independence from Spain, peaceful Apaches reverted to their old ways, and joined hostile Apaches in making life more difficult and dangerous for residents of Tucson. The development of the oasis now proved slow, and in 1846 matters grew worse when war broke out between the United States and Mexico. American troops, meeting no resistance, entered Tucson during the conflict, but the town remained a part of Mexico until the Gadsden Purchase was ratified in 1854.[27]

In the late 1850's Anglos joined Mexicans in Tucson, and the town became the supply depot and distribution point for area forts, farms, ranches and mines. Stage and freight lines maintained contact with the outside world, and Tucson attracted its share of "undesirables," but the most critical problem proved to be the disruption caused by the Civil War. During most of that conflict Union forces occupied the town, and following the war their continued presence inhibited the Apache threat, and Tucson once again became the service center for area civilians and soldiers.[28]

The seat of Pima County, Tucson became the capital of Arizona Territory in 1867. It lost that distinction to Prescott in 1877, but being the "commercial *entrepôt* of Arizona and the remoter Southwest," the oasis continued to grow and prosper. By 1878 Tucson was busy preparing for the arrival of the Southern Pacific railroad, and soon the *Arizona Star* proclaimed:

It is now a settled fact that the city of Tucson is to be the future metropolis of the great Southwest. Railroads, agriculture, mining and stockraising will produce this result, situated as it is upon the direct transcontinental route and the intersecting point of several others, and surrounded upon all sides with the most wonderful mineral ledges known to exist within the United States. In fact, we are the heart of the mineral wealth for sixty miles in every direction. No other spot could be selected in the country which has so many strong points, for we are also the center of grazing interests. North, south and east, thousands of cattle greet the eye of the traveler, and the agricultural products circulate to our city for consumers. From a population of 3,500 we have suddenly advanced to 7,000 and this about two-fifths American. Small retail mercantile houses have become large wholesale and retail establishments.

Specialties in trade are being established, such as wholesale houses in the various branches of business. Manufacturers are being planted in our midst, while banking and real estate dealers have become a part of the established business. Old and new residents are beautifying their homes, while schemes to furnish gas and water for the city fill the air, and the peanut-vendor and the boot-black fill a happy little niche in our onward progress.[29]

In March of 1880 the first Southern Pacific train pulled into the new Tucson depot to a gala reception; the *Star* called it "the most memorable and happy jubilee ever witnessed in this ancient and honorable Pueblo." While the Southern Pacific moved eastward to El Paso, Tucson enjoyed the benefits of being a new railroad center, and the largest city between San Antonio and Los Angeles. Anglos dominated local life, and in 1882 one observer noted that "Tuscon had changed the most appreciably of any town in the Southwest; American energy and capital had effected a wonderful transformation." As a result Anglo-Mexican relations deteriorated.[30]

Tucson's economy declined during the 1880's. With the end of the Apache wars United States troops left the area and the town lost the lucrative military trade. At the same time the collapse of the silver boom in Tombstone and other nearby mining districts had a deleterious effect on Tucson's economy, while periodic droughts and floods limited stockraising and agricultural production in the area. A general climate of business stagnation prevailed, and the population dropped from 7,007 in 1880 to 5,150 in 1890; in 1900 it reached 7,531.[31]

The depression slowed Tucson's rise, but progress occurred. In 1885 the city acquired the Territorial University, destined to become one of its greatest assets in the 1890's. During that decade hinterland activity increased, and the city enjoyed a mild business revival as it continued to be the service center for a sizeable

Arizona Historical Society
Typical resort hotel: El Conquistador in the 1920s, Tucson, Arizona.

region. In the 1890's Tucson's reputation as a health center and winter resort grew and the railroad provided a means of access to the city of "pure air and almost perpetual sunshine." In 1890 the *Arizona Daily Citizen*, noting "the health value of our climate," predicted that "the time is not far distant when it will have a world wide reputation." In 1903 the *Star* could state that "Tucson is known far and wide for two quite distinct reasons: First as a health and pleasure resort, and second as the center of the extensive agriculture, stock-raising, and mining industry of southern Arizona."[32]

The El Paso and Southwestern Railroad brought competition to the Southern Pacific with construction into Tucson in the early 1900's; moreover, a new Tucson to Nogales line facilitated travel to Mexico. Additional railroads made Tucson a more effective service center for area interests, notably the copper mines, cotton farms, and cattle ranches. The city also improved its resort facilities, now including "dude ranches," and by the 1920's Tucson booster organizations advertised the place as "The Sunshine Center of Arizona, the Climate City of the Nation." Another

Arizona Historical Society

Old Main, University of Arizona, Tucson, ca. 1900.

asset, the University of Arizona, became the largest institution of its kind in the Southwest; enrollment climbed from 225 in 1900 to 1,171 in 1920 to 2,164 in 1930.[33]

The "unsettled conditions" caused by the Mexican Revolution limited Tucson's business south of the border, but the loss was offset by World War I prosperity. In the 1920's economic relations with Mexico improved, but the ratio of Mexicans to Anglos in Tucson continued to decline. In 1878 about sixty-seven percent of the inhabitants were of Mexican descent, and by 1901 Mexicans represented about fifty percent of the population. Between 1900 and 1910 the Anglos gained a numerical advantage and they never lost it; by 1930 Mexicans made up but thirty-one percent of the total. As more Anglos arrived in the city they remained in the older neighborhoods south of the tracks. Throughout the period the economic and social distance between the two groups widened.[34]

Significant changes within Tucson during the 1920's included more automobiles and buses, and the decline of the streetcar system. The city became a car sales and service center as "hordes of motorists" traveled into and out of the transportation crossroads, and "auto tourists" spent a million dollars a year in the desert oasis. Air traffic also increased during the decade, and by 1927 Tucson contained two excellent airports, making it an aviation center in the Southwest.[35]

The population of the city rose from 13,193 in 1910 to 20,292 in 1920. In that year Phoenix reached 29,053, and outnumbered Tucson for the first time, but the "metropolis of southern Arizona" survived as an important urban center. In the 1920's Tucson joined in the nationwide boom, and its population jumped to 32,506 in 1930, a sixty percent increase during the decade. The physical expansion of the oasis proceeded apace, and there occurred advances in city services, especially in the structure of local government, public education, the water system, and recreation facilities. In addition the city remained the seat of Pima County, and it served as headquarters for several state and federal agencies.[36]

Compared to El Paso, Albuquerque and Tucson, Phoenix was a latecomer to the southwestern urban frontier. In 1867 a few Anglo pioneers from the small mining camp of Wickenburg moved fifty miles southeast into the Salt River Valley in central Arizona, admired the remains of the canal system of the ancient Hohokam Indian civilization, and sensed the agricultural possibilities of the area. Homesteading land near the Salt, clearing out old irrigation ditches and building new ones, planting crops and negotiating supply contracts with nearby military posts and mining camps, those first settlers, soon followed by others, created an economic base from which to grow and develop.[37]

In 1870 the settlers, numbering about two hundred,

selected a townsite near the geographical center of the valley, and realizing that they were revitalizing the land of an ancient agricultural people, they named it Phoenix, in their view a fitting symbol of life rising anew from the remains of the past. Growth was slow but steady, and by 1872 the valley contained over one thousand residents, one-third of whom lived in Phoenix. By now the seat of Maricopa County, the optimism of the inhabitants was mirrored in the description of Phoenix as "a smart town." One booster predicted that "when it has become the capital of the territory, and when the 'iron horse' steams through our country, the Salt River Valley will be the garden of the Pacific Slope, and Phoenix the most important inland town."[38]

By 1880 Phoenix, population 1,708, was a thriving service center for an active hinterland that included the Salt River Valley, the "most fertile and productive in the Territory" and a superb example of irrigation agriculture at work. Mexicans made up a large part of the unskilled labor force, but Anglos dominated the community. For the most part Mexicans lived apart from the Anglos and they experienced little contact with them except in a subordinate role. Unlike El Paso, Albuquerque and Tucson, Phoenix from the beginning was run by Anglos for Anglos.[39]

During the 1880's the desert oasis enhanced its standing as an urban center by securing a railroad and becoming the capital of Arizona Territory. In July of 1887 a twenty-six mile branch line of the Southern Pacific, the Maricopa and Phoenix, was completed north to the town, thus connecting it to the outside world. In January of 1889 the importance of Phoenix was recognized by the legislature when it removed the capital from Prescott to Phoenix; the move proved to be permanent. The coming of the railroad and the acquisition of the capital, along with the agricultural and commercial progress of the place pleased local promoters and outside investors, and they boosted Phoenix as "the future metropolis of Arizona."[40]

By 1890 some observers were calling Phoenix "the Denver of the Southwest" for they believed that "the wonderful growth and progress of the 'Queen City of the Plains' is to be more than duplicated in the garden belt of Arizona." Actually, growth and development continued to be slow but steady, with the population reaching 3,152 in 1890 and 5,544 in 1900. In February of 1895 another branch railroad, the Santa Fe, Prescott and Phoenix, connected with the Santa Fe main line running across northern Arizona, thus the city enjoyed access to two transcontinental outlets. Among other beneficial services to Phoenix, the railroads provided transportation for the increasing number of health seekers and winter tourists seeking relief and relaxation in the sun. In 1890 it was asserted that "in Phoenix can be found the usual conveniences of Eastern cities," plus some amenities, notably the climate, unavailable in them.[41]

A number of small agricultural towns surrounding Phoenix, including Tempe, Mesa and Glendale, had emerged by 1900 but none of them listed a population exceeding one thousand residents, and none of them ever threatened the prominence of the capital city; it served as the leading urban center in the area, a hub of economic, political, social and cultural activity. Along with progress, however, came problems, especially those dealing with water. Late in the 1890's a severe drought hit the valley, forcing thousands of acres out of cultivation, and many farmers and city dwellers, feeling defeated, moved away in search of a new "garden of the Pacific Slope." Those who remained recognized that progress resulting from growth was doomed unless they solved the water problem. After much debate, they decided that a water storage system was the answer. Joining together, residents formed the Salt River Valley Water Users' Association and this organization, taking advantage of the National Reclamation Act of 1902, supported the federal government in the construction of nearby Roosevelt Dam, completed in 1911. This and similar endeavors brought vital stability, allowed irrigation control, assured agricultural growth, and as the valley prospered so did Phoenix.[42]

With the development of a stable water supply and distribution system, the valley bloomed and Phoenix boomed. The population of the city reached 11,134 in 1910, and the following decaded it almost tripled to 29,053; indeed, by1920 Phoenix had surpassed Tucson in official population, and it was the largest and most important urban center in Arizona. The demands of American participation in World War I and a "cotton craze" in the valley contributed to the boom; also as a service center, the oasis city continued to serve the expanding Phoenix population as well as a vast hinterland of small towns, farms, ranches and mines. The commission-manager government, adopted in 1914, and private developers tried to meet the needs of local residents, including the ongoing influx of newcomers, who were convinced that Phoenix was bound to be "the big city which is to be built between Los Angles and El Paso."[43]

In the 1920's the four "C's" — climate, cotton, cattle and copper — continued to contribute to the advancement of Phoenix and the Salt River Valley. The climate, for example, made the area one of the most inviting winter resort centers in the country, and affluent visitors flocked to the Westward Ho, the Arizona Biltmore and other luxury hotels. The city "where winter never comes" became known as "Delightful Phoenix, the Garden Spot of the Southwest." The desert oasis also became more accessible with the arrival of a Southern Pacific main line in 1926, and the inauguration of scheduled airline service in 1927; these means of transportation made it easier for people to respond to the opportunities and amenities available in the Phoenix area. At the same time local promoters tried to attract affluent Anglo-Americans. As the Chamber of

Arizona Historical Society
The State Capitol Building, Phoenix, about 1900. Winning the battle for the capital affected the rivalry between Phoenix and Tucson in the former's favor.

Arizona Historical Society
Roosevelt Dam on the Salt River Project outside of Phoenix made water available for the Valley.

Arizona Historical Society
An aerial view of Phoenix about 1928. This does less than justice to what later became a "one-floor" city.

Commerce put it, "Phoenix is a modern town . . . and the best kind of people, too. A very small percentage of Mexicans, negroes, or foreigners." Mexicans made up the largest minority group in the city; they numbered 7,293 or 15.2 percent of the population in 1930. Most of them worked cheap labor jobs and lived in the poor neighborhoods of south Phoenix.[44]

During the decade the popularity of the automobile and the bus sent the Phoenix streetcar system into a decline from which it never recovered. As more people and autos arrived, the city experienced increased urban sprawl, considered by residents to be the urban form of the future. Like Tucson, 115 miles to the southeast, Phoenix became a distribution point for the trucking industry in the state. At the same time the city remained a cultural center; it contained "the best of schools" and churches of every denomination, and Arizona State Normal School, later Arizona State University, was located in nearby Tempe. By 1930 Phoenix was a regional urban center of 48,118 inhabitants, the largest city in the Southwest between El Paso and Los Angeles, and local leaders felt justified in calling the desert oasis "truly the capital of Arizona, the hub of new developments. The storehouse and supply house of the state. As Phoenix goes, so goes Arizona."[45]

With the coming of the railroads in the 1880's, the four towns gained great impetus for growth and their populations increased considerably. Railroad contact with the outside world also helped them to overcome rivals and expand as service centers for vast hinterlands. Their development facilitated the refinement of the Southwest, and they played a large role in civilizing the region. They became the home of business districts, military posts and state universities. Stores and factories, schools and churches, banks and hotels, hospitals and court houses, theatres and saloons, and a number of other urban institutions served the people of the four cities and their surrounding areas.

Certain amenities available in the Southwest attracted people to the four centers. The climate, for example, lured visitors as well as permanent residents. Promoters worked diligently to develop El Paso, Albuquerque, Tucson and Phoenix into "ideal places" for those looking for amenities as well as opportunities. Each decade thousands of people from other parts of the country made their way to the sunshine cities of the Southwest in search of "the good life."

Among the successful in the rising cities were those who became effective leaders and boosters of the desert centers. Members of the local business and civic elite who were willing to fuse private interests with community interests, they often directed, with growth and development in mind, the economic, political and cultural life of their respective oases.

The developers of the southwestern urban frontier secured not only advantages especially useful to their cities and the outlying areas, such as water conservation systems, but they also adopted a host of amenities common to cities elsewhere, including street and park development, and other technological innovations. Southwestern urbanites were quick to accept the automobile as a primary mode of transportation. In each of the desert hubs, use of the auto and the bus sent streetcar systems into a decline from which they never recovered. In the four centers, reliance on the automobile and the bus contributed to suburban growth, an urban form considered by residents to be part of "the good life" available to them and others wise enough to move to the cities of the Southwest. In addition, each of the transportation crossroads embraced the airplane and its potential, and they soon became aviation centers.

As the cities evolved and became more "American" there occurred a decline in Anglo-Mexican relations. The Anglos achieved a dominant position in each community, and as they acquired more wealth, power and prestige, they dictated the terms of the ethnic arrangement, one that invariably found the majority of the Mexicans and Mexican-Americans living on the "wrong side of the tracks." For the majority of Hispanics, like the Blacks and Native Americans, upward mobility proved elusive, and poverty remained the norm.

By 1930 El Paso, Albuquerque, Tucson and Phoenix had established themselves as the leading urban centers in the Southwest. Oasis cities, they had acted as spearheads of the desert frontier, and over the years they had exerted an important influence on the development of west Texas, New Mexico and Arizona. The four cities represented the focal points around which the Southwest flourished, and they would maintain their significance in the future; indeed, in the 1930's they would suffer less from the Great Depression than many of their counterparts elsewhere, and during and following World War II they would experience an economic boom and population explosion that would thrust them toward metropolis status.[46]

Bradford Luckingham is Associate Professor of History at Arizona State University, Tempe, Arizona. A graduate of Northern Arizona University, he received his MA from the University of Missouri, Columbia, and his Ph. D. from the University of California, Davis. He has written numerous publications on various western urban history topics.

NOTES

The author wishes to express gratitude to Arizona State University for a 1977 summer grant.

1. D.W. Meinig, *Southwest: Three Peoples in Geographical Change, 1600-1970* (New York, 1971), 3-8.

2. Anne E. Hughes, *The Beginnings of Spanish Settlement in the El Paso District* (Berkeley, 1914), 305-308; Nancy Lee Hammons, "A History of El Paso County, Texas to 1900" (MA thesis, University of Texas, El Paso, 1942), 27-38; C.L. Sonnichsen, *Pass of the North: Four Centuries on the Rio Grande* (El Paso, 1968), 105-106.

3. *Ibid.*, 107-153; Owen White, *Out of the Desert: The Historical Romance of El Paso* (El Paso, 1923), 44-46; *El Paso Herald-Post*, May 28, 1936; *El Paso Times*, April 29, 1956.

4. Sonnichsen, *Pass of the North*, 154-167, 211-230; *El Paso Times*, January 2, 1890, November 6, 1936, April 28, 1956; *El Paso Herald-Post*, May 28, 1936, April 28, 1956; Joseph Leach, "Farewell to Horseback, Muleback, 'Footback' and Prairie Schooner: The Railroad Comes to Town," *Password*, 1 (May, 1956), 34-44; Lillian Hague Corcoran, "He Brought the Railroads to El Paso — The Story of Judge James P. Hague," *Password*, 1 (May, 1956), 45-54.

5. Clyde Wise, Jr., "The Effects of the Railroads Upon El Paso," *Password*, 5 (July, 1950), 91-100; Mildred L. Jordan, "Railroads in the El Paso Area" (MA thesis, University of Texas, El Paso, 1957), *passim*; Sonnichsen, *Pass of the North*, 225, 249-276; Hammons, "History of El Paso County," 137-153.

6. Nadine Hale Prestwood, "The Social Life and Customs of the People of El Paso, 1848-1910" (MA thesis, University of Texas, El Paso, 1949), 29-47; Sonnichsen, *Pass of the North*, 231-248, 277-287, 310-347; White, *Out of the Desert*, 178-186; Eugene O. Porter, "No Dark and Cold and Dreary Days — El Paso, Texas as a Health Resort," *Password*, 4 (April, 1959), 71-78; Richard McMaster, *Musket, Saber & Missile: A History of Fort Bliss* (El Paso, 1962), 36; Rosalie Ivey, "A History of Fort Bliss" (MA thesis, University of Texas, Austin, 1942), 49-55.

7. Pierre W. Berringer, "El Paso — the Gateway to Mexico," *Overland Monthly*, 55 (July, 1910), 120-135; Oscar J. Martinez, *Border Boom Town: Ciudad Juárez since 1848* (Austin, 1978), 32-33.

8. *Ibid.*, 34-37; Mario Trinidad Garciá, "Obreros: The Mexican Workers of El Paso, 1900-1920" (PhD dissertation, University of California, San Diego, 1975), *passim*; Mardee DeWetter, "Revolutionary El Paso, 1910-1917" (MA thesis, University of Texas, El Paso, 1946), *passim*; Department of Planning, City of El Paso, *A Short History of South El Paso* (El Paso, 1967), 13-23.

9. McMaster, *Fort Bliss*, 38-44; Ivey, *Fort Bliss*, 55-60; *El Paso Times*, April 29, 1956, Francis L. Fugate, *Frontier College: Texas Western at El Paso, The First Fifty Years* (El Paso, 1964), 3-55.

10. Martinez, *Juárez*, 57-59; C.L. Sonnichsen and M.G. McKinney, "El Paso from War to Depression," *Southwestern Historical Quarterly*, 64 (January, 1971), 363-369; George Marvin, "El Paso del Norte," *Outlook*, 145 (June 17, 1925), 251-254; Ruth Harris, *Geography of El Paso County* (El Paso, 1930), 14-17, 30-35; *El Paso Times*, April 29, 1956; *El Paso Herald Post*, April 28, 1956.

11. Harris, *Geography of El Paso County*, 30-31, 36; *Christian Science Monitor*, October 11, 1924; Martinez, *Juárez*, 62-64; *El Paso Times*, August 31, 1920, May 16, 1923, September 26, 1930, April 29, 1956; *El Paso Herald-Post*, May 28, 1936, April 28, 1956.

12. *El Paso Times*, September 9, 1928, September 26, 1930, April 29, 1956; *El Paso Herald-Post*, May 28, 1936, April 28, 1956; Harris, *Geography of El Paso County*, 36.

13. Richard E. Greenleaf, "The Founding of Albuquerque, 1706: An Historical-Legal Problem," *New Mexico Historical Review*, 39 (January, 1969), 5-11; Fray Angelico Chavez, "The Albuquerque Story — The First Century," *New Mexico Magazine*, 34 (January, 1956), 22-23, 50; *Albuquerque Tribune*, July 1, 1935, July 4, 1956.

14. *Ibid.*; Chavez, "The Albuquerque Story," *New Mexico Magazine*, 50-51; Fremont Kutnewsky, "From Conquistador to Metropolis," *New Mexico Magazine*, 39 (October, 1960), 18; Alan J. Oppenheimer, *The Historical Background of Albuquerque, New Mexico* (Albuquerque, 1962), 13-22; Paul Horgan, *Great River: The Rio Grande in North American History* (New York, 1954), I, 380-386.

15. Baldwin Mollhausen, *Diary of a Journey from the Mississippi to the Coasts of the Pacific* (London, 1858), II, 9-10; W. W. H. Davis, *El Gringo: or, New Mexico and Her People* (Santa Fe, 1938), 195; Amy Passmore Hurt, "Albuquerque, Old and New," *New Mexico Magazine*, 12 (March, 1934), 8-9; Howard Bryan, "From Wagon Train to Railroad," *Enchantorama* (Albuquerque, 1956), 42; F. Stanley, *The Duke City* (Pampa, Texas, 1963), 71-80.

16. Victor Westphall, "Albuquerque in the 1870's," *New Mexico Historical Review*, 23 (October, 1948), 253-268; Terry Lehman, "Santa Fe and Albuquerque 1870-1900: Conflict in the Development of Two Southwestern Towns" (PhD dissertation, Indiana University, 1974), 124-190; *Albuquerque Review*, April 24, 1880; Lucille Boyle, "The Economic History of Albuquerque 1880-1893" (MA thesis, University of New Mexico, 1948), 3-20.

17. *Ibid.*; Lehman, "Santa Fe and Albuquerque," 140-190; Bernice Ann Rebord, "A Social History of Albuquerque, 1880-1885" (MA thesis, University of New Mexico, 1947), 4-18; Joyce Jane Balch, Jacob Korber, "Early Businessman of Albuquerque, New Mexico, 1881-1921" (MA thesis, University of New Mexico, 1955), 9-11; William C. Ritch, *Aztlan, the History of Attractions in New Mexico* (Boston, 1885), 91-93.

18. Lehman, "Santa Fe and Albuquerque," 157-158, 166-190, 245-270; Gladys Neel, "History (Political) of Albuquerque" (MA thesis, University of New Mexico, 1928), 9-17; Erna Fergusson, *Albuquerque* (Albuquerque, 1947), 18-20; Carolyn Zeleny, "Relations Between the Spanish-Americans and Anglo-Americans in New Mexico" (PhD dissertation, Yale University, 1944), 230-231; Miguel A. Otero, *My Nine Years as Governor of the Territory of New Mexico, 1897-1906* (Albuquerque, 1940), 67-73. As Table A shows, by 1900 Albuquerque had won its urban rivalry with Santa Fe.

19. Charles Raitt, "Albuquerque, Past and Present," *Santa Fe Magazine*, 3 (May, 1910), 630-631; *Albuquerque Morning Journal*, February 12, 1912.

20. *Ibid.*

21. *Ibid.*

22. *Ibid.*; *Albuquerque Tribune*, July 1, 1935; Erna Fergusson, *Our Southwest* (New York, 1940), 227-244.

23. *Albuquerque Daily Citizen*, December 31, 1890; Fergusson, *Albuquerque*, 19-20; Stanley, *Duke City*, 83-106.

24. *Albuquerque Tribune*, July 1, 1935, July 4, 1956; Neel "History of Albuquerque," 65-92; Oppenheimer, *Historical Background*, 41.

25. *Ibid.*, 41-42, 47; *Albuquerque Tribune*, July 1, 1935; Roy Stamm, "First Autos in Albuquerque," *New Mexico Magazine*, 31 (February, 1953), 14-15; Erna Fergusson, "Albuquerque," in Ray B. West, ed., *Rocky Mountain Cities* (New York, 1949), 160-162; Kutnewsky, "From Conquistador to Metropolis," *New Mexico Magazine*, 39.

26. Henry F. Dobyns, *Spanish Colonial Tucson: A Demographic History* (Tucson, 1976), 55-113; Bernice Cosulich, *Tucson*, (Tucson, 1953), 59-61; Sidney B. Brinkerhoff, "The Last Years of Spanish Arizona, 1786-1821," *Arizona and the West*, 9 (Spring, 1967), 10-20.

27. *Ibid.*; Dobyns, *Spanish Colonial Tucson*, 124, 129-130, 201; Cosulich, *Tucson*, 64-68, 87-91; Edward P. Murray, "Tucson: Genesis of a Community," *History Today*, 17 (1967), 843-844; Cameron Greenleaf and Andrew Wallace, "Tucson: Pueblo, Presidio, and American City: A Synopsis of its History," *Arizoniana*, 3 (Summer, 1962), 23.

28. *Ibid.*; 23-24; Cosulich, *Tucson*, 101-107, 197-208; Jay J. Wagoner, *Early Arizona* (Tucson, 1975), 392-401; Frank C. Lockwood and Donald C. Page, *Tucson: The Old Pueblo* (Phoenix, 1930), 34-39; James Officer, "Historical Factors in Interethnic Relations in the Community of Tucson," *Arizoniana*, 1 (Fall, 1960), 13-14; W. Clement Eaton, "Frontier Life in Southern Arizona, 1858-1961," *Southwestern Historical Quarterly*, 26 (January, 1933), 173-192; J. Ross Browne, *A Tour Through Arizona, 1864, or Adventures in the Apache Country* (New York, 1864; Tucson, 1951), 131-139.

29. Cosulich, *Tucson*, 180-181; George H. Kelly, comp., *Legislative History: Arizona, 1864-1912* (Phoenix, 1926), 25-26, 34, 67-70; John Gregory Bourke, *On the Border with Crook* (New York, 1891, 1962), 56. *Arizona Star*, May 23, 1878, February 13, 1879.

30. *Arizona Star*, May 23, 1878, February 13, 1879, June 21, 22, 26, 1879, March 21, 25, 1880; Bourke, *On the Border With Crook*, 450; James Officer, "Sodalities and Systemic Linkage: The Joining Habits of Urban Mexican-Americans" (PhD dissertation, University of Arizona, 1964), 51-58.

31. *Ibid.; Arizona Daily Citizen*, January 1, 1890.

32. Kelly, *Legislative History*, 305-318; Douglas D. Martin, *The Lamb in the Desert: The Story of the University of Arizona* (Tucson, 1960), 22-56; John A. Black, *Arizona: The Land Of Sunshine and Silver, Health and Prosperity, The Place of Ideal Homes* (Tucson, 1890), 71-89; *Arizona Daily Citizen*, January 1, 1890, January 1, 1895; *Arizona Daily Star*, November 26, 1903.

33. David F. Myrick, *Railroads of Arizona: Vol. 1, The Southern Roads* (Berkeley, 1975), 226-231, 303-384, *passim; Tucson Daily Citizen*, September 15, October 1, 1922; *Arizona Daily Star*, August 15, 1915, October 21, 1927, February 22, 1929, February 22, 1930, February 21, 1931.

34. *Arizona Daily Star*, August 15, 1915, February 21, 1936; Officer, Urban Mexican-Americans, 53-61; Harry Getty, "International Relationship in the Community of Tucson" (PhD dissertation, University of Chicago, 1949), 138.

35. *Arizona Daily Star*, August 15, 1915, February 22, March 26, 1929, February 22, 1930, February 21, 1936; *Tucson Daily Citizen*, October 11, 1929.

36. *Ibid.; Arizona Daily Star*, February 22, March 26, 1929, February 22, 1931.

37. Geoffrey P. Mawn, "Promoters, Speculators, and Selection of the Phoenix Townsite," *Arizona and the West*, 19 (Fall, 1977), 207-224; Charles S. Sargent, "Towns of the Salt River Valley, 1870-1930," *Historical Geography*, 5 (Fall, 1975), 103.

38. *Ibid.*; Mawn, "Townsite," *Arizona and the West*, 221; Joseph P. Miller, *Arizona: The Grand Canyon State* (New York, 1966), 220.

39. Patrick Hamilton, *The Resources of Arizona* (San Francisco, 1884), 80-84; Shirley J. Roberts, "Minority-Group Poverty in Phoenix," *Journal of Arizona History*, 14 (Winter, 1973), 347-350.

40. William S. Greever, "Railway Development in the Southwest," *New Mexico Historical Review*, 32 (April, 1957), 168-172; David F. Myrick, *Pioneer Arizona Railroads* (Golden, Colorado, 1968), 24; Kelly, *Legislative History*, 132-135; Black, *Arizona: The Land of Sunshine and Silver, Health and Prosperity, The Place of Ideal Homes*, 54-66.

41. Sargent, "Towns of the Salt River Valley," *Historical Geography*, 3; Myrick, *Pioneer Arizona Railroads*, 14; Greever, "Railway Development," *New Mexico Historical Review*, 168-172; Geoffrey P. Mawn, "Phoenix, Arizona: Central City of the Southwest, 1870-1920" (PhD dissertation, Arizona State University, 1979), *passim*; Sidney R. DeLong, *The History of Arizona to 1903* (San Francisco, 1905), 117-124.

42. Sargent, "Towns of the Salt River Valley," *Historical Geography*, 3-5; Stephen C. Shadegg, *Century One: One Hundred Years of Water Development in the Salt River Valley* (Phoenix, 1969), 10-19; "Water for Phoenix: Building the Roosevelt Dam," *Journal of Arizona History*, 18 (Autumn, 1977), 279-294; H. L. Meredith, "Reclamation in the Salt River Valley, 1902-1917." *Journal of the West*, 7 (January, 1968), 76-83.

43. Mawn, Phoenix, *passim*; Sargent, "Towns of Salt River Valley," *Historical Geography*, 4-6; Joseph C. McGowen, *History of Extra-Long Staple Cottons* (El Paso, 1961), 79-92; Daniel C. Davis, Phoenix, 1907-1913 (Seminar paper, History Department, Arizona State University, 1976), 44-46, 75; Mark Passolt, Phoenix, 1914-1919 (Seminar paper, History Department, Arizona State University, 1976), 10-15, 24-30.

44. Gaylord M. McGrath, The Evolution of Resorts and Guest Ranches in Greater Phoenix (Seminar paper, Geography Department, Arizona State University, 1973), 3-11; Greever, "Railway Development," *New Mexico Historical Review*, 186; *Arizona Republican*, December 26, 1926, December 25, 1927, December 30, 1928, December 29, 1929; *Arizona Republic*, February 25, 1931; *Phoenix City and Salt River Valley Directory, 1920* (Los Angeles, 1920), 3; Roberts, "Poverty in Phoenix," *Journal of Arizona History*, 348-354; Anthony C. Chapelle, "Phoenix, 1920-1925" (Seminar paper, History Department, Arizona State University, 1976), 28, 50-54.

45. *Ibid.*, 79-81; Sam Leopold, "Declaration of Dependence: The Impact of the Automobile on Phoenix in the 1920's" (Seminar paper, History Department, Arizona State University, 1977), *passim; Phoenix City and Salt River Directory, 1930* (Los Angeles, 1930), *passim; Arizona Republican*, May 12, 1920, May 8, 1921, April 30, 1922, December 28, 1924, December 27, 1925, December 26, 30, 1926, November 17, 23, December 12, 15, 1927, December 15, 30, 1928, February 23, June 9, December 29, 1929; *Arizona Republic*, February 25, 1931, November 18, 1934.

46. See the author's forthcoming study entitled "Cities of the Southwest: The Rise of El Paso, Albuquerque, Tucson and Phoenix, 1659-1960."

Downtown Houston in 1905. Men and money poured into the city following the gusher at Spindletop four years earlier.

Houston At The Crossroads:
The Emergence of The Urban Center of The Southwest

Harold L. Platt

Current responses to the mushroom growth of the "Sunbelt" cities have given new emphasis to concepts of regionalism. Because contemporary technology and culture have virtually erased the boundaries between urban, suburban, and rural, today's urbanologist is becoming a regional planner. Fresh perspectives on the regional configurations of growth are also encouraging scholars to take a closer look at the relationship of town and country in the past. Until recently, however, historians highlighted only the contrasts that separated urban and rural areas into mutually antagonistic groups. Several popular studies of the city slicker versus the country bumpkin have reinforced a literary tradition which reflected real but one-sided views of the city's ties with its surrounding hinterland.[1] A more balanced picture is now appearing, as previously ignored facets of regional history, especially the intimate economic, demographic, and political bonds of the city and the countryside are given more careful scrutiny. These investigations show that the reciprocal interactions of town and country collectively molded a characteristic pattern of development for every section and stamped a unique imprint of regional culture on each of them.[2]

The origins of Houston's rise to the preeminent position in the Southwest throw important new light on the regional context of urban growth. Before 1901, neither the Bayou City nor its old nemesis, Galveston, could fairly claim to be the central place of the Texas Gulf Coast in spite of over fifty years of rivalry for this coveted title. Unlike New York in the East, Chicago in the Midwest, and Denver in the Rocky Mountains, no city in Texas had emerged that clearly dominated the vast hinterland of the area. Then, two spectacular chance events in close succession — a hurricane and an oil gusher — dramatically overturned the local balance of power in favor of the Bayou City. The first, the devastating storm and tidal wave of September 1900, literally eliminated the island port of Galveston, but not its regional economic functions of trade and transportation. These the safer, inland entrepôt eagerly absorbed — Galveston's loss was Houston's gain. Only four months later, the surprising discovery of an ocean of black gold under the coastal plain rapidly boosted the nearest urban base, Houston, into national prominence. These two quirks of nature set off a still uninterrupted surge of growth that insured Houston's place as the commercial hub of the Southwest's agricultural wealth as well as the industrial headquarters of the nation's energy business.

The upheaval on the Texas Gulf Coast in the early 1900s offers an useful test case for analyzing the interdependence among the cities and the countryside of a region. Long term trends of the section's urbanization

before the storm can be measured quantitatively against sudden shifts which followed in the wake of the catastrophe. In addition, the juxtaposition of a crucial new ingredient, the oil boom, provides a means of accurately assessing the qualitative impacts of both radical changes on the responsible decision-makers. Their reactions inhibited the recovery of Galveston in irreversible ways. By 1910, the inland rival gained such an indisputable command over the economy of the local area that its power began affecting the larger balance of forces in the region. Although Houston's emergence as the urban center of the Southwest remained somewhat obscured until 1930, the crossroads towards that goal had been passed at the turn of the century.

From their founding in the 1830s to the dawn of the 1900s, Houston and Galveston followed remarkably parallel paths of urbanization. The two cities seemed curiously bound together as if magically defying the statistical laws of probability. In such basic steps of city building as the demographic character of the settlements, nature of the local economies, climate of entrepreneurial activity, distribution of wealth and power, tone of the cultural milieu, and evolution of urban public services, the sister cities marched in cadence. Even their differences underscored their essential similarities. City planning in Galveston was directed by a close-knit group of families while Houston's strategy

Houston in 1894, on the eve of an economic boom. Looking northeast from the center of town, homes and businesses still intermixed in the downtown area.

of growth was wrought by a more diverse commercial-civic élite. After the 1840s, the two entrepôts were pitted against each other in a constant state of competition, but only because they both sought the same goal, the urban crown of the Southwest.[3]

During their formative stages, Houston and Galveston grew in tandem because a common regional setting nurtured both commercial outposts with the same Southern peoples and agricultural wealth. On the eve of the Texas revolution from Mexico in the mid-thirties, Northern speculators planted several townsites on Galveston Bay, the only good natural harbor on the Gulf Coast from the Mississippi to the Rio Grande. Galveston, on the eastern tip of a low-lying island stretching nearly across the bay's entrance, possessed the best location as a transshipment point between the interior's super-rich cotton and sugar lands and the world's markets. But a surrounding wall of sandbars meant that cargoes had to be transferred, or lightered, offshore between ships and barges. They could then shuttle just as easily up narrow bayous for fifty miles to Houston, at the headwaters of navigation.[4] For forty years, a complete dependence on waterborne means of transportation to Texas guaranteed a preponderance of Southern migrants on the coastal beachhead. Moreover, other "forward linkages" from the plantations of the fast expanding hinterland to the two budding entrepôts gave almost identical characters to their physical environments and their rising merchant elites. By the prewar decade, Houston and Galveston were booming frontier towns, Southern communities filled with cotton factories and planters, saloonkeepers and gamblers, dock workers and teamsters, and German immigrants and Negro slaves.[5]

In the fifties, the coming of the railroad sparked a sharp urban rivalry that exposed distinct differences between the commercial-civic élites of the central nodes of the area. Debate in Austin over the state's role in financing and managing the railroad polarized Texans into supporting either a Houston or a Galveston plan. On the one hand, Bayou City representatives called for a conventional program of mixed enterprises whose lines would inevitably connect into a national transportation network. This policy alternative reflected a relatively open structure of business leadership that continued to retain flexibility in the postbellum period. On the other hand, the islanders advocated a state-centered system of public ownership which would fan out from their docks and warehouses into the hinterland. Houston, however, rallied enough rural support to win this crucial duel and consequently to become the rail hub of the region. Rejected on a state level, Galveston's elite families would soon forge their own public-private monopoly of local port facilities, the "Octopus of the Gulf" as it would become known to embittered shippers throughout the interior after the war.[6]

For the remainder of the century, distinctive groups of entrepreneurs from the sister cities fueled the race for a permanent lead in urban growth and renown. At various times, water or rail technologies held the competitive edge, but businessmen from neither city were able to translate these marginal differences into a decisive victory. Before the opening of an overland route to New Orleans in 1879, Galveston slowly outpaced its rival because of its superior site as a seaport. Yet, the commercial-civic élite of the Bayou City successfully offset most of the island's locational advantage. Typically, Houston's established leadership forged an alliance with a powerful outsider, Commodore Charles Morgan, who carved an improved ship channel up to the inland rail hub.[7] In the eighties, as the completion of the regional system of railroads began tipping the flow of trade to Houston, Galveston's élite families took aggressive strides to neutralize these gains by constructing a deep-water port. They mobilized shippers from as far away as Denver into an effective sectional lobby that finally secured Congressional support in 1890 for the expensive, six-million-dollar project. At the same time, they stymied their competitor's alternative bid for a federally financed modernization of the increasingly obsolete ship channel. On the eve of the catastrophe, Galveston threatened to surge ahead to a commanding position as the commercial center of the sprawling farm, cattle, and timber lands of the Southwest.[8]

Until the island city's promising future was tragically cut short in 1900, the two coastal entrepôts had been locked in a duel for regional hegemony that neither could win. For over sixty years, the similarities resulting from the twin cities' shared setting on the Texas Gulf had far outweighed the variations produced by different stuctures of élite leadership. Even these peculiarities had been more in the nature of style than substance. Compared to élite groups of urbanities in other sections of the United States, the contrasts between the luminaries of the two Southwestern ports blur into insignificance. More important, the basic sources of urban growth that demark one place from the next had been drawn from the same regional wellsprings. The origins of the twin cities' populations, functions of their economies, pace of their city building, and tone of their societies had formed a common context for development. Cultivated by driving, albeit individual, groups of city boosters, these pervasive influences had kept the process of urbanization on the Texas Gulf evenly matched.[9]

Between 1900 and 1910 however, Houston emerged victorious as the central place of the coastal area. Galveston's misfortune and the skill of Bayou City businessmen in taking advantage of the rich new opportunities presented by the oil boom completely upset the previously balanced configuration of local forces. The island city's growth was seriously retarded while its rival's was significantly accelerated. Incredibly large finds of petroleum in the vicinity added national

A typical oilfield on the Texas Gulf Coast in the early 1900s. Many similar discoveries nearby boosted Houston into national prominence.

urgency to needs for a safe, deep water port on the Texas Gulf. The Galveston disaster convinced Congress to abandon the island port in favor of refurbishing the now decrepit ship channel. Old lines of trade and transportation were indelibly redrawn in the coastal area. Two years later in 1904, a second major discovery of black gold in the Humble field, just a few miles outside of Houston ended any question about the location of the oil industry headquarters in Texas, if not the entire country. By the end of the decade, two traumatic events and men's responses to them combined to create novel patterns of urban-rural relationships throughout the Southwest.

Washing away 6,000 people and $30,000,000 in property, the Galveston hurricane of 8 September 1900 is still regarded as the worst natural disaster in the nation's history. The fierce storm and tidal wave hit the exposed city of 38,000 residents squarely, cutting a wide path of death and destruction right through the middle of the community.[10] In the days following the catastrophe, stunned civic leaders groped to restore not only law and order but also public credit to finance relief and recovery efforts. Within a month, the prestigious Deep Water Committee, the élite inner circle of fifteen who represented half of the island's wealth, were formulating bold plans for the reconstruction of their vanquished urban enterprise.[11] Although Houston suffered considerable property damage, the fifty mile buffer of land diminished the fury of the storm to below lethal levels. The inland town was fully prepared to react with dispatch when that most famous of all oil gushers came in at Spindletop four months later.

The size of the energy reserves found seventy five miles east of Houston was also unprecedented in the annals of American history. On the outskirts of Beaumont, one of Houston's satellite towns, the original Lucas well spilled 800,000 barrels of petroleum into jerry-built reservoirs in the first ten days, more than Texas' 300 existing rigs had pumped out in the past four years. In the ensuing mad rush to get rich quick, money and speculators poured into the coastal area almost as rapidly as the liquid gold flowed out. In 1902, for instance, oilmen extracted over 17 million barrels from Spindletop alone, while wildcatters were tapping big new pools in fields nearby. The immense size of the reserves insured the quick intervention of investment bankers and oil moguls from the U.S. and Europe. But local businessmen could still occupy key positions as their managers, besides organizing competition as independent producers.[12]

At base then, Houston's success in capturing the oil boom rested on the abilities of its business leaders to recognize the far-reaching implications of Spindletop for the cities of the region. In fact, civic spokesmen had been debating vigorously for over a year about the best way to make a "Greater Houston." On the eve of the energy revolution in the Southwest, former mayor H. Baldwin Rice, timberland baron John H. Kirby, and other members of the influential Business League agreed that there were two essential ingredients in the prescription for achieving metropolitan status. Speaker after speaker called for the modernization of the ship channel and the attraction of more foreign investment in local manufacturing enterprises.[13] Giving top priority to growth, city planner-engineer George Porter, for example, argued that

> industrial development is the important factor in city building. . . . The world is now a neighborhood, made so by rapid transit and competition in the carrying trade by rail and water.[14]

He advocated the establishment of more factories to exploit the countryside's diverse bounty of cotton, grains, rice and lumber. The golden opportunities opened by the hurricane and the oil boom galvanized Houston's businessmen into a powerful, united front behind this perceptive, if traditional, vision of progress.[15]

The immediate reactions of Houstonians to Spindletop revealed a keen appreciation of the intimate relationship between the natural resources of a region's hinterland and the man-made expansion of its urban nodes. Within two weeks of the Lucas gusher, the Business League was organizing a pipeline consortium to bring the fuel to the city. Houston's major consumers of energy realized that dramatic reductions in material and labor bills would result if they converted their furnaces from expensive, imported coals to less costly fuel oils. Local railroad and shipping executives were reaching similar conclusions which were to greatly lower transportation costs throughout the Southwest.[16] Kirby, B.F. Bonner and other incorporators of the Consumers' Gas and Fuel [Pipeline] Company drew even broader connections between cheap energy, industrial development, and urban growth. In March, with the satisfactory conversion of the city's largest energy user, the American Brewing Association, the Houston *Post* announced triumphantly

> The fuel problem for manufacturing in Houston

has been solved. . . . Houston has now reached a point where expansion will be made a business.[17]

The rise of John Kirby epitomized the creative business leader who readily combined the pursuit of personal fortune with the "business" of promoting Houston's growth. Besides his pivotal role in bringing oil into the city, Kirby adroitly played the part of power broker between the resource developers of the Southwest and the investment bankers of the North. In 1890, the ambitious young lawyer had become a regional planner when he convinced Boston money managers to purchase a hundred thousand acres of prime forest land in the pine thickets of east Texas. Growing up there in a family of poor farmers, Kirby personally understood what the breaking of the hill country's isolation and poverty would mean to its people. His success as a regional planner and an inter-regional broker gave him tremendous prestige throughout the state. This influence allowed him to amass control of over one million acres in less than three months after the Lucas gusher. Kirby seized the opportunity of the moment by making a quick change from timberland agent to oilfield dealer. Acting again as the middleman, the city booster persuaded Easterners to finance a multimillion dollar scheme for funneling the region's natural wealth through Bayou City lumber yards and oil refineries.[18] Kirby's Houston Oil Company represented one of several instant giants such as Texaco and Humble Oil Company that Houstonians helped organize during the first decade of the century.

While imaginative entrepreneurs like Kirby were laying industrial foundations for the city's economic growth, they were also undertaking shrewd political maneuvers aimed at absorbing their rival's share of the region's commerce. As in the past, this meant the construction of a deep-water canal which would neutralize Galveston's superior location. Throughout the nineties, Houston's Congressional representative, Thomas Ball, had spearheaded a concerted lobbying campaign by serving on the strategic Rivers and Harbors Committee. Nevertheless, its all powerful chairman, Theodore Burton, had frustrated every effort of the Texans because the Army Corps of Engineers had already chosen Galveston as the best transshipment point in the Southwest. What years of intense lobbying failed to achieve however, the terrible storm accomplished almost miraculously. In 1902, Burton relented and Congress dutifully appropriated one million dollars to begin dredging a modern shipping lane to the safer, inland port.[19]

The importance of this crucial decision cannot be overestimated. If Galveston had become the site of the port, Houston might have been by-passed in the twentieth century. As the historian of the inland waterway notes

> Deep water at Galveston [in 1896] brought Houston to a major crisis in its economic development. Houstonians could either sit still and

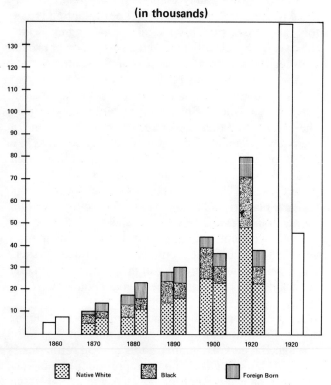

Chart Number 1

THE GROWTH OF POPULATION, HOUSTON AND GALVESTON, 1860-1920

(in thousands)

Native White   Black   Foreign Born

Sources: U. S. Bureau of the Census. Census of the United States, Population: 1860, 1870, 1880, 1890, 1900, 1910, 1920.

regaining its commercial momentum. Instead, Galveston went into permanent eclipse behind the steady ascendancy of its long time rival.

These conclusions gain strong support from an examination of the sister cities' rates of growth before and after the storm. A statistical comparison of three fundamental indicators of urbanization is sufficient to show the irrevocable nature of the tumultuous events at the crossroads of the twentieth century. Population figures and the assessed valuations of property within municipal borders supply two reliable measures of city building (see charts 1 and 2 respectively). In a similar way, the value of products from manufacturing provides a good test of industrial vitality (see chart 3). Where the differences between the cities remained relatively small before 1900, a large gap opened dramatically between each pair of variables over the course of the decade. From 1900 to 1910, Galveston stood still statistically; Houston exhibited accelerated rates of expansion in all three categories. During the following decade, the Bayou City's lead widened rapidly. Its rise to metropolitan status completely overshadowed Galveston which was now relegated to the backwaters of the region.

Taken together, the impacts of the two fortuitous incidents in the winter of 1900-01 shifted the traditional commercial functions of the twin cities almost exclusively to Houston. In 1902, the island city had irretrievably lost its competitive edge as the best location for a modern port when Houston won federal funding for its ship channel. Thereafter, Galveston's recovery was seriously retarded by the presence of a nearby rival which readily diverted the disrupted flow of trade through its matching facilities. The reversal of Congressional policy had resulted primarily from the lessons of the hurricane, but local promoters of the waterway had never stopped agitating for the project. The conjunction of the catastrophe and the oil rush had suddenly opened new opportunities for the civic élite to fulfill the Business League's formula for metropolitan success. This kind of aggressive leadership turned momentary opportunities into permanent advantages. In addition, national attention began focusing on the Bayou City, the closest and safest urban base for the exploitation of the area's rich resources.

After 1910, the repercussions from Houston's singular position of urban supremacy on the Texas Gulf spread inexorably throughout the Southwest. The solid foundations of industry and commerce that had been laid in the early 1900s contributed to this steady ascendancy. The following decade, however, served as an incubation period, a coming to maturity of both the city's new roles in the region and the nation's consumer markets for petroleum products. During the 1920s, the automobile created an insatiable demand for oil that sparked a process of self-sustaining growth in Hous-

watch many of their commercial advantages disappear, or they could build a channel that would again put their town on par with Galveston.[20]

However, the destruction of Galveston diverted the flow of trade at least temporarily to Houston. Perhaps the innovative responses of the island's commercial-civic élite might have produced a recovery analogous to Chicago's rise from the ashes in the 1870s, or San Franscisco's revival after the earthquake in 1906. The creation of America's first commission government and the erection of a mighty sea wall clearly demonstrated the abilities of the island's leaders to adapt to change. Galveston did not lack local supporters, but outside backers.[21]

The knowledge that protected shipping facilities were becoming available near Houston offered Galveston's traditional customers an attractive alternative to returning to the dangerously exposed island. With its vunerability still fresh in everyone's mind, moreover, the managers of the region's newly emerging industries such as oil, lumber, and rice rejected Galveston in favor of the more secure inland site.[22] In short, the ship-channel project prevented the island city from ever

Chart Number 2
THE GROWTH OF PROPERTY VALUES,
HOUSTON AND GALVESTON, 1880-1920
(in millions)

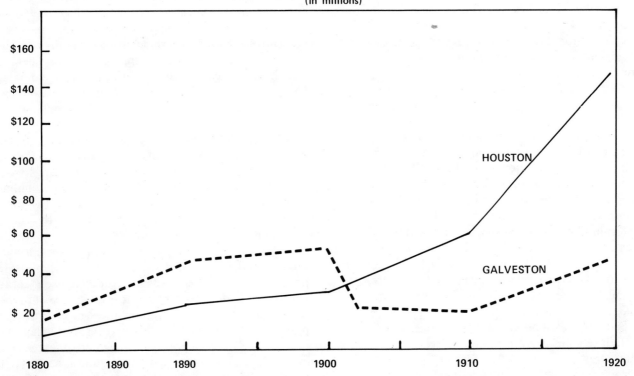

Sources: U. S. Bureau of the Census. Census of the United States, Report on the Valuation, Taxation and Public Indebtedness in the United States: 1880, 1890, 1900; ibid., Special Reports, Financial Statistics of the Cities: 1910, 1920.

Chart Number 3
THE GROWTH OF MANUFACTURED PRODUCTS,
HOUSTON AND GALVESTON, 1880-1920
(in millions)

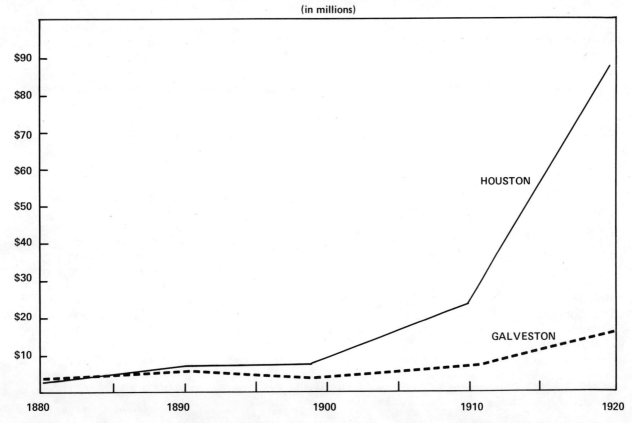

Sources: U. S. Bureau of the Census. Census of the United States, Manufacturing: 1880, 1890, 1900, 1910, 1920.

ton's urban economy. These dynamics fueled Houston's drive to rise above all its commercial competitors: Dallas, San Antonio, and New Orleans. By 1930, the advantages gained at the turn of the century reached a decisive culmination. Houston emerged with an undisputed hegemony over the entire Southwest.

Before the twenties, the Port of Houston paid few dividends but then the rewards became handsome indeed. It took until 1914 to complete the deep-water channel, just as war in Europe was jarring world trade patterns out of their nineteenth century molds. Yet, even during this difficult period of political and economic adjustment to novel conditions of interdependency, Houston began combining oil and trade to bootstrap itself up to metropolitan proportions. To advance construction of the inland waterway for example, civic leaders in 1909 had proposed a major innovation in city-federal relations, a plan of matching funds between local and national units of government. The resulting navigation bonds were purchased by Houston bankers, whose families formed the inner core of the urban élite. The bankers could afford to finance these debts entirely at home because the oil boom was rapidly raising their deposits to levels far above the national average.[23] At war's end, this kind of self-reinforcing process of economic expansion left the Gulf Coast entrepôt ready to reap the benefits of the era of prosperity that followed.

The dawning of the Automobile Age consolidated Houston's preeminence in the region. In the twenties, the internal combustion engine and Henry Ford's techniques of mass production transformed the petroleum business from a supplier of kerosene lamp oils into one of America's biggest and fastest growing industrial giants. By 1930, oil exports from the Gulf made Houston the third largest port in the nation, topped only by New York and Los Angeles. Accounting for three

quarters of the channel's tonnage, the liquid gold brought the city's commercial promise to realization and fulfilled its industrial potential.[24] Since the Army Engineers could not bring the waterway up to the central business district, a surging urban economy sent the city sprawling down to the shipping corridor. There, a massive refining and manufacturing complex extended back towards the Gulf, ironically beginning the linkage of the old rivals into a single, urbanized conglomeration.

By 1930, Houston clearly dominated both the urban centers and the hinterland of the Southwest. In national terms, the Bayou City jumped in the rankings from fifty-first to twenty-sixth biggest. More than doubling its population to 292,000 people during the twenties, Houston became the largest city in Texas by finally overcoming its last serious competitor, Dallas.[25] In the postwar decade, new discoveries of oil all around this rail hub to the North had also given it a sharp boost in population to 260,000 residents. But the close identity in the size of the two cities was less indicative of future trends than their very different rates of growth: 111 percent for Houston versus 64 percent for Dallas. Although the Great Depression slowed urban expansion everywhere, the coastal port witnessed a healthy, 30 percent increment in the thirties while the inland city continued to show only about half of Houston's rate of increase.[26] An explanation for these differences lies rooted in the same kind of regional geography of cities that had earlier applied to the Houston-Galveston axis.

In the twentieth century, Dallas experienced locational drawbacks analogous to Houston's in the previous century. First, the Bayou City's site on the Gulf put the truly inland distribution center at a distinct, commercial disadvantage. With Texas oil helping to reduce transportation costs, Houston became the entrepôt for the vast Transmississippi West. Its port functioned as

TABLE 1
POPULATION OF SOUTHWESTERN CITIES, 1900-1940

	1900	1910	1920	1930	1940
Amarillo	1400	10,000	15,500	43,100	51,700
Beaumont	9400	20,600	40,400	57,700	59,000
Dallas	42,600	92,100	159,000	260,500	294,700
El Paso	15,100	39,300	77,600	102,400	96,800
Fort Worth	26,700	73,300	106,500	163,500	177,700
Galveston	37,800	37,000	44,300	53,000	60,900
Houston	44,600	78,800	138,300	292,400	384,500
Oklahoma City	10,000	64,200	91,300	185,400	204,400
Phoenix	5500	11,100	29,000	48,100	65,400
San Antonio	55,300	96,600	161,400	231,500	253,900
Tulsa	1400	18,200	72,100	141,300	142,200

SOURCE: U.S. Department of Commerce. Bureau of the Census. *Statistical Abstract of the United States: 1946.*

The Houston Ship Channel and Wharf in 1914. Sea-going vessels fifty miles inland ended the urban rivalry between Houston and Galveston.

the small end of a huge funnel that eventually reached out to encompass the grain bowl of the North Central region. Second, Dallas had to contend with an active rival nearby, Fort Worth, which created a divisive counterpoint for urban growth within the local area (see table 1). To be sure, a combination of several factors contributed to Houston's victory over Dallas. Yet, the urban configurations of the region undoubtedly had a profound influence on the final outcome.

Houston's climb to the coveted status of the urban center of the Southwest followed the two strange quirks of nature that had totally upset the region's equilibrium at the turn of the century. Before the destruction of Galveston, the sister cities had marched in cadence to the rhythms of commercial growth produced by a shared setting on the coastal plain. Perceptive urban planners from the Bayou City had recognized and

seized the opportunities of 1900-01 to replace this tandem development with an accelerated drive to local preeminence. After the hurricane convinced Congress to reconsider the boosters' ambitious scheme for a safer, inland waterway, Houston suddenly became the only logical location for the petroleum industry that Spindletop richly nurtured. The city's new advantages in trade and manufacturing accumulated steadily to a point where the expansion of the local economy turned into a self-sustaining process in the early twenties. Outpacing all its remaining competitors by 1930, Houston has continued to maintain its hold on the urban crown of the Southwest down to the present.

For the city planner of the late twentieth century, at least two broad conclusions emerge from this historical examination of the regional context of urban growth. The Houston example suggests that the interplay between urban and rural areas continue to exert a powerful influence on the well-being of the city dweller as well as his country cousin. Although city-suburban relationships have been receiving more careful scrutiny lately from urban planners, they should further widen their scope to include the regional configurations of all three types of areas. If nothing else, increasing signals of ecological distress are painful reminders that the city and its hinterland still interact in ways vital to everyone. Of course, the American economy has undergone great transformations since the early part of the century. But whether cotton, coal, or "Sunbirds," who flock to outlying retirement villages, fuel the urban economy, the impacts of change can be brought into better balance by applying regional perspectives to current problems.

A second, related conclusion arises from the interplay of the cities of the Southwest in the past. In this case study, the urban geographer provides an accurate explanation for the evolution of an heirarchy or pyramid of larger to smaller places within the region. Their central place models of growth fit well here, especially the notion of the bigger city's accumulating advantages over smaller rivals nearby.[27] The example of Galveston's loss becoming Houston's gain can be extended profitably to present circumstances. As technological advances in transportation continue to shrink time and space, more and more cities come into a direct interdependence. These trends imply that students of the city should analyze urban configurations not only on a regional scale but also on inter-regional ones as well. The chronic drain of resources from Northeastern to Sunbelt centers has recently given urgency to the need for this kind of approach to urban planning.

Dr. Harold L. Platt has been an assistant professor at Loyola University of Chicago since 1974. A graduate of the University of Illinois (Urbana), he received his Ph.D. from Rice University. He is the author of an esay on progressivism in Houston, which appears in *The Age of Urban Reform*, eds., Michael Ebner and Eugene Tobin (New York: Kennikat, 1977). He is completing a monograph on the city building process during the second half of the nineteenth century.

FOOTNOTES

1. Two classic studies are Morton and Lucia White, *The Intellectual versus the City: From Thomas Jefferson to Frank Lloyd Wright* (Cambridge: Harvard University Press and M.I.T. Press, 1962); and Anselm L. Strauss, *Images of the American City* (Glencoe, Illinois: Free Press, 1961).

2. See for example, James T. Lemon, *The Best Poor Man's Country, A Geographical Study of Early Southeastern Pennsylvania* (New York: Norton, 1972); Carville Earle and Ronald Hoffman, "Urban Development in the Eighteenth Century South," *Perspectives in American History* 10(1976):7-78; and David R. Goldfield, "Urban-Rural Relations in the Old South: The Example of Virginia," *Journal of Urban History* 2(February 1976):146-168.

3. Several excellent studies of Texas cities during the antebellum period now exist. For comparative perspectives, see Kenneth W. Wheeler, *To Wear a City's Crown — The Beginning of Urban Growth in Texas, 1836-1865* (Cambridge: Harvard University Press, 1968); and Earl W. Fornell, *The Galveston Era: The Texas Crescent on the Eve of Secession* (Austin: University of Texas Press, 1961). No monograph adequately covers Galveston during the postwar era but David G. McComb, *Houston — The Bayou City* (Austin: University of Texas Press, 1969), provides a recent, urban biography.

4. James P. Baughman, "The Evolution of Rail-Water Systems of Transportation in the Gulf-Southwest, 1836-1890," *Journal of Southern History* 34(August 1968):357-381; Marilyn McAdams Sibley, *The Port of Houston: A History* (Austin: University of Texas Press, 1968), Chaps. 1-3.

5. Wheller, *City's Crown*, pp. 104-150; Fornell, *Galveston Era*, Chaps. 3,6.

6. St. Clair G. Reed, *A History of the Texas Railroad* (Houston: St. Clair, 1941), pp. 53-87; Sibley, *Port of Houston*, Chaps. 4-5; Earl F. Woodward, "Internal Improvements in Texas in the Early 1850s," *Southwest Historical Quarterly* 76(October 1972):160-182.

7. Baughman, "Water-Rail Systems," pp. 357-381; ibid., *Charles Morgan and the Development of Southern Transportation* (Nashville: Vanderbilt University Press, 1968).

8. Robert H. Peebles, "The Galveston Harbor Controversy of the Gilded Age," *Texana* 12(1974):74-83; Sibley, *Port of Houston*, p. 114.

9. Two otherwise excellent studies by Kenneth Wheeler, [*City's Crown*, pp. 90, 161-163]a d Earl Fornell [*Galveston Era*, pp. 10-21]a s ert erroneously that Houston's victory over Galveston was discernable clearly before the Civil War. They argue that the social environment of the entrepreneurial élite was more open and mobile in Houston. In Galveston, a closed circle of families completely monopolized the power and wealth in the port city. But Mary S. Jackson neatly refutes these claims in her sensitive analysis of the census manuscripts for 1850 and the following decade. Actually, the distribution of income in the two cities showed closely similar patterns. See her important and well written Ph.D. dissertation, "The People of Houston in the 1850s," (Indiana University, 1975).

10. For a modern account of the hurricane, consider Herbert Mason, Jr., *Death From the Sea* (New York: Dial, 1972). For damage estimates, Cf. Bradley Rice, "The Galveston Plan of City Government by Commission: The Birth of a Progressive Idea," *Southwest Historical Quarterly* 73 (April 1975):383-385.

11. *Ibid.*, pp. 367-408; E. R. Cheesborough, *Galveston's Commission Form of City Government* (Galveston, Texas: Reprint for the Deepwater Committee, 1910), provides the best contemporary account. A different, perspective is presented by James Weinstein, "Organized Business and the City Commission and Manager Movements," *Journal of Southern History* 28(May 1962):166-182.

12. Harold F. Williamson et. al., *The American Petroleum Industry*, vol. 2: *The Age of Energy 1899-1959* (Evanston: Northwestern University Press, 1963):17-24; Seth S. McKay and Odie B. Faulk, *Texas After Spindletop* (Austin, Texas: Teck-Vaughn, 1965), Chap. 1; Carl Coke Rister, *Oil-Titan of the Southwest* (Norman: University of Oklahoma Press, 1949).

13. "To Make a Greater Houston," *Houston Post*, January 4-10, 1901.

14. *Ibid.*, January 9, 1901.

15. On the contrary, the majority of Houstonians favored community oriented policies which gave primary emphasis to improving the quality of the local environment. In the March 1900 elections, their mayoralty can-

didate triumphed again in spite of the establishments's complaints against the incumbent's "nagging" posture towards outside capital and corporations. But the forces of localism won only a short-lived victory that ended with the 1902 elections. For further insight into the political conflicts over the direction of city planning, see my "City Building and Progressive Reform: The Modernization of an Urban Polity, Houston 1892-1905," in *The Age of Urban Reform*, eds. Michael H. Ebner and Eugene M. Tobin, (Port Washington, N.Y.: Kennikat, 1977) pp. 28-42.

16. Houston *Post*, January 27, 29, 1901; McKay and Faulk, *Texas*, pp. 9-10.

17. Houston *Post*, March 24, 1901. For the formation of the company, see *ibid.*, February 17, 1901, and March 24, 1901.

18. John O. King, "The Early History of the Houston Oil Company of Texas, 1901-1908," (Master's Thesis, University of Houston, 1958). For a look into Kirby's business philosophy see George T. Morgan, Jr., "The Gospel of Wealth Goes South: John Henry Kirby and Labor's Struggle for Self-Determination, 1901-1906," *Southwest Historical Quarterly* 75(October 1971):158-185.

19. Thomas M. Ball, *The Port of Houston: How It Came To Pass* (Houston: n.p., n.d.); Sibley, *Port of Houston*, pp. 123-127.

20. *Ibid.*, p. 114.

21. See above, nn. 10-11.

22. Williamson, *Age of Energy*, pp. 74-90; McComb, *Houston*, pp. 114-116; Sibley, *Port of Houston*, pp. 151-152.

23. *Ibid.*, pp. 134-138; McComb, *Houston*, pp. 118-119.

24. Sibley, *Port of Houston*, pp. 160-162, 168.

25. U.S. Department of Commerce. Bureau of the Census. *Fifteenth Census of the United States, 1930: Population*, vol. 1.

26. *Ibid.*

27. A helpful introduction to central place theory is Allan R. Pred, *The Spacial Dynamics of U.S. Urban-Industrial Growth, 1800-1914* (Cambridge: M.I.T. Press, 1966).

Dick Kent Photography

Aerial view of downtown Albuquerque and the East Mesa 1978. Following the destruction of several landmark buildings, the flight of major retailers such as Sears to regional shopping centers, and the construction of Interstate 40, Central Avenue (the broad street starting in the lower lefthand corner) has been overshadowed by "Urban Renewalized" sectors to the north and south. The downtown as a whole, however, has lost its position as the main retail and entertainment center, but retains its 8:30 to 5:00 role as the hub of government and finance.

Growth Trends In The Albuquerque SMSA*, 1940-1978

Howard N. Rabinowitz

World War II helped transform numerous small western towns into sprawling metropolises. Although journalists and politicians have recently discovered the shift of people and political power to the so-called Sunbelt, historians have been slow to seek the causes and consequences of the urban West's remarkable postwar

expansion, Western historians rarely venture past the turn of the twentieth century and when they do, it is usually to examine non-urban matters. And with few exceptions, urban historians have limited themselves to the history of a handful of large eastern and midwestern cities in the years prior to 1920. As a result, economists, political scientists, and sociologists have taken the lead among social scientists in examining such issues crucial to the postwar development of western cities such as

*Standard Metropolitan Statistical Area

city-suburb relations, annexation, land-use planning, and growth policies.[1] Yet each of these issues requires careful historical investigation if we are to understand the phenomenon of rapid growth in the urban West.

The experience of the Albuquerque Standard Metropolitan Statistical Area since 1940 reflects what has been happening throughout most of the urban west. In 1940 New Mexico's Bernalillo County had 69,391 residents, 35,449 of whom were concentrated in Albuquerque, the state's largest city. Ten years later when the county was designated the Albuquerque SMSA, its population had grown to 145,673 on its way to 262,199 in 1960 and 315,774 in 1970.[2] In the latter year it ranked 96th out of 233 SMSAs, although Albuquerque itself was the nation's 58th largest city with a population of 243,751.[3] Along with the rapid growth so typical of western cities has come a relationship between city and suburb that not only separates the Albuquerque SMSA from most eastern and midwestern counterparts, but even for many older Sunbelt SMSAs. A look at Albuquerque's recent history will reveal much about the forces shaping the patterns of growth throughout metropolitan America.

During the late nineteenth century, the railroad created a network of new or expanded communities throughout the West. With obvious exceptions such as Los Angeles and Denver, most of these places enjoyed only moderate growth until World War II. Like her Sunbelt contemporaries Tucson and Phoenix, Albuquerque on the eve of the war was basically what it had been since the railroad brought it into being in 1880, little more than a small town that attracted tourists and health seekers and served as a trading and distribution center for a limited hinterland. The World War and Cold War that followed, however, led to the establishment and rapid expansion of Kirtland Air Force Base and the Sandia and Mazano establishment which concentrated on special weapons development and atomic research. By the mid-1950s the military and military activities so common in the region had replaced the declining Santa Fe Railroad as the city's most important source of economic growth. The federal government further stimulated the local economy by continuing its pre-war policy of establishing regional offices for numerous agencies, a policy that had already given the city the nickname "Little Washington." Growth was also generated by the expansion of the University of New Mexico from 1800 students in 1940 to over 5000 in 1950 and more than 20,000 by the mid-1970s, the opening of the University's School of Medicine which, together with the construction or enlargement of numerous public and private hospitals, enhanced the city's long-standing reputation as a health center, and finally, by the continued success of the tourist industry, especially after the rediscovery of Indian crafts. In short, Albuquerque can be classified as a typical post-industrial city dependent upon a government- and service-oriented economy that in 1970 had only 7 percent of its workforce in manufacturing jobs.[4]

The SMSA is atypical, however, in that as late as 1970 it consisted of a single county totally dominated by a central city whose share of the SMSA population had grown from 51.1 % in 1940 to 77.2% in 1970. During the same period the percentage of residents in the central cities of most of the country's 85 largest metropolitan areas declined so that by 1973 in only 21 did central-city population represent as much as 60% of the total metropolitan population. The percentage was only 34% in the major eastern cities, but even in the sample's 18 western cities the mean was only 44%. Although the South, including Texas, had the greatest concentration of metropolitan population in its central cities, less than half of its 27 cities exceeded the 60% mark.[5]

The city of Albuquerque was also only one of two incorporated places in the entire SMSA, the other being the village of Los Ranchos de Albuquerque, population 1,900 in 1970. The absence of incorporated suburbs, so troubling to most other cities, was due to several factors including a 1963 law (recently repealed) that forbade the incorporation of communities within five miles of the central city.[6] the poverty of the small villages in the

Albuquerque Public Schools
John A. Milne, Superintendent of Schools 1910-1955. In addition to overseeing successfully a rapidly expanding school system, Milne helped determine the course of the city's growth through acquisition of sites for future schools long before the surrounding areas were developed.

Alvarado Hotel with the Fred Harvey Indian Museum in the center foreground circa 1955. Located just north of the Santa Fe Railway station, the cupolaed Alvarado Hotel became the city's most famous landmark following its construction in 1901. Its demolition in 1970 marked the nadir of local interest in historic preservation and dealt the entire downtown a severe blow whose effects are still evident today.

Shop #5 of Santa Fe's Centralized Work Equipment Shop 1968. Rather than repairing locomotives as in the pre-diesel days, Albuquerque's shops now work on assorted railroad equipment.

Santa Fe's Super Chief making a service stop at the Albuquerque station circa 1952. Albuquerque welcomed several trainloads of visitors a day until the interstate highway and expanded air travel reduced rail traffic to a trickle after the early 1960s. Amtrak is presently planning to cancel the city's last scheduled passenger train.

Santa Fe Railway Station circa 1952. Sharing an architectural style and long platform with the Alvarado Hotel, the railroad station welcomed several trailoads of visitors a day until the interstate highway and expanded air travel reduced rail traffic to a trickle after the early 1960s. Amtrak is presently planning to cancel the city's last scheduled passenger train.

area, and the fact that many areas outside of the city were satisfied with their access to city and county services. As recently as 1976, the last in a series of attempts to incorporate the adjacent South Valley failed dismally.[7]

A final cause for the absence of incorporated communities also helps account for the remarkable growth of the central city. This of course, has been an aggressive policy of annexation so typical of Sunbelt cities. As early as 1940, the city administration, local newspap-

ers, and the Chamber of Commerce expressed concern about the proliferation of new subdivisions just outside the city limits. In response, they launched a "Greater Albuquerque" campaign to bring these areas into the city in time for the taking of the 1940 census. "Not only should Old Town be a part of the present city of Albuquerque, but so should all the territory adjacent to the city," declared the *Albuquerque Journal* in one of its frequent editorials on the subject. "To all intents and purposes," it continued, "the entire built up commun-

Santa Fe Railway roundhouse and shops circa 1945. The Santa Fe shops operated around the clock during World War II and provided the city with its largest payroll. Their importance declined, however, after the Santa Fe converted to diesels in the early 1950s.

ity that surrounds Albuquerque IS Albuquerque, and should officially become so."[8] The failure to bring in these new areas encouraged the city commission to revise its previously liberal policy of extending services to non-city residents. As one commissioner put it, "If we continue to extend water and fire protection outside the city, why will people want to come inside the limits?"[9] The withholding of city services did lead to a few small annexations,[10] but as late as 1946 the *Journal* was still complaining that

> The growth in the last few years has been more rapid outside the city than within. It has resulted in areas being developed without adequate water, sewer and other services. It is becoming a detriment to health and physical appearances of greater Albuquerque . . . We need some program

whereby we can be brought together in one big municipality and improvements extended to all areas.[11]

With the aid of favorable state legislation,[12] such a program was soon undertaken with dramatic results. In 1940 the city comprised an area of 11 square miles. This was increased to 16 square miles in June 1946 and to 24 square miles in October 1948. By 1950 the city limits had more than doubled and by 1973 they covered an area of 82.2 square miles. Today Albuquerque sprawls over 92 square miles.[13] Prior to 1950 much of the annexed land already contained sizeable populations but after 1950 and especially during the early 1960s, much of the land was empty and brought into the city at the request of developers who hoped that city services would make their subdivisions more attractive. There are no accu-

The University of New Mexico

The central mall at the University of New Mexico looking eastward toward the Sandia Mountains. With its distinctive pueblo revival architecture, the university is a symbol of Albuquerque's effort to retain its rich heritage in the face of unprecedented growth.

rate figures with which to gauge the impact of annexation on city population growth during the 1940s, although at least 20,000 residents were immediately added when the city tripled in area between 1946 and 1950.[14] Census data for subsequent years provides a firmer picture of annexation's role, although in this case most of the new residents arrived after annexation had occurred. In 1960, 23,646 of the city's 201,189 residents lived in areas annexed during the previous decade; ten years later, however, 234,036 of the city's 243,751 people lived within the boundaries of the 1960 city.[15]

Not surprisingly, widespread annexation produced a socio-economic pattern quite unlike that found in most SMSA's outside certain parts of the Sunbelt. The central city was able to maintain a strong middle-income base either by annexing already heavily populated middle-class "Anglo" subdivisions or else by annexing largely undeveloped land before it drew middle-class migrants from within the city's original boundaries. Unlike most cities, particularly those in the East and Midwest, Albuquerque was able to catch most members of the fleeing middle class.[16] It is true that generally low-income areas such as Barelas, Martineztown and Old Town were also added to the city, but their presence was more then balanced by the addition of middle- and upper-income areas and by the number of semi-rural, low-income districts still outside the city. As a result, the socio-economic status of central-city residents (as expressed in median years of schooling completed, median income of families and unrelated individuals, and percentage of persons employed in managerial and professional jobs) has been consistently higher than that of the rest of the SMSA. (See Tables 3-5)

It needs to be added that although the city's indicators have improved with each census, those of the surrounding territory have increased more rapidly, thus steadily reducing the gap since 1940. Nevertheless, the 1970 census still found city residents with a median income of \$7737 vs. \$7371 for the entire SMSA; 12.6 years of schooling vs. 12.5; and 34.9% employed in professional and managerial positions vs. 32.3% The contrast with the central city was greatest in the urban fringe. Almost three-fifths of the fringe's 53,000 people were concentrated in the heavily Chicano South Valley where residents had 10.3 years of schooling and a median income of \$5543. Almost 30% of the residents were under the poverty level compared to only 14.2% within the city. The North Valley, which contained over 10,000 residents, enjoyed much higher socio-economic status than the South Valley, due mainly to the presence of several wealthy Anglo enclaves, but as a whole still lagged considerably behind the city.[17]

These findings support sociologist Leo Schnore's hypothesis as to the likelihood of finding higher socio-economic status for residents of central cities in younger SMSAs in contrast to the suburban superiority generally found elsewhere. The so-called "Tucson-Albuquerque" type is isolated in the 1950s and 1960s is still alive and well in the Albuquerque of the 1970s, even though as he predicted, the gap is narrowing between city and suburbs.[18] As the contrast between the North and South valleys suggests, however, we must not lose sight of the significant disparities within the suburban ring. But that is a subject for another essay.

What can be examined here, however, is the general character of city-suburb relations. This has already been touched on in the discussion of annexation, but it needs to be emphasized that the process has not always occurred without opposition. As one county resident put it in 1940, "Up to date I haven't heard of people living outside the city begging to be admitted.[19] And indeed many residents of places annexed during the late 1940s were practically dragged into the city after prolonged court battles, petition drives and lobbying efforts. There was especially strong resistance from residents of Old Town, the original settlement of Albuquerque founded in 1706 but later overwhelmed by the new railroad town. Proponents of annexation stressed the benefits of improved public services for Old Town and the impact of sanitary advances, "[a] bigger 1950 census total," and a richer historical heritage for Albuquerque.[20] Opponents countered that "annexation will substantially increase taxes on every owner of real property in Old Town, will mean payment of a sewer tax, [and] will mean higher occupation license fees for business." For good measure they added that "The present city administration is arrogant, overbearing, and dictatorial."[21] This opposition proved un-

Table 1

Population Statistics 1930-1975

	1930	1940	1950	1960	1970	1975[1]
Bernalillo County (SMSA as of 1950)	45,430	69,391	145,673	262,199	315,774	362,087[2]
Urbanized Area	NA	NA	NA	241,216	297,451	NA
Albuquerque	26,570	35,449	96,815	201,189	243,751	279,401
% of SMSA	58.5	51.1	66.5	76.7	77.2	77.2[3]
Urban Fringe	NA	NA	NA	40,027	53,700	NA
Los Ranchos de Alb.	NA	NA	NA	NA	1,900	NA
North Valley (U)	NA	NA	NA	NA	10,366	NA
Sandia (U)	NA	NA	NA	5,431	6,867	NA
South Valley (U)	NA	NA	NA	NA	29,389	NA
Rural Nonfarm	NA	24,071	NA	19,892	17,678	NA
Rural Farm	NA	9,871	NA	1,091	526	NA

1. estimate as of July 1, 1975
2. does not include estimated 22,576 in Sandoval County
3. 72.6 if Sandoval County is included in SMSA

Table 2

Median Age

Population Statistics 1930-1975

	1950	1960	1970
Bernalillo County (SMSA as of 1950)	26.0	23.8	24.4
Urbanized Area	NA	24.0	24.5
Albuquerque	27.4	24.8	25.1
Urban Fringe	NA	NA	21.7
Los Ranchos de Alb.	NA	NA	27.9
North Valley (U)	NA	NA	27.6
Sandia (U)	NA	NA	20.7
South Valley (U)	NA	NA	21.1

Table 4

Percentage of Employed Persons in Managerial and Professional Jobs

	1940[1]	1950[1]	1960[1]	1970[2]
Bernalillo County (SMSA as of 1950)	22.6	24.6	28.8	32.3
Urbanized Area	NA	NA	29.5	32.5
Albuquerque	28.2	27.9	31.4	34.9
Urban Fringe	NA	NA	15.4	17.4
Outside Central City	13.9	16.3	NA	NA
Rural Nonfarm	NA	NA	20.5	29.0
Rural Farm	NA	NA	8.2	31.5
Ratio Alb/SMSA	1.25	1.13	1.09	1.08
Ratio U.F./Alb	NA	NA	.49	.50

1. persons 14 yrs. and over
2. persons 16 yrs. and over

Table 3

Median Income for All Families and Unrelated Individuals

	1950	1960	1970
SMSA	$2,794	$5,456	$7,371
Urbanized Area	NA	5,613	7,369
Albuquerque	3,021	5,894	7,737
Urban Fringe	NA	4,254	5,879
North Valley	NA	NA	6,814
South Valley	NA	NA	5,543
Rural Nonfarm	NA	3,726	7,350
Rural Farm	NA	5,200	8,526[1]
Ratio Alb/SMSA	1.08	1.08	1.05
Ratio U.F./Alb.	NA	.72	.78

1. for 152 families and 32 unrelated individuals

Table 5

Median School Years Completed for Persons 25 yrs. and Over

	1940	1950	1960	1970
Bernalillo County (SMSA as of 1950)	9.2	11.7	12.2	12.5
Urbanized Area	NA	NA	12.3	12.4
Albuquerque	11.6	12.1	12.4	12.6
Urban Fringe	NA	NA	10.6	11.5
North Valley (U)	NA	NA	NA	11.4
South Valley (U)	NA	NA	NA	10.3
Rural Nonfarm	8.0	NA	NA	12.2
Rural Farm	6.6	NA	NA	12.5
Ratio Alb/SMSA	1.26	1.03	1.02	1.01
Ratio U.F./Alb.	NA	NA	.85	.91

Table 6
Percentage of Persons Employed in
Manufacturing and White Collar Jobs

	% Manufacturing			% White Collar	
	1950	1960	1970	1960	1970
SMSA	8.0	9.6	7.6	54.9	60.7
Urbanized Area	NA	9.5	7.4	56.2	61.3
Albuquerque	7.2	9.4	7.0	59.1	64.4
Urban Fringe	NA	10.6	NA	34.7	NA
North Valley	NA	NA	10.4	NA	41.6
South Valley	NA	NA	8.7	NA	34.4

successful, but non-city residents subsequently have been better able to resist several other efforts at annexation and especially to thwart attempts at city-county consolidation.

Consolidation was considered at least as early as 1940,[22] but the issue came to a head during a lackluster campaign in 1973. Advocates of consolidation argued that the rapid growth of the previous thirty years had produced a wasteful duplication of urban services. City voters in a light turnout cast a slight majority in favor of consolidation, but irate county voters turned out in large numbers overwhelmingly to defeat the proposal.[23] The negative arguments were those generally found in such campaigns and centered around a feared increase in taxes and loss of political power. More interestingly, though, were the fears of county residents that their semi-rural way of life would be destroyed by rigid city building restrictions and by the fact that these residents already enjoyed most city services including libraries, busses, and water.[24] In short, county residents, be they Anglo or Chicano, rich or poor, felt and continue to feel along with most suburbanites that the ideal situation is proximity to city life so as to enjoy its benefits while at the same time avoiding the burdens which city residents must bear.

Consolidation is not a dead issue, however, although there are signs that if it is to be successful, it will have to be done on a piecemeal basis that involves specific governmental functions rather than an immediate wholesale merger. Some functional consolidation has already taken place. In 1940 there were separate and totally independent boards of education and superin-

tendents for the city and county schools. Five years later the county system turned over its largest district to the city board and in 1949 the two systems were consolidated under the leadership of the city superintendent, John Milne.[25] Currently there is a good deal of discussion about the value of combining the Albuquerque Police Department and the Bernalillo County Sheriff's Office in the name of economy and greater efficiency. Such a merger would be particularly significant since during the 1973 referendum the county sheriff was one of the most vocal opponents of city-county consolidation because of the effect it would have had on his position and his patronage-ridden department. The recent leasing of the Bernalillo County Medical Center to the University of New Mexico for $1 per year could be a further factor in any consolidation effort. Removing education, hospital administration, and, possibly, police protection from the purview of county government would leave that government with little reason to exist. The fact that inefficiency and scandal characterize the administration of its remaining functions would further weaken the forces opposing consolidation.

The consolidation issue has implications for the broader issues of planning and controlled growth. As early as 1947, the *Albuquerque Journal* observed that

Albuquerque in its years of rapid growth has been built without any planning. The result has been that the city has not the physical appearance that it should possess. Blighted areas exist where they should not have been allowed. Business or commercial areas have encroached upon residential districts. It will take years of effort to overcome these defects.[26]

Yet despite the passage of state legislation in 1947 allowing municipalities to establish planning commissions, the city did not have a permanent planning department or zoning ordinance until the early 1950s and until the late 1960s developers and boosters controlled land-use policy.[27] As elsewhere, however, the late 1960s brought an increased awareness of the weakness of uncontrolled growth. Calls for limited growth came from environmentally-conscious migrants and longtime residents who claimed that urban sprawl, pollution, and

Table 7
Black Population

	1940		1950		1960		1970	
	No.	%	No.	%	No.	%	No.	%
Bernalillo County (SMSA as of 1950)	849	1.2	1605	1.1	2,445	0.9	6,689	2.1
Urbanized Area	NA	NA	NA	NA	2,318	1.0	6,614	2.2
Albuquerque	547	1.5	1223	1.3	1,751	0.9	5,425	2.2
Urban Fringe	NA	NA	NA	NA	NA	NA	1,189	2.2
North Valley (U)	NA	NA	NA	NA	NA	NA	25	0.2
South Valley (U)	NA	NA	NA	NA	NA	NA	414	1.4
Sandia (U)[1]	NA	NA	NA	NA	NA	NA	583	9.0

1. includes military bases

Sandia Laboratories and Dick Ruddy Photography

The Z Division Technical Area 1946-47. An offshoot of Los Alamos Scientific Laboratory and the forerunner of Sandia Laboratories, the Z Division represented the federal government's growing interest in Albuquerque as a site for special weapons and energy research. The planes in the upper right are part of the thousands stockpiled at Kirtland Air Force Base after World War II.

Sandia Laboratories

Sandia Laboratories 1978. Operated by a division of Western Electric with the Departments of Energy and Defense as major contractors, Sandia Laboratories has replaced the Santa Fe Railway as the city's largest private employer.

Table 8
Indian Population

	1960 No.	1960 %	1970 No.	1970 %
SMSA	1617	0.6	5839	1.8
Urbanized Area	903	0.4	3712	1.2
Albuquerque	824	0.4	3351	1.4
Urban Fringe	NA	NA	361	0.7
North Valley (U)	NA	NA	111	1.1
South Valley (U)	NA	NA	172	0.6

Table 9
Spanish Language
or
Surname Population

	1970 No.	%
SMSA[1]	123,814	39.2
Urbanized Area	115,863	39.0
Albuquerque[2]	85,032	34.9
Urban Fringe[3]	30,831	57.4
North Valley (U)	5,984	57.7
South Valley (U)	21,512	73.2
Rural Nonfarm[4]	7,832	44.3
Rural Farm[5]	119	22.6

1. If "Persons of Spanish origin or descent" definition is used the figures are 96,465 and 30.5%.
2. If alternate definition used, the figures are 67,041 and 27.5%.
3. If alternate definition used, the figures are 24,530 and 45.7%.
4. If alternate definition used, the figures are 4,748 and 26.9%.
5. If alternate definition used, the figures are 146 and 27.8%.

Albuquerque City Government

Mayor David Rusk. Since taking office in late 1977, Mayor Rusk has sought to overcome the detrimental effects of more than thirty years of largely unplanned rapid growth.

destruction of old landmarks were undermining the quality of life. One outcome of this reaction was the adoption of the city's first comprehensive plan in 1975.[28]

Another manifestation of this increased interest in limited growth and greater public planning was the conflict between the city commission and city manager over growth policies that led to the adoption of a new charter in 1974. Four months after voters rejected the more radical remedy of city-county consolidation, city residents decided to return to the council-mayor form of government they had abandoned in 1917, though this time it was to be on a non-partisan basis.[29] And capping this era of re-examination of the traditional "bigger is better" approach of the public and private sectors was the election in the fall of 1977 of Mayor David Rusk, the son of the former Secretary of State. Rusk ran on a platform supporting the comprehensive plan, downtown revitalization, improved mass transit, and strong mayoral leadership and opposing mass transit, and strong mayoral leadership and opposing construc-

tion of another bridge across the Rio Grande that separates the city's populous east side from the developing West Mesa. Already since taking office, he has pushed ahead with plans to make downtown a thriving commercial, cultural, and residential district, sought to encourage a sense of neighborhood identity, and announced a slowdown in the extension of city services to prospective leap-frog subdivisions. Whether or not he will be able to accomplish his goals will depend on his ability to rally a politically apathetic public and to overcome somehow the decentralization of power in the metropolitan area. Though power is not as fragmented as in most metropolitan areas, the lack of coordination among city government, the autonomous Albuquerque Public Schools, county government, two flood control districts, and the inter-county Council of Governments has made it difficult in the past to institute positive measures and prevent destructive tendencies.

The immediate future will bring little change in the dominance of the central city in the Albuquerque SMSA. The Census Bureau's population estimates for 1975 indicated a 14.7% gain over 1970 for Bernalillo County and 14.6% for the city, while the area outside

Dick Kent Photography

Albuquerque's Northeast Heights 1959. Almost all of the subdivisions pictured were developed after 1953. The two almost empty squares in the center are the future sites for the city's two largest regional shopping centers, Winrock (nearest the bottom) and Coronado.

Dick Kent Photography

Albuquerque's Northeast Heights 1978. Both Winrock (bottom middle), opened in 1961, and Coronado, opened in 1963, have doubled in size as a result of recent expansion. Interstate 40 immediately south of Winrock was completed in 1964 and has been a strong decentralizing force, helping to fill in this area's checkerboard pattern of settlement as well as encourageing similar development farther east. Scheduled hotel and office construction adjacent to the shopping centers will solidify the sector's status as a satellite downtown.

the city showed a similar slight gain in the rate of increase of median income.[30] Nevertheless, the socioeconomic gap between the city of Albuquerque and the rest of the SMSA has actually increased as a result of the post-1970 addition of Sandoval County to the Albuquerque SMSA.[31] Its estimated population of 22,500 in 1975 contained some high-status residents in the small incorporated villages of Corrales and Jemez Springs and in the unincorporated developer's dream of Rio Rancho, but overall its socio-economic indicators in 1970 were much lower than those of the SMSA as defined in 1970. Sandoval, for example, had 41.2% of its workers in white collar jobs vs. 60.7% for Bernalillo County; median years of schooling completed were 10.3 vs. 12.5; and median income was 60% of Bernalillo's.[32] Sandoval is growing faster than Bernalillo largely because its percentage increase in net migration is twice as great, but even the continued influx of high-status people will require at least another decade for it to match Bernalillo indicators. By that time some form of metropolitan consolidation may well have taken place.

Meanwhile the critical issues in local politics will continue to revolve around the often conflicting claims of the economy and the environment and will pit against each other the proponents and opponents of planned growth. What is most interesting here is that the low-income areas of the suburban ring will have the most to gain economically and the most to lose culturally. Will the heavily Chicano, native-born New Mexicans currently tied to a semi-rural way of life join with developers and Chamber of Commerce boosters in the fight against middle-and upper-income Anglo newcomers dedicated to the preservation of what is unique about Albuquerque? The answer to that question will determine much of what happens to the Albuquerque SMSA during the remainder of the century.

Howard N. Rabinowitz graduated from Swarthmore and received his Ph.D. from the University of Chicago. He has been on the faculty of the University of New Mexico at Albuquerque since 1971 and is now an Associate Professor. He is the author of *Race Relations in the Urban South, 1865-1890* (1978).

Notes

The author wishes to thank Professor David R. Goldfield for his comments on an earlier version of this essay and the National Endowment for the Humanities for financial assistance during its preparation.

1. For example, there are no historians among the thirteen contributors to David C. Perry and Alfred J. Watkins (eds.), *The Rise of the Sunbelt Cities* (Beverly Hills: Sage Publications, 1977). An exception among historians is Kenneth T. Jackson, "Metropolitan Government Versus Political Autonomy: Politics on the Crabgrass Frontier," in Kenneth T. Jackson and Stanley K. Schultz (eds.), *Cities in American History* (New York: Alfred A. Knopf, 1972), 442-462. The ongoing work of Carl J. Abbott and Roger W. Lotchin, represented elsewhere in this work, also suggests, that urban historians are finally responding to Horace Greeley's injunction to "turn your face to the great West." See especially Abbott's "Social Geography in the Metropolitan West: Denver, Portland and San Antonio since 1940," (unpublished paper delivered to the Council of University Institutes of Urban Affairs, Denver, Colorado, 10 March 1978). Also worth noting is Robert M. Fogelson, *The Fragmented Metropolis: Los Angeles 1850-1930* (Cambridge: Harvard University Press, 1967) which considers for an earlier period many of the issues discussed in this article.

2. U.S. Bureau of the Census, *Sixteenth Census of Population: 1940* (Washington: U.S. Govt. Printing Office, 1943), II, Part 4, 980, 995; *Seventeenth Census of Population: 1950* (Washington: U.S. Govt. Printing Office, 1952), II, Part 31, 6; *Eighteenth Census of Population: 1960 Vol. I, Characteristics of the Population* (Washington: U.S. Govt. Printing Office, 1963), Part 33, 11; *Nineteenth Census Population: 1970: Number of Inhabitants New Mexico* (Washington: U.S. Govt. Printing Office, 1971), Part 33, 17. The Census Bureau defines an SMSA as "a county or group of contiguous counties [cities and towns in New England] which contains at least one city of 50,000 inhabitants or more, or 'twin cities' with a combined population of at least 50,000. In addition . . . [other] contiguous

Kirtland Air Force Base

Albuquerque Municipal Airport circa 1940. Since construction of new terminal facilities in 1963, the old terminal has had many uses, most recently serving as the home of the Museum of Albuquerque.

counties are included . . . if, according to certain criteria, they are socially and economically integrated with the central city." *Ibid.*, 1970, vii.

3. U.S. Bureau of the Census, *Statistical Abstract of the United States 1970* (Washington: U.S. Govt. Printing Office, 1970), 839; *Ibid.*, 1971, 21, 830. By 1973, the SMSA was estimated to be the nation's 92nd largest and the city was estimated to be the 54th largest. *Ibid.*, 1975, 21, 23.

4. The percentage of employed persons in manufacturing jobs had risen from 7.2% in 1950 to 9.4% in 1960 before plant closings produced the decline in 1970. In 1970, 7.6% of the employed in the entire SMSA were in manufacturing jobs. U.S. Bureau of the Census, *Seventeenth Census: 1950*, II, Part 31, 15; *Eighteenth Census: 1960*, I, Part 33, 63; *Nineteenth Census: 1970, General Social and Economic Characteristics*, Part 33, 97. Useful background material on Albuquerque can be found in: Erna Fergusson, *Albuquerque* (Albuquerque: Merle Armitage Editions, 1947); *idem*, "Albuquerque: A Place to Live In," in Ray B. West, Jr., (ed.), *Rocky Mountain Cities* (New York: W.W. Norton & Co., 1949), 151-178; "Albuquerque: Bombs Build Boom Town," *Business Week*, 1080 (May 13, 1950), 58-61; Neil M. Clark, "The Cities of America: Albuquerque," *Saturday Evening Post*, 222 (April 8, 1950), 26-27, 139, 141-142, 144-145; Alan J. Oppenheimer, "The Historical Background of Albuquerque, New Mexico," mimeographed (Albuquerque: City Planning Department, 1962). See also the numerous "theme issues" of *Albuquerque Progress* published by the Albuquerque National Bank beginning in 1934.

5. In 1973 the only cities with a larger percentage of their area's population than Albuquerque were San Antonio, Memphis, Austin, Jacksonville, and El Paso. *Trends in Metropolitan America* (Washington: Advisory Commission on Intergovernmental Relations, February 1977), 3, 14-16. Although the Albuquerque SMSA grew by 20.4% between 1960 and 1970, the urban part grew by 23.3% while the rural part declined by 12.7%. U.S. Bureau of the Census, Nineteenth Census: 1970, Number of Inhabitants, Part 33, 13.

6. *New Mexico Laws of 1963*, chapter 160.

7. For the forces undermining two earlier attempts at South Valley incorporation, see *Albuquerque Journal*, November 5, 1960, A-8; September 20, 1963, September 22, 1963, A-4. For the failure due to economic constraints of a still earlier attempt to incorporate Alameda, an old settlement north of Albuquerque, see *ibid.*, November 11, 1945, 1, 2; December 6, 1945, 2. For a good, if somewhat romanticized picture of one of the valley's semi-rural villages (Los Griegos) during the 1930s, see Irene Fisher, *Bathtub and Silver Bullet* (Placitas, N.M.: The Tumbleweed Press, 1976).

8. *Albuquerque Journal* editorial, January 30, 1940, 6. See also *ibid.*, January 23, 1940, 6.

9. *Ibid.*, February 21, 1970, 1, 7, quote, 7.

10. See, for example, *ibid.*, June 12, 1940, 1, 7.

11. *Ibid.*, January 9, 1946, 6. See also *Albuquerque Progress*, XIII (June 1946), 3, 13.

12. See *New Mexico Status Annotated 1953*

Kirtland Air Force Base

Kirtland Field barracks and offices circa 1943. Attracted by the abundant open land, ideal climate, and the lobbying efforts of local boosters, the Army constructed the Albuquerque Air Force Base in 1941. Renamed Kirtland Field and finally Kirtland Air Force Base, its spectacular growth has had a tremendous impact on the city's economy while its spread towards the mountains has blocked further urban expansion to the south.

Kirtland Air Force Base

Aerial view of Kirtland Field looking east circa 1945. For caption see above.

Compiliation, secs. 14-6-1 through 14-6-13.

13. E. H. Chacon, *Annexations to the City of Albuquerque, New Mexico* (Albuquerque: Albuquerque City Engineers Office, Department of Public Works, 1967); U.S. Bureau of the Census, *Statistical Abstract of the United States 1975*, 23; *Albuquerque Journal*, February 24, 1978, A-3.

14. *Albuquerque Journal*, August 22, 1948, section 2, 1. An indication of future trends, however, was the annexation in early 1950 of a "sparsely settled area" consisting of 3300 acres and 15 to 20 residents. *Ibid.*, January 25, 1950, 1.

15. U.S. Bureau of the Census, *Eighteenth Census: 1960*, I, Part 33, 10; *Nineteenth Census: 1970, Number of Inhabitants*, Part 33, 12.

16. For a good introduction to the effect of annexation on city growth and well-being, see Jackson, "Metropolitan Government Versus Political Autonomy," 442-462 and *Metropolitan Trends*, 3 and *passim*. See also Arnold Fleischmann, "Sunbelt Boosterism: The Politics of Postwar Growth and Annexation in San Antonio," in Perry and Watkins (eds.), *Rise of the Sunbelt Cities*, 151-168.

17. U.S. Bureau of the Census, *Nineteenth Census: 1970, General Social and Economic Characteristics*, Part 33, 131, 139, 142, 144-146, 149, 171, 179.

18. Schnore's work is quite extensive, but see especially Leo Schnore, "Measuring City-Suburban Status Differences," *Urban Affairs Quarterly*, III (September 1967), 95-

74

108 and *Class and Race in City and Suburbs* (Chicago: Markham Publishing Co., 1972). It should be noted, however, that as far as income is concerned, Tucson has been steadily losing ground to its suburbs so that as of 1973 per capita income in the city was 88% of its suburbs whereas Albuquerque's was 144% of its suburbs, the highest differential in the nation. Meanwhile in Phoenix the suburban per capita income was equal to that of the city and will no doubt soon surpass it. The eighteen largest western cities had a mean of 104% with only 11 having equal or greater per capita incomes than their suburbs. The only cities in the country even approaching Albuquerque's per capita income dominance over its suburbs were El Paso, Corpus Christi, Memphis, Tulsa, Mobile, Columbus (Ga.), Shreveport, and Jackson. The mean for the largest 85 cities was 96% (*Metropolitan Trends,* 39-43). See also John D. Kasarda and George V. Redfern, "Differential Patterns of City and Suburban Growth in the United States," *Journal of Urban History,* 2 (November 1975), 43-66; John J. Harrigan, "A New Look at Central-City Suburban Differences," *Social Science,* 51 (Autumn 1976), 200-208.

19. Letter of Sarah Yott to the editor, *Albuquerque Journal,* June 21, 1940, 12.

20. See, for example, *ibid.,* February 18, 1948, 1; April 11, 1949, 1.

21. Quoted *ibid.,* April 11, 1949, 1; see also City Commission Minutes, January 17-18, 1949, Vol 49, 23-24, 27-29 (Office of the City Clerk, Albuquerque Municipal Building). For opposition to annexation to other areas, see City Commission Minutes, August 3, September 7, 1948, Vol. 48, 363-366, 422-423; *Albuquerque Journal,* January 27, 1950, 3. By the late 1940s opponents of annexation often had the support of two members of the five-man commission who feared the financial costs of annexing vacant land on the one hand and the political costs of bringing into the city numerous unwilling suburbanites on the other. For similar opposition to annexation among Phoenix sub-

urbs, see the report of F. B. Blandford, Jr., an Albuquerque city planner who had just returned from Phoenix, in City Commission Minutes, June 7, 1955, Vol. 55, No. 2, 319.

22. See, for example, *Albuquerque Journal,* December 5, 1940, 1; December 7, 1940, 10; September 21, 1950, 4; November 16, 1950, 5; December 24, 1950, 1, 2. See also petitions from various local civic and business organizations calling for consolidation in City Commission Minutes, July 8, August 5, 12, 1952, Vol. 52, 330, 384, 390-391. They resulted in appointment of a City and County Consolidation Committee. City CommissionMinutes, September 9, 1952, Vol. 52, 426; January 6, 1953, Vol. 53, 3.

23. City residents cast 12,533 votes in favor of consolidation and 10,072 against; county residents cast 1,392 votes in favor and 7,477 against. Daniel D. Weaks, "An Analysis of the Consolidation Effort in Albuquerque-Bernalillo County," mimeographed (Studies in Urban Affairs Number 19; Albuquerque: Albuquerque Urban Observatory, 1973), 86.

24. *Ibid., passim.* For the longstanding opposition of county residents to stricter building regulations, see *Albuquerque Journal,* January 10, 1940, 5; January 14, 1940, 1, 5; January 23, 1940, 6; June 19, 1950, 5. Unlike most recent consolidation campaigns elsewhere, neither race nor class were issues due to the relatively even distribution of the SMSA's few blacks and to the heavy concentration in the county of low income people, most of whom were Chicano.

25. *Albuquerque Journal,* December 11, 1940, 4; December 12, 1940, 4; March 21, 1945, 2; April 28, 1945, 7; May 1, 1945, 1; May 2, 1945, 9; Tom Wiley, *Public School Education in New Mexico* (Albuquerque: Division of Government Research of the University of New Mexico, 1965), 91.

26. *Albuquerque Journal* editorial, June 20, 1947, 10. See also *ibid.,* August 28, 1948, 6.

27. Oppenheimer, "Historical Background," A-16; for the adoption and content of the city's first comprehensive zoning ordinance, see City Commission Minutes,

November 17, 1953, Vol. 53, No. 3, 666-667. Prior to the organization of an official city planning department, there was first a weak City Planning Advisory Board and then a stronger citizen-run City Planning Commission aided by the city's first Director of Planning. See City Commission Minutes, January 25, February 15, June 7, June 14, 1949, Vol. 49, 42, 71-72, 260-261, 272-274. For earlier interest in planning and zoning in Albuquerque during the teens and 1920s, see Dorothy I. Cline, *Albuquerque and the City Manager Plan 1917-1948* (Albuquerque: Division of Research of the Department of Government of the University of New Mexico, 1951), 33; S. R. DeBoer, "A Tentative Zoning Ordinance for Albuquerque, New Mexico," typescript, ca. December 1928 (Planning Department Archives, Albuquerque Municipal Building).

28. The Albuquerque/Bernalillo County Comprehensive Plan consists of four parts that were approved separately between February and August 1975 by the city and county governments. The four parts are: *Guidelines for Public Systems West of the Rio Grande* (February-March 1975); *Policies Plan* (April 1975); *Metropolitan Areas and Urban Centers Plan* (April 1975); *Plan for Major Open Space* (August 1975).

29. Paul L. Hain, F. Chris Garcia, Judd Conway, "From Council-Manager to Mayor-Council: The Case of Albuquerque," *Nation's Cities,* 13 (October 1975), 10-12.

30. U.S. Bureau of the Census, *Current Population Reports: Population Estimates and Projections* Series P-25 No. 679 (Washington: U.S. Govt. Printing Office, April 1977), 9.

31. U.S. Bureau of the Census, *Current Population Reports: Federal-State Cooperative Program for Population Estimates* Series P-26 No. 75-31 (Washington: U.S. Govt. Printing Office, August 1976), 3.

32. U.S. Bureau of the Census, *Nineteenth Census: 1970: General Social and Economic Characteristics,* Part 33, 98-99.

Equality of Opportunity On the Urban Frontier:
Access to Credit in Denver, Colorado Territory, 1858-1876

Lyle W. Dorsett

Horace Greeley's popularization of the challenge "Go West, young man, go forth into the Country," put into words a faith embraced by many nineteenth-century Americans. In short, the belief maintained that the West was a land of opportunity. It was a place for new beginnings. A region across the Alleghenies, even beyond the Mississippi, the West was an area where hard-working, strong people could get ahead regardless of their birthplace, family name, education or wealth. Students of myths in history correctly point out that what is true is not always as important as what people assume is true. If people fervently believe in something they will act on it, reality notwithstanding.[1]

In this essay my concern is less with what people assumed and more with what actually existed. Obviously people supposed opportunities were plentiful in the West. Settlers who moved to the territories in the nineteenth century were legion. But once they reached the promised land, did they find equality of economic opportunity? Freedom to earn money, after all, motivated most emigrants.

A fundamental factor in measuring equality of op-

Denver Saloons and Taverns.

Fred Z. Salomon

demographic trend was so great that it became a problem. William Byers, the editor of the *Rocky Mountain News* and an important promoter of Denver and its hinterland, urged newcomers to farm as well as search for gold and seek employment in the city. As early as 1859 he suggested that the most certain route to wealth was in farming. Thousands of prospectors and urban dwellers, Byers noted, needed food that was still being imported long distances at great expense from the east and the Salt Lake Valley. By the mid-1870s, promoter Byers was using his newspaper office in Denver as a clearing house. From there he tried to direct Denver's newcomers to other towns and parts of the territory. Denver was already crowded and other communities needed workers.[3]

Most clearly, then, pilgrims to Colorado Territory believed that there were economic opportunities in Denver. To what extent were they correct? If access to credit provides insight, the R. G. Dun credit reports, housed in Harvard University's Baker Library, are a valuable source for furnishing some answers.

Because there was an increasing demand for capital in Colorado during the territorial years, wholesalers, bankers and other investors in the "states" wanted to know who the credit applicants were and to what extent they were reliable. Such information was needed so that intelligent decisions could be made about loans. The company that could supply the data after 1859 was R. G. Dun and Company. Originally employed in a mercantile agency owned by Lewis and Arthur Tappan, Robert Graham Dun worked for the company eight years prior to 1859. That year the thirty-three year old entrepreneur bought the company that would become Dun and Bradstreet in 1933.

During the late nineteenth century R.G. Dun made a national reputation as a dependable credit investigator. With an organization of scores (ultimately hundreds) of correspondents in the states, territories and foreign countries, the agency described its system to prospective clients in this way in 1858:

> The principal object of the Agency is to supply to annual subscribers information respecting the character, capacity and pecuniary conditions of persons asking credit . . . . correspondents are selected for their integrity, long residence in the county, general acquaintance, business experience and judgment.[4]

Local correspondents sent information about people seeking credit to the home office in New York. Also, the agency had travelling reporters who checked up on the accuracy of the correspondents. The reports were ultimately copied in ledgers at the home office, and it is those volumes that are housed at Baker Library.

The correspondents each had a code number which identified them. The key no longer exists so it is impossible to know who in Colorado sent in the reports. We

portunity is access to credit. In Colorado Territory, for example, the bulk of the prospectors and settlers were people of modest or no material means. If they had been well established back east they never would have moved (health-seekers excepted) to the Great American Desert. Credit was essential if they were to buy land, get a grub stake, or start businesses in the urban communities. The actual choices available to prospectors and residents of mining towns have been thoroughly researched by Duane Smith. Other scholars, particularly Gene Gressley, Lewis Atherton, Fred Shannon and John Hicks, have studied the opportunities and hardships of ranchers and farmers.[2] What has not been focused on specifically is the availability of credit in important territorial cities such as Denver.

During the middle ages the city represented freedom to the rural peasant. Indeed, the phrase "Die Stadt Luft macht Frei" (city air makes you free) became a slogan of hope in medieval Europe. That the city was viewed as a place of economic opportunity in nineteenth-century America is apparent also. Not only do we have census data to support Fred Shannon's thesis that many rural dwellers moved to the cities; in Colorado that not only cannot expose the informant, we do not know if a favorable report meant that the person actually received the loan, or if an unfavorable report meant denial of credit. What we do know is the type of judgment being passed, and we can assume that Dun's agency's recommendations were followed and found to be reliable. What else accounts for the growing number of R. G. Dun and Company subscribers, and the increasing popularity of the company among creditors?

If one of the reasons for going West was to escape an environment where established people had marked advantages, Colorado Territory must have disappointed some pioneers. When a newcomer to Denver had eastern connections or had already built a good reputation in the east, that advantage traveled with him. One man was lauded as "a grad [uate] of . . . Law School in NY City," and another applauded for being "successful . . . [and] well known in St. Louis." Another man was celebrated for doing "a fine exchange bus [iness] with the East."[5] If a prospective borrower had maintained a business establishment elsewhere, as three people had done at Leavenworth, Kansas, St. Louis and Boonville, Missouri, such experience was clearly an advantage.[6] One man was cited approvingly because he owned property in Chicago, and a woman was given a favorable report because business houses in St. Louis knew her and had confidence in her.[7]

More than good reports followed the transients who went to Colorado. Bad reputations traveled long distances too. They undoubtedly prevented some immigrants from wiping the slate clean and getting a new start (with credit anyway) in the new land. Joseph Arnold was listed this way: "Came here from Cairo, Ill [inois] where he bore a bad reputation and was regarded as a bad man."[8] Of two partners it was noted that "there are sevl [several] claims here for collection from Kansas and also from Kansas City Mo."[9] One escapee from the east was cited for skipping out on debts in St. Louis and another for defrauding creditors in Meadville, Pennsylvania.[10]

It is difficult to generalize about access to credit for minorities. There were not many blacks in Colorado Territory, and thus not many can be identified as credit applicants. In one case where a mulatto named Barney Ford was cited, he was labelled "a yellow man" by the correspondent. Despite the widespread prejudice against Afro-Americans in the United States at that time, Ford was most favorably endorsed by the agency's employee. "He is good. Owns Valuable RE [real estate] and is one of the oldest residents and stands No. 1 at home." On a different date the correspondent continued in the same laudatory vein: "Man of excellent char [acter] and stdg [standing] proverbial for his honesty and square dealing."[11]

Jewish settlers were often labelled as such, but apparently not denied credit. A. Zodiag, according to a Dun reporter, "appears to be an active wide awake young hebrew." Joseph Gottlieb, a pawnbroker, was

Edward Chase.

listed as a "Jew wor [th] 10-15m [thousand dollars] . . . safe . . . good credit."[12] Two merchandisers, the Salomon brothers, were given one of the strongest recommendations in the ledger. "It is one of the best firms in the territory. They may be credited to any extent that their trade may require."[13]

Catholics were never identified in the reports. Italians were not labelled either, but perhaps that was because their names made their ethnic identity clear. R. Gandalfo and C. B. Serventi were fruit dealers in Denver. When they moved on to California they were reported to be "paid up here and left in good shape."[14] Unlike these Italians, however, Germans did not always fare well. German-born Charles Boettcher did receive highest ratings, but a Denver soap manufacturer was stigmatized as "quite an ordinary ignorant old German . . . . not recommended for credit."[15]

If ethnicity in some cases abridged access to credit, equality of opportunity was certainly restricted for those who did not measure up to the dominant society's view of worthiness. Those who embodied the traits of honesty, frugality, hard work, temperance, and marital fidelity — virtues urged on every school child who learned to read from William Holmes McGuffey's readers — got the most favorable recommendations.[16] Dun's measuring stick was applied in all cases. If the potential borrower scored well, the descriptions were adulatory: "High character and standing and very enterprising . . . good habits . . . strictly honora-

William Newton Byers.

could have a profitable business and substantial assets including real property, and he still would be downgraded. Edward Chase, for example, one of Denver's wealthiest men and wisest investors in real estate, was written up in the following derisive way: "Keep [s] a drinking and gambling [establishment] in community and not to be trusted more than any of the occupation . . . worth perhaps 30m [thousand dollars] or more."[19] A saloonkeeper who became deputy sheriff was listed as a man who, when he came here, "bore a bad reputation and was regarded as a bad man."[20] Another Denver saloonkeeper, noted as one who "owns RE [real estate] here worth 3 to 5m [thousand dollars] carries very small stock [in his saloon] . . . he has made money . . . had the reputation of being a hard citizen . . . not recommended for credit."[21]

Woe to loan-seeking saloonkeepers and even to men who had other occupations, if they led a life that fell short of Dun's moral standards. Weighed in the balances and found wanting was one chap because "he lives up to his income," and another for being too "disposed to take his ease."[22] But the most thunderous wrath of the mercantile agency was reserved for men who drank alcohol to excess and maintained mistresses. A Denver lawyer was described as "separate from his wife . . . char [acter] on acct [account] of unmoral habs [habits], keeps a mistress, etc. . . . he is now morally, socially, physically, mentally and legally a wreck."[23]

ble . . .," were some of the key phrases that the most fortunate found on their recommendations. Another high mark came for investing in real estate. The ledgers are full of applause for putting money into property, whereas holding mining stocks without substantial real property was viewed as careless, even reckless.[17]

Women, too, if they had good character and habits, fared extremely well. Indeed, women without collateral could usually get recommendations for credit where men could not, even when everything was equal except their sex. No doubt this was due in part to the Denver correspondents' desire to attract and keep decent and morally upstanding women in the predominantly male territory. In any case, between 1859 and 1877 women were not denied equality of economic opportunity when it came to finding credit endorsements. On the contrary, they had an edge over men as far as collateral requirements.[18]

By far the people most discriminated against were neither women nor ethnic minorities, they were saloonkeepers. Excessive drinking, laziness, and loose morals were associated with this business. A saloonkeeper

Barney Ford.

Denver Public Library.

Drawing conclusions from the R.G. Dun materials is speculative at best. With some certainty it can be said that women had equal access to credit. Other minorities such as Jews, Germans, and blacks usually were not denied good recommendations, but how disadvantaged they were by the labels placed on them is impossible to say. F. Z. Salomon was Jewish. He was so labelled by a Dun correspondent who nevertheless recommended him highly. Salomon became one of Denver's most prominent and wealthy businessmen. The German Charles Boettcher's story was strikingly similar to Salomon's as was the fate of one black man, Barney L. Ford.

With the exception of Edward Chase, most of Denver's saloonkeepers sank into obscurity, just as the agency's investigators assumed they would do. On the other hand, men such as Walter Cheesman, John Evans, David Moffat and James Archer were noted by these same investigators to have the habits and inner qualities that would vault them to positions of wealth and prominence and that is precisely how they ended up. Were the Dun correspondents men of vision — nineteenth-century prophets who recognized men of quality when they saw them? Their recommendations and predictions seem to say so. But then, maybe their biases toward territorial settlers with certain life styles became self-fulfilling prophesies. If you got credit, after all, your chances of getting ahead in a boom community were markedly increased.

An important question relating to this story involves

the credit-rating standards. In brief, who set these guidelines? Certainly R. G. Dun had a voice here. However, it should be noted that, according to James D. Norris, Dun's most recent and able biographer, Dun did not practice what he preached. A high-living man who spent everything that he earned, the credit magnate also drank liquor to excess and died of cirrhosis of the liver. R. G. Dun also recklessly speculated in silver mines. He lost $300,000 that he gambled on Colorado's Caribou Mine.[24]

Even if Dun in effect said "do as I say, not as I do," his rules applied in general. Beyond this, on the other hand, local correspondents obviously set standards. For instance, women got credit in Colorado when they could not have found it back east — for local reasons. Also, saloonkeepers were an exceptionally unsavory lot in Colorado Territory. They were loathed by most influential people in early Denver, but this attitude did not prevail in eastern and southern parts of the United States during the same years.[25] Finally, it should be underlined that the essence of the R. G. Dun character and life-style evaluation grew out of much more than Dun's personal views and the notions of local investigators — it came out of nineteenth-century American culture. Churches, schools, novelists and textbook authors all played a part in stressing the importance of Victorian respectability and behavior.

Surpassing the impact of R. G. Dun and Company on equality of opportunity and the propagation of the nineteenth-century value system, this credit reporting enterprise had a powerful effect on urban and business development. Local money for mining, smelting, commercial farming, and transportation was almost nonexistent in the territorial years. The economic development of Denver and its vast mining and agricultural hinterland could never have occurred so rapidly without a system of credit reporting. Denver's growth was inextricably tied to investments from Boston, New York and Britain. Outside capital was the Queen City's lifeblood. Without it the region's resources would not have been exploited, and the vast throng of settlers would never have emigrated to the central Rockies.[26] But the money was forthcoming because investors could learn — with more than a fair degree of accuracy — what kinds of risks they were taking. So in the last analysis it is difficult to determine the importance of what was written down over one hundred years ago in those bulky credit ledgers without access to records which would allow us to see the loans granted and the results achieved of those Dun rated.

Lyle W. Dorsett has been Professor of History at the University of Denver since 1972. A graduate of the University of Missouri, he received his Ph.D. in 1965. Among his publications are five books in urban history: *The Pendergast Machine, The Challenge of the City, 1860-1910, Franklin D. Roosevelt and the City Bosses, The Queen City: A History of Denver, K. C.: A History of Kansas City, Missouri.* The Kansas City volume was co-authored with A. T. Brown whom Dorsett serves with as co-editor of a series entitled "Western Urban History."

FOOTNOTES

1. Henry Nash Smith, *Virgin Land: The American West as Symbol and Myth* (Cambridge, 1950).
2. Duane A. Smith, *Rocky Mountain Mining Camps: The Urban Frontier* (Bloomington, 1967); "The San Juans: A Computerized Portrait" *Colorado Magazine*, LII, 2, (Spring, 1975), 137-52; Gene M. Gressley, *Bankers and Cattlemen* (New York, 1966); Lewis Atherton, *The Cattle Kings* (Bloomington, 1961); Fred A. Shannon, *The Farmer's Last Frontier: Agriculture, 1860-1897* (New York, 1945); John D. Hicks, *The Populist Revolt*, (Minneapolis, 1931). There is good material in James E. Wright, *The Politics of Populism: Dissent in Colorado* (New Haven, 1974), but most of his data and conclusions relate to the post-territorial period (1876-   ).
3. *Rocky Mountain News* April 19, 1859; Lyle W. Dorsett, *The Queen City: A History of Denver* (Boulder, 1977).
4. This quotation is from Edward N. Vose, *Seventy-five Years of the Mercantile Agency, R. G. Dun and Company, 1841-*

1916 (New York, 1916), 63. This volume has a brief history of the agency. For more background or material on the agency and its function see James H. Madison, "The Credit Reports of R. G. Dun and Company as Historical Sources," *Historical Methods Newsletter*, VIII, (1975), 128-131; and Madison, "The Evolution of Commercial Credit Reporting Agencies in Nineteenth-Century America," *Business History Review*, XLVIII, 2, (Summer, 1974), 164-86; and Robert W. Lovett, "Nineteenth-Century Credit Information" in John Lawton, ed., *Shop Talk: Papers on Historical Business and Commercial Records of New England Delivered Before a Symposium held November 2, 1973 at the Boston Public Library* (Boston, 1975).
5. The R. G. Dun and Company ledgers I used are labelled "Colorado Territory." I will cite only the volume number, date, and the name on the entry. Vol. I, December 3, 1877, Platt Rogers; Vol. I, November 14, 1871, James Archer; Vol. I, May 3, 1870, Jerome B. Chaffee.

6. Vol. II, December 19, 1874, L. Reuben; Vol. II, October 11, 1875, Ch. B. Patterson; Vol. II, October 14, 1874, Mrs. M. A. Simpson.
7. Vol. II, December 7, 1874, John Evans; Vol. II, October 14, 1874, Mrs. M. A. Simpson.
8. Vol. II, December 1, 1874, Joseph Arnold.
9. Vol. II, June 17, 1876.
10. Vol. II, December 1, 1874, Charles E. Leichenring; Vol. II, September 25, 1873, Mrs. E. H. Perkins.
11. Vol. I, October 4, 1870, November 14, B. L. Ford.
12. Vol. II, February 23, 1875, A. Zodiag; Vol. I, June 19, 1873, Joseph Gottlieb.
13. Vol. I, August 19, 1863, Salomon Bros.
14. Vol. II, April 2, 1875, R. Gandolfo and Co.
15. Vol. II, March 8, 1874, C. Boettcher; Vol. II, October 26, 1875, June 27, 1876, Wm. Bender.
16. For an analysis of the McGuffey readers see Harvey C. Minnich, *William Holmes McGuffey and His Readers* (New York, 1936); and Irvin G. Wyllie, *The Self-Made*

Man in America: The Myth of Rags to Riches (New Brunswick, 1954).

17. Vol. I, November 14, 1871, James Archer; Vol. I, October 27, 1871, W. H. Buchtel; Vol. I, August 4, 1875, David H. Moffat, Jr.; Vol. I, October 24, 1872, R. W. Woodbury; Vol. II, June 21, 1875, C. Boettcher.

18. Examples of reports on women are: Vol. I, May 27, 1873, Mrs. A. L. Williams; Vol. II, October 14, 1874, Mrs. M. A. Simpson; Vol. I, July 3, 1873, Mrs. John Evans; Vol. II, September 30, 1873, Mrs. A. Stimson; Vol. II, April 10, 1874.

19. Vol. I, November 16, 1865, April 19, 1866, January 2, 1867, Heatly and Chase.

20. Vol. II, December 1, 1874, December 6, 1875, Joseph Arnold.

21. Vol. II, March 16, 1874, December 1, 1874, O. H. Woodward.

22. Vol. I, December 4, 1880, Jas. T. Weborn; Vol. I, November 16, 1871, Hughes and Morrison.

23. Vol. I, October 18, 1871, November 14, 1871, J. B. Smith.

24. For raising the question posed in this paragraph, I thank Professor Duane A. Smith, Fort Lewis College, Durango, Colorado. See James D. Norris, *R. G. Dun and Co., 1841-1900: The Development of Credit-Reporting in the Nineteenth Century* (Westport, Ct., 1978) and Duane A. Smith, *Silver Saga* (Boulder, 1974). Also relevant to this subject was Norris's paper, "R. G. Dun and Co. and the Development of Credit Reporting in the Nineteenth Century," as well as his comments, presented at the Pacific Coast Branch of the American Historical Association, San Francisco, August 18, 1978.

25. For this insight I am indebted to Professor Roger Ransom of the University of California, Riverside, who made this point at the Pacific Coast Branch Meeting in San Francisco, August 18, 1978. See also Roger Ransom and Richard Sutch, *One Kind of Freedom: The Economic Consequences of Emancipation* (Cambridge, England and N. Y., 1977).

26. For detailed evidence on investing in Denver and its hinterland see Lyle W. Dorsett, *The Queen City: A History of Denver* (Boulder, 1977).

Los Angeles Aqueduct:
A Search for Water

By William K. Jones
Museum Curator, Dwight D. Eisenhower Library

Water has always been a problem to Los Angeles. This major city, founded in 1781 as Pueblo de Nuestra Senora la Reina de Los Angeles, received most of its water until 1913 from the Los Angeles River by means of a primitive municipal system.[1] In 1868, a private company, the Los Angeles City Water Company, ob- tained a franchise to operate the public water works for thirty years. After four years of litigation, beginning in 1898, the city recovered control of the system. In the period 1868 to 1900, Los Angeles' population increased from less than 5,000 to more than 100,000 people.[2]

Most of Los Angeles' growth took place in the two

The builders (left to right) — J.B. Lippincott, Fred Eaton and William Mulholland.

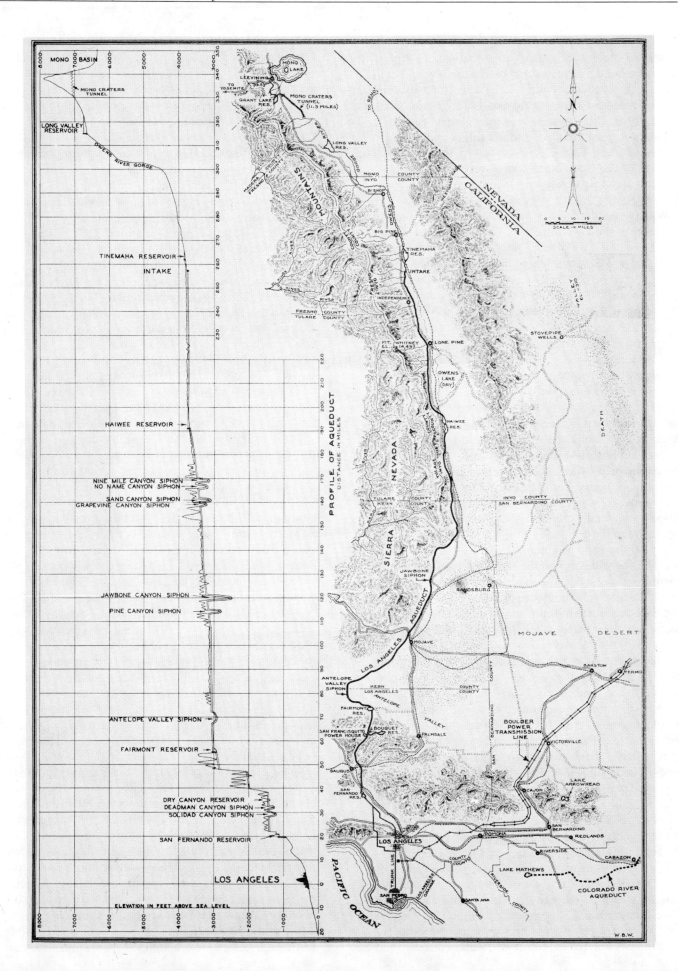

decades preceding 1900, doubling in the ten years from 1880 to 1890, and again from 1890 to 1900. City planners, assuming that the astonishing growth would continue, estimated that with conservative use existing water resources would be adequate until about 1920. But four years after the turn of the century, the city's population again doubled, and the safety margin of fifteen years was cut to four years. At this time two surveys of the Los Angeles area were made to determine the quantity of water that could be obtained near the city.[3]

William Mulholland, Chief Engineer and General Manager of the City Bureau of Water Works and Supply, examined the water resources of the southern part of the state. His report stated that a ten to twenty year supply could be obtained at a reasonable cost by building reservoirs in the San Gabriel Valley or on the coastal plain. He pointed out, however, this would lead to rapid exhaustion of water resources required by communities commercially and politically tributary to Los Angeles.[4]

Joseph B. Lippincott, survising engineer of the United States Reclamation Service for the Southwest, prepared the second report for the city. His survey pointed out that water sources tapped in the Los Angeles area would be expensive and temporary.[5]

The Mulholland-Lippincott reports suggested that the municipality should go to a remote region where a minimum of injury would be caused by the acquisition and removal of water. After considerable searching Los Angeles city leaders selected the Owens River, situated between the eastern base of the Sierra Nevada Mountains and the Inyo Mountain Range, as the new water source. The valley is about 120 miles long, from two to ten miles wide, and lies at an elevation of between 3,500 and 6,000 feet. It is situated approximately in the center of California, north to south and is isolated from the San Joaquin Valley by the "High Sierras" and from Los Angeles by the Mojave Desert.[6]

The Owens River has its source in the Sierra Nevada Mountains. The snowfall on western slopes is extremely heavy and nearly every canyon carries a fine stream of water throughout the year. These gentle brooks become veritable rivers in the spring and summer months. Thirty-five such tributaries flow into Owens River from a drainage area of 2,800 square miles. The 150 mile long river is supplied entirely by this run-off. There is enough water in the river to irrigate the Owens Valley, and according to one report the water wasted, which runs into the Owens Lake, a salt *playa* of about seventy-five square miles at the end of the Owens River, could amply supply a city of two million people.[7]

Fred Eaton, engineer, rancher and ex-mayor of Los Angeles, first suggested to Los Angeles water officials that they turn to the Owens River. Eaton had been Chief Engineer and Superintendent of the Los Angeles City Water Company, and his experience working for both the city and the old franchised water company had

given him insight into water needs. Thirteen years before the valley was chosen, Eaton had seen its potential and had begun to buy water options and land in the area. In the fall of 1904 he began extensive purchasing of contracts and options on water-bearing property, so that by the time he presented his idea to the representatives of the city, he had obtained over 30,000 dollars worth of property. Eaton first proposed a combined private and municipal project in which the city would receive 10,000 miner's[8] inches of water for domestic uses with the surplus water to be available to Eaton and his associates for disposal outside the city.[9]

Mulholland accompanied Eaton to Owens Valley in September of 1904. As the two engineers traveled by wagon over the 250 miles of desert to the valley, Eaton pointed out that in some past geologic period a river had apparently flowed from the eastern foot of the Sierras to within a few miles of the Southern California Plain. The flow of this river had been cut off by volcanic action which had formed a barrier across the southern end of Owens Valley. The two men say, however, that the barrier was low and that after it was passed the only obstacle in the way of an aqueduct would be the mountain range north of Los Angeles. They decided that if the city could take advantage of this old river course, a water line could be built at a minimum cost and without the use of a single pump.[10]

Because of the growing interest in water and electrical power in the West, Los Angeles met competition in Owens Valley. Two other groups had seen the possibilities of the Owens River. One, a local electrical power company, made plans to build an aqueduct and a power transmission line to Los Angeles, but this endeavor was being checked by the city's second rival, the United States Reclamation Service. The Reclamation Service presented the greatest obstacle to Los Angeles' bid to obtain water from the Sierras.

As early as June, 1903, J. C. Clausen, an engineer for the Service, had surveyed Owens Valley as a possible location for a federal irrigation project. Although this examination was merely preliminary and the local residents were warned that the survey might result in the condemning of the area, they doubted that the federal project would materialize. When Los Angeles eventually won Owens Valley, the local farmers and ranchers believed that the Reclamation Service had sold out their interests. In 1904, one month before his trip to the valley with Mulholland, Eaton had accompanied a Reclamation Service crew on a survey into this area. Eaton realized that he and city officials must act quickly to obtain it as a source of water for Los Angeles.[11]

To resolve the conflict of interest with the Reclamation Service, the city had to show a definite need for the area and to receive a commitment from Los Angeles taxpayers indicating their support of such a project. On his return from the valley, Mulholland began a detailed study of the proposed line. He plotted an approximate route and made an estimate of the cost and time that would be involved. He believed that 25,000,000 dollars would cover the purchase of land and water rights and the cost of construction and that it could be built in five years. Mulholland completed the plans by early 1905 and presented them to the Los Angeles Water Board. After approving them the Board announced that Lippincott had sent word that the government might step aside if the city's project were publicly owned from one end to the other. The ruling made in May of 1905 stated:

> Against a private enterprise, the Reclamation Service could exercise the right of condemnation. As against a municipality seeking water for a large urban population, the government would not persist in its project, its policy being to promote the good of the greatest number.[12]

Eaton, after being notified of this ruling, decided to sell.

This presented still another problem for the Los Angeles Water Board. Because the options were about to expire, there was no time for a bond issue to raise the money to purchase Eaton's holdings. If the city allowed the options to expire, the cost of re-purchase would be exorbitant. The city's plans for Owens Valley were not publicly known, but there had been enough activity and interest in the area to arouse curiosity and to raise the price of water options. With these problems in mind the city water board authorized William H. Workman, City Treasurer, to take 150,000 dollars from the board's funds to purchase Eaton's property. Had the bond issue which was held later in the fall failed, city leaders having used public funds to buy land over 200 miles from Los Angeles would have been in an embarrassing position. On May 22, 1905, the city bought out Fred Eaton.[13]

As soon as the water board notified the Reclamation Service that it had taken steps to make the planned water project entirely a public venture, the Service called a meeting of a board of engineers to decide the fate of the federal plan for Owens Valley. This three man board met in San Francisco in late July and held hearings on the Owens Valley Reclamation Project. Testifying at these meetings were Clausen, who had supervised the survey of the area, and Lippincott. Clausen's testimony favored continuation of the federal government plans, but Lippincott urged that regardless of the plan's feasibility the government should not continue surveys and the whole idea should be abandoned in favor of Los Angeles. The board issued its decision on July 28, 1905. The engineers stated that they favored the federal project and believed it should be completed, but that since Los Angeles had made it impractical by purchasing land and water options in the area, the government should stop work in the valley.[14]

On the last day of July, 1905, the Los Angeles *Times* released the news of the proposed aqueduct. Previously the water board had informed the newspapers of their actions but had requested that the project be kept out of the news. The official explanation of the board's secrecy was that:

> Any advance knowledge of the intentions of the City of Los Angeles to purchase great tracts of land and water rights in Owens Valley would certainly have led to local excitement and loss to the City. The City officials, therefore, conducted preliminary negotiations in this quiet and business-like manner before making public announcements.[15]

Not only were the people of Los Angeles and Owens Valley not publicly informed of what was happening, but neither was the City Council which had no advance notice of the plans.[16]

In trying to keep their plans for Owens Valley secret and to prevent exploitation of the city by valley land owners and speculators, the water board unknowingly allowed a syndicate of newspapermen, realtors, and one of their own board colleagues to make a fortune by giving them privileged information. This wealth was made not in Owens Valley but almost 200 miles away in the San Fernando Valley. As early as 1903 investors had seen the possibilities of the San Fernando Valley as an agricultural area to supply Los Angeles, but the lack of water presented a problem. Despite this drawback a group of investors, including Harrison Gray Otis, owner of the Los Angeles *Times,* Edwin T. Earl, owner of the Los Angeles *Express,* L. C. Brand, president of the Title Guarantee and Trust Company, and Henry Edwards Huntington, owner of the electric inter-urban railroad that served Los Angeles, began purchasing land in the San Fernando Valley. They planned to extend an electric railroad line into the valley and to subdivide the land for sale to settlers.[17]

On November 28, 1904, General Moses Hazeltine Sherman, a member of the Los Angeles Water Board, joined the San Fernando developers in a syndicate to buy land in the valley. Their company, the San Fernando Mission Land Company, purchased over 16,000 acres of land at thirty-five dollars per acre. When the proposed Los Angeles Aqueduct was announced the following July, the price of the same land went to over three hundred dollars per acre. This jump was caused because existing water laws stated that Los Angeles had to find a current use for its future water supplies. If the city failed to use the water, it would relinquish its claims to it and would have to re-negotiate for more when the demand increased. Because of this law Mulholland suggested that the surpluses be used to irrigate sections of the San Fernando Valley.[18] He also recommended locating the terminal reservoir of the aqueduct in the valley.[18]

Soon after the water board plans for an aqueduct from Owens Valley were made public, Mr. J. O. Koepfli, President of the Chamber of Commerce of Los Angeles, was asked for his support and for the backing of the Chamber of Commerce. In August of 1905 this city body and other commercial interests sent a special committee to investigate the Owens River Valley. This group took samples of the water for analysis, made an estimate of construction costs, and examined the general feasibility of the project. On their return these men made public their finding in a report presented to the Chamber of Commerce. They outlined six reasons why Los Angeles had to turn to Owens Valley and stated they "heartily" approved the entire plan and urged public support for the bonds needed to finance the water line.[19]

In September the water board asked the city to issue bonds for 1,500,000 dollars for the purchase of land and water and to inaugurate work on the aqueduct. Support for these bonds came from the city government, the Chamber of Commerce and all city newspapers except one, the *Daily News*.[20] On September 7, 1905, by a vote of 10,787 to 755 or over fourteen to one, the citizens of Los Angeles approved the bonds and endorsed the Owens River Project.[21]

While consulting engineers examined the valley, the water board sent a delegation to Washington, D. C. to obtain a right-of-way across government lands for the aqueduct and to gain permission for Los Angeles to control surplus water in Owens Valley. Since Congress would have to pass on Los Angeles' request, the leader chosen for this delegation was Senator Frank P. Flint. This veteran lawmaker from Los Angeles enjoyed a prominence in the national Republican Party that made him valuable to the city's cause. The people of Owens Valley presented the city with its major obstacle in Washington. Unhappy with the Reclamation Service and demanding Lippincott's removal from the Service, valley farmers felt they had been robbed of their future by a great thirsty giant. Most of them believed that both the valley and the city could use water from the Owens River and that plans to obtain control of the surplus was merely a "water grab" to make San Fernando Valley speculators rich. To act for them in Washington they enlisted the aid of Representative Sylvester C. Smith from the Inyo District which includes part of Owens Valley.[22]

Smith was unable to stop Flint who, with the aid of Secretary of the Interior Ethan A. Hitchcock, Chief of the Forest Service Gifford Pinchot, and President Theodore Roosevelt, received both the right-of-way for the line across federal lands and the right of use of the Owens River surplus flow. Pinchot went so far as to declare 298,880 acres of treeless land in Owens Valley a national forest, thus closing it to homesteading. Taft later reversed Pinchot's move, but by that time Los Angeles had completed its aqueduct.[23]

On June 20, 1906, Congress passed an act known as "Public Law Number 395" which granted to Los Angeles all necessary rights-of-way for canals and reservoirs for carrying and storing water and the rights-of-way for electric plants and transmission lines. This act also provided for the sale of public land and reservoir sites to the city at a rate of $1.25 per acre. Besides this federal grant the Southern Pacific Railroad Company sold about 1,000 acres it held in the San Fernando Valley to Los Angeles for five dollars per acre.[24]

After approval by consulting engineers and the federal government were received, the next step for William Mulholland and the water board was to obtain approval for a final bond issue for 23,000,000 dollars by Los Angeles voters. The city charter stated that this was the maximum amount for which the city could bond itself. Such a bond would place a tax of eighty-eight dollars on every man, woman, and child within the corporate limits.[25] Opposition to the aqueduct project came from a small group of Los Angeles citizens led by newspaperman Samuel I. Clover who felt the plan was a water grab to help the Otis-Huntington syndicate. Clover published articles stating that water from Owens River held too much alkali to be used for municipal purposes and that city water shortages had been created by the water department to scare the people into backing the Owens Valley Plan.

Mulholland had the backing of the Los Angeles Chamber of Commerce, the Merchants and Manufacturers Association, newspapers and most civic organizations. The opposition unintentionally promoted passage of the bond issue by rallying supporters. Pamphlets were distributed, slide shows were presented in theaters, school children debated the subject, Mulholland made speeches and Owens Valley water was used at tea parties to disprove Clover's alkali story. On June 12, 1907, the electorate passed the aqueduct bond issue by a vote of ten to one.[26]

The project was then taken out of the hands of the water board and placed under a newly formed Board of Public Works. This new body worked closely with the Water Commissioners. Because of public trust in them, Mulholland and Lippincott were appointed to an advisory committee to handle the details and supervise building the Los Angeles Aqueduct.

Preparations for construction of the aqueduct began soon after the June 12, 1907 bond issue election. The preliminary work rivaled in magnitude the actual excavation and pipe-laying. Mulholland divided the route of the aqueduct into eleven sections which varied in length from six to twenty-three miles depending upon the nature of the terrain.[27] For each of these divisions roads, telephone and power lines, and quarters and offices had to be constructed and, most important, water had to be supplied.

Only one road, a dusty wagon trail, connected Los Angeles and Owens Valley. It led through the little desert town of Mojave, which for half a century prospectors had made their last stop before entering Death Valley, and ore wagons laden with gold and silver from the Sierra Nevada Mountains made it their first stop. Mulholland decided on Mojave as his central distribution point.

Tons of freight and machinery had to be moved by mule train and railroads to the construction sites. Each day the railroad carried detachments of engineers, laborers and equipment. Workmen who lacked train fare walked along the railroad right-of-way. All the men and equipment went first to Mojave and then were distributed to division headquarters along the line.[28]

When the crews began to arrive for work assignments, they built construction camps at various points along the line of stakes that marked the route of the aqueduct. The engineers had planned camp buildings well adapted to the climatic conditions of the region with many windows and doors. Some were portable to allow them to be moved from point to point as construction progressed. The city spent an average of twenty-five dollars to house each man. One hundred eighty-five major buildings were constructed on the line, all lighted by electricity from the city's hydro-electric plants in Owens Valley.[29]

Each camp consisted of an office building, which also included quarters for the engineers and their assistants, a row of bunk houses and a camp store constructed half of wood and half of canvas to supply the necessities of desert living from clothing to tobacco. Each bunkhouse, built to withstand the extremes of desert temperatures, was divided into rooms with two men sharing each room. Every camp also had a mess hall with enough room to feed the hundreds of men who composed each working shift; corrugated iron warehouses and machine shops to store and repair heavy steam shovels, caterpillars, traction engines and drills, and barns and corrals for the livestock. In addition, each major camp had a hospital staffed with a surgeon and steward.[30]

While some crews built the camps, others were hard at work searching out water and laying lines to supply men, animals and equipment. This precious liquid was found in streams and springs in the mountains along the course of the aqueduct. Four systems with three and four inch mains were laid across the desert giving the appearance that men had walked along dragging them as though they were hoses. These four original systems served the whole project for the five-year construction period.[31]

While not discounting the importance of thorough planning and preparation, the engineers believed that completion of the water carrier within five years depended on the speed with which the tunnels could be driven. In September, 1907, at the same time other preparations were beginning, a crew of forty men set up

Los Angeles Department of Water and Power

Section of open canal work showing "stakers" and steam shovel.

camp in San Francisquito Canyon and broke ground at the south portal of the five mile Elizabeth Tunnel. Early in October a second crew started on its north face. While digging this tunnel, the crews set several American records for hardrock tunnel driving, the last being 604 feet in one month. Mulholland and his engineers had estimated it would take five years to complete the tunnel; it took only forty months.[32]

When construction began, the engineers projected that a reasonable progress for each end of the tunnel would be eight feet per day with three crews of eight hours each making one day's work. Soon after work started, the Board of Public Works set up a system of bonuses in which each man in the tunnel received forty cents above his regular wage for every foot exceeding the eight foot quota. The effect of the bonuses was to increase the daily wage of the laborers about thirty percent and to decrease the cost of digging from ten to fifteen percent. Besides the savings made in tunnel construction, the equipment that had been used in the tunnel was released for some other phase of the aqueduct much earlier than had been anticipated.[33]

By October 1, 1908, the date construction officially began, the preliminary work was finished. At this time 215 miles of road, 230 miles of pipeline, 218 miles of power transmission line and 377 miles of telegraph and telephone line were in service. Also, the problem of transporting material from Mojave to Owens Valley had been overcome by building a branch of the Southern Pacific Railroad, known as the Nevada and California Railroad. Finally, a cement plant had been built with a daily capacity of 1,000 barrels of Portland cement.[34]

The army of men who started work on the line came from every level of society. Among them were highly experienced engineers like Mulholland and Lippincott, young engineers just out of college, clerks and draftsmen, mechanics and miners, heavy equipment operators and mule skinners, but most of them were rank and file laborers. These men known as "stakers" worked in the ditch. To maintain a high level of competence, everyone on the payroll except day laborers had to be certified by the City Civil Service Commission of Los Angeles. City officials believed this would minimize political jobs and help remove unproductive laborers.[35]

Los Angeles Department of Water and Power

General work scene on the canal section of the Aqueduct, showing "staker" laborers.

The stakers, over 4,000 of them, came mainly from the gold fields of California and Colorado. They were experienced in digging and tunneling. The work force was domestic. Not a single foreign laborer was imported to work on the project.[36] The workers were soon tagged with the name "hobo" labor because of their habit of working at one division only long enough to be eligible for a bonus. The bonus system, started at the Elizabeth Tunnel, was soon extended to the whole project. It was based on a ten working day period, at the end of which time all bonuses were paid. On payday many took their blanket rolls and bottles and water and set out for the nearest ragtown. After walking at least four miles they would reach these half-wood, half-tent towns made up almost entirely of saloons and bawdy houses. The long walk was required because Los Angeles had persuaded the state legislature to pass a law that saloons and brothels had to be at least four miles from the construction project. After several days of pleasure, the staker would set out for the next division to start the pattern all over again. The tunnel crews usually stayed at their divisions longer than the ditch laborers, but one tunnel foreman recalled in a newspaper interview that he regularly had "one crew drunk, one crew sobering up, and one crew working."[37]

Wherever the stakemen worked along the line, they found one condition that had not existed in the mines, overall use of the most modern construction equipment and techniques. Mulholland believed that if the line were to be completed in five years — and for under 24,000,000 dollars — he must remain aware of the newest construction methods and be ready to use anything that would improve the efficiency of his workers. Mulholland's foresight and that of his assistants paid off for the city. His decision to use the Leyner air hammer drill in the tunnels saved some twenty months of hard rock driving. These light weight drills, designed and built by J. George Leyner of Denver, Colorado, used a light, high-speed oscillating piston or "hammer," striking the end of the drill rod, to drive the drill into the rock rather than the slow action of the piston drill, then standard, in which the entire drill rod was driven in and out.[38]

In addition to the air drill, a new kind of blasting cap was introduced, first in the Elizabeth Tunnel and then over the entire project. This German-made fuse proved

Los Angeles Department of Water and Power

The Soledad inverted siphon, one of the longest sections of the Los Angeles Aqueduct.

more reliable and much safer than the American-made blasting cap. Over 6,000,000 pounds of blasting powder were used in building the aqueduct, yet only five men were killed by accidents due to explosives in underground work.[39]

Also pioneered on the aqueduct was the electricity-driven shovel. Due to the scarcity of water in the desert, steam power was not always practical. The two hydroelectric plants that had been built in Owens Valley to supply power to the camps were used to run much of the heavy equipment, making this the first major engineering project in America to utilize electricity in this way. These electric shovels reduced expenses by cutting down the need for coal and fuel oil.[40]

Not all of the new equipment proved successful. One example was the Caterpillar tractor. Before its introduction all material for the project had been carried over the precipitous mountain roads and across the desert on wagons pulled by jerk-line mule teams. Moving materials and heavy equipment this way was slow and difficult. The shovels had to be dismantled and packed in several wagons before they could be transported from one location to another. To overcome this

Mulholland decided to try the newly invented traction engine, called by its manufacturer the "Caterpillar" because of its resemblance to a caterpillar as it moved across the ground. With this new tractor a shovel could be moved easily by simply hooking on two "Cats" in tandem and pulling it. Here again the savings were substantial since one tractor could do the work of hundreds of animals at less than half the cost. But after several months of work in the desert the Caterpillars began to cost more and more to maintain as fine blowing sand destroyed vital parts. After repeated breakdowns and repairs, Mulholland abandoned them. The slower but more reliable mule once more became the method of transportation in the desert.[41]

Construction was not the only phase of the Los Angeles Aqueduct in which new techniques were used. In designing the water carrier, engineers employed the inverted siphon, a new method for transporting water across ravines and canyons. The inverted siphon is a steel or concrete pipe designed to handle extremely high heads of water pressures that build up as water descends into and rises out of canyons. Before their development water had to be gradually lowered into a

Jerk-line mule teams pulling section of steel pipe used on the Soledad siphon.

Los Angeles Department of Water and Power

canyon by a long sloping decline. With the inverted siphon the water could be dropped over the edge of a canyon wall. It had limited use on the Catskill Mountain Aqueduct and at Niagara Falls. Construction design called for a total of over nine miles of siphon, with three sections over a mile in length and twenty shorter ones. One of the longest sections, called the Soledad siphon, was 8,060 feet long and eleven feet in diameter and was, except for a steel main imbedded in concrete near Madrid, Spain, the largest steel pipe in use by 1912.[42]

Eastern companies that supplied steel for the siphons built thirty-foot sections of large diameter pipe with one-half inch thick steel walls and shipped them to the project on railroad flat cars. Each of these sections made up a full carload. Some of the steel for the smaller siphons was cut and shaped at the factory and shipped unriveted. This reduced shipping expense by making it possible to place more than one section on a railroad car.[43]

Trouble developed with the siphons after their installation. At Sand Canyon where the design called for a steel siphon, the engineers decided to experiment by drilling a pressure tunnel in rock on both inclines. The rock formation of the canyon walls seemed to be massive granite. But when the first pressure hit the siphon, fissures and leaks began to appear. When full pressure was turned into the conduit, the south incline blew out spectacularly, and the whole side of the mountain crashed to the canyon floor.[44]

Another problem occurred soon after completion of the aqueduct when unusually heavy rains washed out concrete piers which supported the siphon across Antelope Valley. When the siphon sagged from loss of these supports, a circular seam broke. Water burst out at a head pressure of 200 pounds per square inch. As the water left the lower portion of the siphon a vacuum was created in the upper portion subjecting the pipe to atmospheric pressure and "the steel pipe collapsed like an emptied fire hose for nearly two miles of its length."[45] In places the top and bottom of the pipe were forced to within a few inches of each other. On examining the damage, many engineers pronounced it a total loss, saying that the thick pipe would have to be taken up, the 1/4 to 5/16 inch thick steel plate rerolled and the siphon rebuilt.

The section was repaired, however, by turning water slowly into the pipe after the break had been mended. The hydraulic pressure created as the water started down the siphon restored its circular form. By gradually increasing the head of water the engineers allowed the pipe to take its original form without breaking joints or shearing rivets. Common sense and ingenuity saved the city over 245,000 dollars in repair expense, and the line was working in less than a month.[46]

With excellent supervision, new building techniques and bonus incentives, the aqueduct was far ahead of the construction timetable. Work had been going so well

Los Angeles Department of Water and Power
Collapsed inverted siphon at Antelope Valley

that the New York investment companies were buying bonds ahead of schedule. In mid-May, 1910, a currency shortage caused the financing firms to stop purchasing bonds in advance and to inform the city that they would supply no more money until the construction schedule caught up with the bonds already purchased.

This financial stricture hit at a time when there was only enough money on hand for one month's work at the regular pace. In order to conserve funds, Mulholland reduced the size of his crews, retaining only enough men to prevent completed work from falling into disrepair. Only in the tunnels did he maintain full work gangs. In a few days the work force dropped from over 4,000 men to less than 1,000. Whole divisions were shut down, and Mojave, ordinarily booming with the trade of 3,000 workers, became a dead camp. Since he was ahead of schedule, Mulholland believed he could ride out the money strain, but his well-organized crews were broken down and scattered.

During the slow-down, trouble erupted among the remaining workers. On July 19 the mess contractor asked to raise the price of food in order to compensate for the smaller number of boarders. Aqueduct officials, in answer to these demands, raised the price of meals five cents on condition that the food would be improved. This rate increase went into effect in November, 1910, and was branded by the Western Federation of Miners, who were trying to organize the aqueduct workers, as unfair. The union, at this time, linked with the Industrial Workers of the World, had already made considerable headway in organizing the tunnel crews of the Little Lake, Grapevine and Elizabeth Divisions. The union gained enough strength to call a strike two weeks after the meal price increase. More that seven hundred men walked off the line leaving only skeleton crews at most construction sites and closing Elizabeth tunnel completely.[47]

By the end of 1910 the financial crisis was over, and Mulholland was able to weaken the hold of the union by lowering meal prices and raising bonuses. The temporary slowdown cost Los Angeles more than 250,000 dollars but did not necessitate an extension in construction time.

After a slight delay in May, 1913, when a section of the pipeline burst, Owens River water arrived at the San Fernando reservoir on November 5, 1913. After being treated at the reservoir, the water was pumped into city mains. Over 30,000 people watched as the water poured out of the last tunnel and down an artificial waterfall. As the water rushed in, Mulholland is quoted as saying, "There it is. Take it."[48]

Los Angeles did take the water, and virtually overnight the city turned from water famine to water flood. The San Fernando Valley, where the aqueduct dumped its precious load into the Upper Van Norman Lake, changed from a grain growing center dependent on intermittent rainfall to one of the richest truck garden and orchard communities in the United States. By 1915 most of the valley was annexed by Los Angeles. With the lure of what was thought to be an inexhaustible water supply, one community after another joined Los Angeles. The belief that they had solved their water problems was short lived for Angelenos. While it lasted, they made the most of it.

For William Mulholland the period following completion of the line was a time of reward. Most of the population is Los Angeles and the nation believed that his boundless energy and confidence had made the aqueduct a reality. All the animosity for his role in the acquisition of water rights in Owens Valley seemed to

Los Angeles Department of Water and Power

Typical construction camp located in the Grapevine Division, in the Mojave Desert.

South portal of the Elizabeth Lake Tunnel during construction.

dissolve. National magazines acclaimed the aqueduct to be a "splendid monument to Chief Engineer Mulholland and his assistants" and an engineering feat second only to the Panama Canal.[49] The University of California gave Mulholland an honorary doctorate in engineering, and wherever he went he was introduced as the "Goliath of the West" and as "California's greatest man."[50]

Leaders in Los Angeles now felt that they were totally independent of the limitations nature placed on their region. As early as 1905 they realized that because of the uncertain condition of their water supply, it was unlikely factories, mills and other long term investment enterprises would be located in the Los Angeles area. Also, because a large percentage of the city's income was from tourism which would be one of the first activities to be curtailed during a depression, Los Angeles would be directly affected by every shift in the national economy. Many people now believed that even if no new industry moved to the area a large population could support itself on the irrigated land in the suburbs. One engineer estimated that he could sustain himself and his family on only one acre of irrigated land in the Hollywood area. With over a hundred thousand acres of such land to be irrigated this would mean that Los Angeles could now maintain over a half a million people living in a radius of twenty-five miles of City Hall.[51]

Unfortunately, despite the engineering genius that had gone into the aqueduct, one vital feature of the Owens Valley project had been omitted — a major reservoir. With the pressing need for water, Los Angeles simply built the aqueduct and tapped into the lower end of Owens River. The only reservoirs built were small ones that served the month-to-month operation of the aqueduct. During normal climatic conditions there was enough water in Owens River for both Owens Valley farmers to irrigate their fields and the water board to supply the city. But without a major reservoir water could not be stored during wet years to provide for dry ones.[52]

In a normal year most of the water that flowed into Owens Valley from the Sierra Nevada Mountains went unused.[53] Most of the precipitation in this area occurs in the form of snow. As a result streams feeding Owens River are at their minimum discharge between September and April although about eighty percent of the moisture falls in this period. During early April snow begins to melt and between June 15 and July 15 the river reaches its maximum flow. The discharge then begins to decline until by mid-September it once again reaches its minimum which remains regular because of percolating ground water.[54]

Between 1913 and 1920 exceptionally heavy snowfall in the mountains provided enough water to allow the ground water level to remain high, thus insuring a supply during the long months when stream discharge into the river was low. But beginning in 1922 a succession of abnormally dry years started to affect the flow of Owens River making it inadequate to supply both the needs of the valley and the demand of the rapidly growing city. Had Los Angeles followed early recommendations to built a major reservoir at Long Valley in the upper reaches of Owens Valley above Bishop (see map) problems of later years could have been avoided.[55]

This decrease in water came at a time of unprecedented and unforeseen population growth in both Owens Valley and Los Angeles after World War I. William Mulholland's intolerant attitude toward valley residents, and a feud between Mulholland and several Los Angelenos, including Fred Eaton, who had large ranches in Los Valley, gave rise to a violent period in Southern California history. The events of the next few years have been described as "California's Little Civil War"[56] or simply as the "Water War."[57]

Trouble broke out in the summer of 1922 when water reaching the aqueduct intake proved to be insufficient to meet the city's needs. More water was required. The first step taken by the city was to buy irrigated lands and the ditches that served them and allow the water allotted for that property to go on down river toward the intake.[58] This action by the city caused deep alarm among the valley people. They feared that their oasis would soon return to desert. The remaining farmers countered the city first by diverting more water into their fields[59] and second by attempting to form the Owens Valley Irrigation District to hold all remaining water rights. Late in 1922 the plan for the formation of this irrigation district was approved by a vote of the farmers. Before the water titles could be turned over to the new district, two agents from Los Angeles moved along the McNalley Ditch, one of the oldest and largest irrigation canals, offering high prices for water rights.[60]

During 1922 and 1923 Los Angeles spent over 12,000,000 dollars purchasing water-bearing lands, but this did not help the ever decreasing water supply in Los Angeles and the San Fernando Valley. Early in 1923 farmers in the San Fernando Valley were told that supplying domestic needs of the city had priority over irrigating the valley, therefore, they would have to curtail the watering of their fields. Mulholland protested this move, holding that water once put on the land should never be removed.[61]

In the summer of 1923 Los Angeles began drilling water wells near the aqueduct intake. An effort was made by the overlying farmers to block this action, but for each case that was tried and an injunction issued, the city would buy out the landowner.[62] At this same time the Los Angeles Department of Public Service tried to purchase the water rights along the Big Pine Canal, the last big ditch out from the mouth of the aqueduct. All water that was not taken by canals upstream was being siphoned off by Big Pine. When their move to buy the land failed, the city resorted to more "primitive measures." The Big Pine intake was on a U-bend in the meandering river. A construction crew was sent into the area with instructions to cut a canal across the bend, diverting the river and leaving the Big Pine Canal high and dry.

When the Big Piners discovered the city workmen, they formed a posse of about twenty armed men and moved on the construction site. They charged across the river and with what one of them called a "shotgun injunction" told the laborers that if the work stopped no one would be shot. The farmers took all the city equipment and dumped it into the river. Faced with armed force the city reopened negotiations for purchase of water rights and soon met the farmers' demand of 1,100,000 dollars, thus making many of the farmers wealthy.[63]

By October, 1923, the water problem was so critical in Los Angeles that Mulholland recommended to the Department of Public Service that another area would have to be opened up to serve the city's increasing needs. He proposed that a survey be made of the Colorado Rover to determine the feasibility of importing water from it. This recommendation was approved, and on October 29, 1923, William Mulholland led the first reconnaissance party of the Colorado River aqueduct survey into the field.

Colorado River water was many millions of dollars and a decade away. What Los Angeles needed was immediate help. By 1924, water flowing into the aqueduct had dropped from 355 to 262.5 cubic feet per second. The local rainfall in Owens Valley had declined from an average of over sixteen inches per year to 6.67 inches.[64]

By March, 1924, farmers in the San Fernando Valley faced the possibility of financial ruin if Los Angeles did not receive enough water to allow them to irrigate their fields. They sent a delegation up to Owens Valley to buy water. The delegates were escorted along brim-full irrigation canals and were told that not a drop of it was for sale but that they could buy out the entire upper valley in forty-eight hours for 8,000,000 dollars. At this point the controversy changed from farmers fighting to keep their homes and lands productive to farmers trying to get as much money from the city as they could possible force them to pay. The Owens Valley farmers told the San Fernandoans that if they needed the water so badly they should be willing to pay what was asked for it.

The delegation returned home and within two months the city gave its answer. A suit was filed against the upper valley in an effort to recover the McNally and Big Pine water that Los Angeles had purchased. Fearing they could never defeat the city in court, the Owens Valley people prepared for violence.[65]

The suit was filed in early May, 1924. On May 20, three boxes of dynamite were taken from a Bishop powder house owned by Wilfred and Mark Watterson, leaders of the settlers fighting Los Angeles. Wilfred Watterson owned five banks in eastern California and dominated the economic life of Owens Valley. The destination of the dynamite was a section of the aqueduct a few miles north of the town of Lone Pine.

Here shortly after one a.m. on May 21, 1924, a charge was set off that shook the lower valley like an earthquake. Almost before the dynamiters could leave the scene, the aqueduct employees were swarming over the area. They found that a forty-foot section of the line had been blown away.[66]

The water crisis had reached another turning point. It now became a shooting war. Soon after the dynamiting an attorney representing Los Angeles in Owens Valley was kidnapped and ordered to leave the valley.[67] Mulholland, enraged by the attack on his aqueduct, hurled a diatribe at the Owens Valley ranchers calling them "yellow" and "barking dogs." The ranchers countered this name calling with a warning that if he set one foot in Bishop he would be lynched.[68]

In the valley demands that the city buy all of the ranches grew to include demands that the town properties be included in Los Angeles' purchasing and that reparation be made to the business communities for intangible damage done by the loss of customers due to their moving after selling out to the city. In July, 1924, Los Angeles mayor George E. Cryer went to Owens Valley to investigate the problem and to try to bring it to a reasonable solution. Upon his return to Los Angeles he recommended that the city purchase all of the remaining land in Owens Valley. To this Mulholland, who questioned the integrity of the valley leaders, answered that most of the water-bearing land in the area had been purchased and that the settlers were trying to force the city to buy land it did not need.[69]

Two months later Mulholland, in open defiance of the Bishop settlers' threats, led a party of reporters, committeemen, engineers and the entire Los Angeles Water Board to Owens Valley. They were met by Watterson and were told that the only fair solution was to buy the whole district. On their return to Los Angeles the commissioners drew up a plan of compensation for losses accrued by business by previous land purchases and promised to aid the valley economy. This plan submitted by the Los Angeles Board of Public Service Commissioners to the Owens Valley residents in October proposed:

> ...a reservation of thirty thousand acres in the upper part of the valley for agricultural purposes, the development of surface and underground water supplies, the construction of paved highways, and a systematic plan for the upbuilding of the valley towns.[70]

This proposal was aimed at increasing tourist travel in the area besides improving the farmers' situation. But this effort was met by criticism and was denounced in the valley as a "vague declaration . . . that in effect, said nothing, meant nothing and guaranteed nothing."[71]

The valley leaders saw that this fairly generous proposal and early snowstorms which promised more water for the next spring were diminishing their prospects for forcing the lucrative sale of their properties. They felt that more vigorous steps were needed to coerce the city to buy their land. Early on the morning of November 16, 1924, Mark Watterson led a force of between sixty and a hundred men in autos down the length of Owens valley. When this parade neared the town of Lone Pine (see map) it turned eastward toward the aqueduct which lay in the tortuous Alabama Hills. Here these men, many of them prominent Valley citizens, seized a set of waste gates and turned the water out of the aqueduct through an overflow spillway to flow into the Owens River. This water, amounting to 200,000,000 gallons per day, flowed downriver, eventually to be evaporated as it lay in the dry basin of Owens Lake.

The first representative of the city to reach the scene was Edward F. Leaney, who was Los Angeles' chief delegate in Owens Valley. Although warned not to leave his car, he climbed into the main wheelhouse. Here, while swinging a noose in front of him, the settlers explained their reasons for forcibly taking the Alabama Gates. In essence the demonstration was aimed at publicizing their demands throughout California. Also they hoped that direct action might help force Los Angeles to make a decision to buy out the valley. Their hopes for publicity were soon fulfilled by the arrival of a large number of reporters from throughout the nation.[72]

After Leaney's unsuccessful attempt to reason with the settlers, Los Angeles turned to legal action. Seventy-five copies of a restraining order were issued and given to the sheriff of Inyo County, Charles Collins. Armed with these orders he arrived at the gates the day after they had been taken. He found that the settlers had strung barbed wire around the gates and wheelhouse and were waiting for a contingent of detectives and investigators that were rumored on their way to the site from Los Angeles. Collins' efforts were at best half-hearted. The documents he issued were thrown into the river, and he was picked up and carried to his car.[73]

By the second day the siege at the waste gates had become a valley-wide picnic. Wives of the insurgents brought baskets of food; children played in and around the wheelhouse; and in store windows were signs that read, "If I am not on the job, you will find me at the Aqueduct." A similar sign was flown from the flagpole in Bishop. One preacher who was asked why he was condoning this act of lawlessness by being present at the site answered that his whole congregation was there. This holiday was costing Los Angeles an estimated 15,000 dollars per day.[74]

In desperation Los Angeles sent out a request to sheriffs throughout southern California for their aid. Once these law officers agreed to give their support to the sheriff of Inyo, word was sent to Sheriff Collins. His office reported that he had left the county to go to the state capitol to plead with Governor F.W. Richardson to call out the National Guard. The Governor steadfastly refused to take any such action.[75]

The Owens Valley farmers' hopes that Los Angeles businessmen would not stand behind the water department when the reputation of the city for fair dealing was questioned were thwarted. The water supply was not immediately cut off because of reservoirs near the city, and most Angelenos believed that the valley action was an attempt to terrorize them. The attitude of the city went against the farmers' cause, and instead of aiding them, it was the businessmen who finally broke the beleaguerment.[76]

The farmers were finally driven from the Alabama Gates by economic pressure. When the demonstration broke out, Wilfred Watterson was meeting with fellow bankers of the Clearinghouse Association in Los Angeles. At this meeting Watterson called for the adoption of a resolution supporting the "embattled farmers" and calling for the outright purchase of all the land in question. But instead of supporting Watterson the bankers told him that unless he got the gates closed, they would cut off his bank's credit.[77] He immediately returned to Owens Valley, and on the evening of the nineteenth he met with a twelve-man delegation from the spillway at his soda works at Keeler on Owens Lake. He explained that the business community in Los Angeles had agreed to aid the farmers, and he advised them to return to their homes. Before sunup the next morning, the settlers broke camp and turned the Alabama Gates to city employees, who promptly diverted the water back into the aqueduct.[78]

No legal action was taken against the men who had seized the spillway, but their return of it to city control did not end hostilities. Though tempers seemed to cool during the rest of 1924 and 1925, the following year a new series of dynamitings began on the line. These continued in the valley. These crimes too went unpunished.[79] Between May and August of 1927, dynamitings were almost a weekly if not a nightly affair. City agents armed with Winchesters, tommyguns and sawed off shotguns raced up and down the line only to have the saboteurs slip in behind them and blow gaping holes in the aqueduct.[80]

What Los Angeles could not do by offering to buy all the land in Owens Valley at appraised prices and by sending great armies of armed World War I veterans into the valley was accomplished by a simple newspaper notice that appeared in a Bishop newspaper on August 4, 1927. The announcement stated that N.N. and M.G. Watterson were closing their banks in Owens Valley. An audit by State Superintendent of Banks Will C. Woods showed a shortage in excess of two million dollars.

The collapse of the banks in Inyo County coupled with the arrest of their leaders stunned the valley farmers and delighted Los Angeles citizens. The failure of the Wattersons' banks explained why the brothers had been so eager to get Los Angeles money and why they had not allowed the farmers to carry their fight to the courtroom. Both the Wattersons were convicted of thirty-six counts of embezzlement on November 11,

1927, and sentenced to long prison terms in San Quentin. Los Angeles quickly moved to clean up Owens Valley by starting a program of land and business purchasing.[81] Under this program, augmented by a twelve million dollar bond issue, Los Angeles, by the mid-1930's, had bought more than ninety percent of the privately-owned land, both business and rural in Owens Valley.[82]

The conviction of the Watterson brothers marked the end of organized resistance to Los Angeles in Owens Valley. Most of the families that had remained in the valley were ruined financially by the failure of the banks. Los Angeles offered jobs to many men as a measure to relieve the wide-spread distress in the area. In some cases they were set to work repairing the damage they had done on the aqueduct. Also, though the nation was suffering a severe depression in the 1930's, Los Angeles continued to offer and to pay land prices that it had originally set in the early 1920's. As another method of stabilizing the supporting area's economy, the city, working with the people of Inyo County, began leasing its properties for continued operation. In many cases these properties, both rural and business, remained in the hands of the former owners.[83]

The disaster that broke Owens Valley's will to fight was soon equalled by a disaster that broke the spirit not only of William Mulholland but of the entire Los Angeles Water and Power Department. In August of 1924, Los Angeles had begun construction of a reservoir in San Francisquito Canyon. This reservoir was to catch and store water that had been used to create electricity. Formerly the water that was released from the San Fernando Reservoir power generator had been lost. Mulholland suggested that the city build a dam on the Santa Clara River to save this water. Also, concern over the fact that the Elizabeth Tunnel pierced the San Andreas Fault and that emergency storage was needed below the fault was a prime factor in the need for a dam.[84]

By May, 1926, work was completed, and the structure was christened the St. Francis Dam. Almost as soon as it was finished, problems arose. The dam site lay along the San Andreas Fault, and the rock formation on which the base of the dam sat was permeated by fractures and cracks. The fact that these hazards were overlooked or ignored can probably be explained by the constant pressure that was on the Department of Water and Power to find new sources of water to supply Los Angeles. Soon after construction was completed, leaks

began to develop, and by the end of 1927 it was evident that the valley walls, made up of mica schist and conglomerate, were soaking up water and swelling, causing two major dam cracks. Appearing in January of 1928 they started at the top center of the structure and sloped out to each side, indicating that the sides of the dam were being forced upward.[85]

Early in March the water below the dam turned muddy, indicating to many that the abutment ground was giving way. On March 12, 1928, Mulholland and Harvey A. Van Norman, Mulholland's assistant, inspected the dam. They explained that the muddy water was due to a nearby road construction project, and although the dam leaked, all concrete dams leak slightly. A few hours later at 11:57½ a.m. the entire structure gave way, sending a hundred and eighty-five foot wall of water down the San Francisquito Canyon. Five hours later, the crest, now twenty-five feet high, rushed out of the mouth of the Santa Clara River into the Pacific Ocean, some sixty miles from the dam, leaving a wake of terror and destruction that destroyed the towns of Piru, Castaic Junction, Fillmore, Santa Paula and Ventura plus several construction camps and numerous isolated farms and ranches. The official death toll was fixed at between 385 and 420, but there was no way of knowing the exact number. Over 1,250 homes and 7,900 acres of farmland lay desolated, making it one of America's worst flood disasters.[86]

William Mulholland bore the brunt of the wrath of the people in the Santa Clara Valley. At the coroner's inquest that followed the tragedy, Mulholland accepted full responsibility for the dam. "Don't blame anybody else," his statement began. "You just fasten it on me. If there was an error of human judgment, I was the human."[87] It is interesting to note the use of the word "if" in Mulholland's testimony. He believed that the dam had been dynamited by Owens Valley hotheads. This belief was shared by only a few experts, one being Frank Rieber, consulting engineer for San Francisco. No definite proof was ever presented for this theory.[88]

The St. Francis Dam experience left the Los Angeles Department of Water and Power without the leadership of Mulholland. He retired immediately after the coroner's inquest, much mellower toward the Owens Valley problem. From March 1928 the rift between the valley farmers and the city seemed to lessen. There were occasional flareups and dynamitings, but nothing to compare with the previous hostilities.

REFERENCES

1. Robert Glass Cleland, *From Wilderness to Empire: A History of California* (New York: Alfred A. Knopf, 1959), 336.
2. U.S. Census Office, 9th Census, 1870, *Ninth Census of the United States, Statistics of Population* (Washington: Government Printing Office, 1872), 90; and U.S. Census Office, 12th Census, 1900, *Twelfth Census of the United States, Population, I*

(Washington: Government Printing Office, 1901), 126.
3. Charles Anaden Moody, "Los Angeles and the Owens River," *Out West*, XXIII, No. 4 (October, 1905), 428.
4. City of Los Angeles, *Complete Report on Construction of the Los Angeles Aqudeuct* (Los Angeles: Department of Public Service, 1916), 9.

5. Joseph B. Lippincott. "William Mulholland—Engineer, Pioneer, Raconteur —Part II," *Civil Engineering*, II (March, 1941), 162.
6. City of Los Angeles, 51.
7. Henry Z. Osborne, "The Completion of the Los Angeles Aqueduct," *Scientific American*, CIX, No. 19 (November 8, 1913), 364.

8. A miner's inch of water is equal to one and one-half cubic feet per minute or 13,000 gallons per day.

9. U.S. Congress, House, *Fourth Annual Report of the Reclamation Service, 1904-1905*, 59th Cong., 1st sess., 1906, House Doc. 86, 97.

10. City of Los Angeles, 13.

11. Remi Nadeau, *The Water Seekers* (New York: Doubleday and Co., 1950) 12.

12. City of Los Angeles, 10.

13. Margaret Romer, "The Story of Los Angeles," *Journal of the West*, III (January, 1964), 17.

14. U.S. Congress, House, 97.

15. City of Los Angeles, 48.

16. William R. Stewart, "A Desert City's Far Reach for Water," *The World's Work* XV, No. 1 (November, 1907), 9538-39.

17. Nadeau, 33.

18. Remi Nadeau, "Water War," *American Heritage*, XIII, No. 1 (December, 1961), 32.

19. City of Los Angeles, 14.

20. Romer, 17.

21. City of Los Angeles, 14.

22. Nadeau, *Water Seekers*, 35.

23. Oscar Osburn Winther, "Los Angeles: It's Aqueduct Life Lines," *The Journal of Geography*, XLIX (February, 1950), 48.

24. City of Los Angeles, 71-72.

25. Burt A. Heinly, "Carrying Water Through A Desert: The Story of the Los Angeles Aqueduct," *The National Geographic Magazine*, XXI (July, 1910), 585.

26. Vincent Ostrum, *Water and Politics: A Study of Water Policies and Adminstration in the Development of Los Angeles* (Los Angeles: The Haynes Foundation, 1953), 55.

27. Burt A. Heinly, "Carrying Water Through a Desert: The Story of the Los Angeles Aqueduct," *The National Geographic Magazine*, XXI (July, 1910), 585.

28. Roscoe E. Schrader, "A Ditch in the Desert," *Scribner's Magazine*, LI, No. 5 (May, 1912), 541.

29. Burt A. Heinly, "The Longest Aqueduct in the World," *The Outlook*, XCIII (September 25, 1909), 218.

30. Schrader, 544.

31. *Ibid.*, 542.

32. Remi Nadeau, *The Water Seekers*, 47.

33. City of Los Angeles, *Complete Report on Construction of the Los Angeles Aqueduct* (Los Angeles: Department of Public Service, 1916), 21.

34. City of Los Angeles, 22.

35. Heinly, "Carrying Water Through...," 588.

36. Morrow Mayo, *Los Angeles* (New York: Alfred A. Knopf, 1933), 238.

37. Heinly, "The Longest Aqueduct...," 219; and Nadeau, 47.

38. City of Los Angeles, 21.

39. *Ibid.*, 25.

40. Schrader, 544.

41. Nadeau, 49.

42. Heinly, "The Longest Aqueduct...," 476.

43. "Nine Miles of Siphons," *The Literary Digest*, XLVI, No. 9, Whole No. 1193 (March 1, 1913), 452.

44. City of Los Angeles, 26.

45. *Ibid.*, 29.

46. *Ibid.*, 29.

47. Nadeau, 52-53; and City of Los Angeles, 26.

48. Remi Nadeau, "Water War," *American Heritage*, XIII (December, 1961), 35.

49. Henry Z. Osborne, "The Completion of the Los Angeles Aqueduct," *Scientific American*, CIX, No. 19 (November 8, 1913), 372.

50. Remi Nadeau, "Water War," *American Heritage*, XIII, 35.

51. William E. Smythe, "The Social Significance of the Owens River Project," *Out West*, XXIII, No. 4 (Octtober, 1905), 443-45.

52. Nadeau, 35.

53. Morrow Mayo, *Los Angeles* (New York: Alfred A. Knopf, 1933), 230.

54. Vincent Ostrum, *Water and Politics: A Study of Water Policies and Administration in the Development of Los Angeles* (Los Angeles: The Haynes Foundation, 1953), 55.

55. In 1941 a reservoir was finally built at Long Valley.

56. "California's Little Civil War," *Scribner's Magazine*, LI, No. 8 (May, 1912), 15.

57. Nadeau, 30.

58. A Special Correspondent, "The Owens Valley Controversy," *The Outlook*, CXLVI, No. 11 (July 13, 1927), 342.

59. Robert Glass Cleland, *California in Our Time, 1900-1940* (New York: Alfred A. Knopf, 1947), 185.

60. Nadeau, 103.

61. Joseph B. Lippincott, "William Mulholland—Engineer, Pioneer, Raconteur —Part II," *Civil Engineering*, II (March, 1941), 163.

62. Ostrum, 132.

63. Nadeau, 103.

64. Ostrum, 15-16.

65. Nadeau, 104.

66. "California's Little Civil War," 15.

67. *Ibid.*

68. Nadeau, 104.

69. Ostrum, 62.

70. Cleland, 188.

71. *Ibid.*

72. A Special Correspondent, 343.

73. Nadeau, 87.

74. *Ibid.*, 88-89.

75. Nadeau, "Water War", 104.

76. A Special Correspondent, 343.

77. Nadeau, "Water War", 105.

78. "California's Little Civil War," 15.

79. Cleland, 189.

80. Nadeau, "Water Seekers", 104-107.

81. Nadeau, "Water War," 106.

82. Inyo County Board of Supervisors, *Inyo 1866-1966* (Bishop, California: Chalfant Press, 1966), 70.

83. *Ibid.*

84. Charles Outland, *Man-Made Disaster: The Story of the St. Francis Dam* (Glendale, California: The Arthur H. Clark Co., 1965), 30.

85. *Ibid.*, 49-58.

86. *Ibid.*, 79, Appendix v, vi.

87. *Ibid.*, 211.

88. *Ibid.*, 193.

Gold and the Growth of a Metropolis: A Comparative Study of San Francisco and Melbourne, Australia

By Diane Kirkby

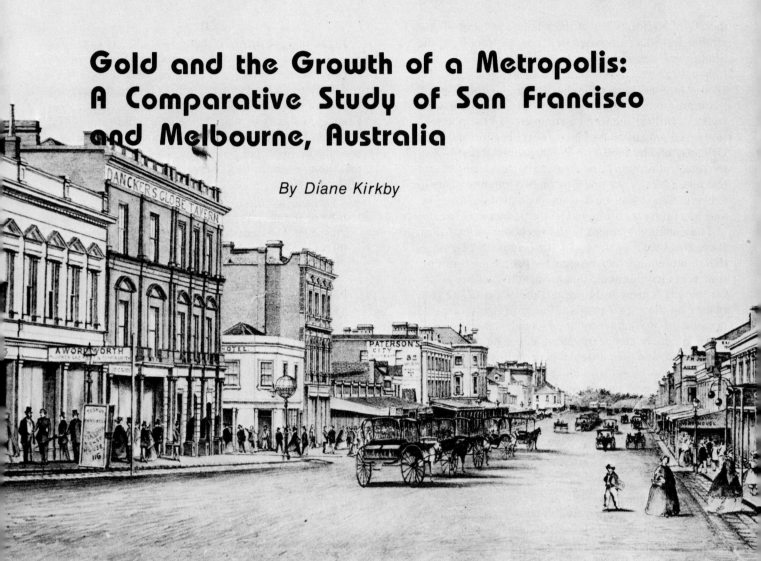

Swanston Street, Melbourne, 1863, Charles Troedel, **Melbourne Album** *(Melb., 1863).*

Of all the mad pursuits any people ever took up gold digging was the maddest and stupidest. If they get as much gold as would make a bridge from Australia to Europe it would not be worth a mealy potato to mankind.

Thomas Carlyle.

I

When the war with Mexico ended in February, 1848, the little settlement of Yerba Buena on the coast of California had been officially called San Francisco for one year and had a population of approximately 800-1,000 people.[1] At the same time, across the Pacific in the British colony of Victoria, Melbourne, though younger than Yerba Buena, was already a thriving settlement patterned in the mother country's towns as well established as the county seat of Port Phillip.[2] Within ten years both these cities, despite their differences, were thriving metropolises and their names were familiar throughout the world. Melbourne had grown from a town of 23,000 inhabitants in July 1851, to a proud city of 126,000 by 1861 and 200,000 just nine years later. It was, by 1870, the financial and commercial pivot not merely of Victoria, but of the whole continent of Australia, and was recognised as "The Metropolis of the Southern Hemisphere".[3]

San Francisco, too, had grown astonishingly. By 1856 it was no longer a small frontier outpost, but a "complex city without peer on the American west coast."[4] In 1851 the foreign commerce of the port was surpassed only by that of New York, Boston and New Orleans,[5] and by 1860 with 56,000 people, it had 14% of the total Californian population.[6] The development that had taken New York and Boston two hundred years to achieve, San Francisco had accomplished within eight, and her future as a major U.S. city was assured.[7]

The common element in the phenomenal growth of these two urban centres was the discovery of gold in their hinterlands which brought the people, institutions, transport facilities and commercial activities necessary for the city's growth. However, the effect of the gold rushes on these two towns differed in many respects because of the nature of their initial settlement, the stage of each city's development when gold was discovered, and the particular geographical and historical circumstances surrounding them. In each case the discovery of gold merely speeded up (albeit remarkably) an already evolving process of growth. Both cities were initially established as ports on the coast, partly for strategic reasons and partly because they were also important entries to the interior pastoral country. The effect of the gold rushes was forcibly to encourage the growth of this agricultural hinterland and likewise the necessary transport and port facilities which put each of these cities ahead of their rivals and secured their place as major urban centres. To understand this fact further it is necessary to look closely at the growth of Melbourne and San Francisco and to determine the ultimate impact of the discovery of gold in each case.

II

Richard Wade, in his introduction to Roger Lotchin's *San Francisco 1846-1856*, points out that however reasonable the growth of a "great and unique metropolis here on the Pacific...sitting on the shimmering beauty of the Bay" may now appear in retrospect, San Francisco's growth was neither inevitable nor tidy.[8] Bayard Taylor, that most popular of chroniclers, thought in 1849 that San Francisco's growth was remarkable, even for that one year, considering its drawbacks.

> The increase in that time had been made in the face of the greatest disadvantages under which a city ever labored; an uncultivated country, an ungenial climate, exorbitant rates of labor, want of building materials, imperfect civil organisation — lacking everything, in short, but gold dust and enterprise.[9]

The cause of this unbelievable growth in the face of such difficulties was, of course, the needs of the gold rush; San Francisco's location was a port in contrast to the interior location of the other gold rush cities, Sacramento and Stockton, meant that San Francisco benefited in quite an individual way. There was no competition to the sea-going trade from railroads to and from the east, and as the incoming clipper ships had to unload their cargoes at San Francisco to be carried into the interior on smaller boats, San Francisco developed rapidly as a service centre to the hinterland. Gold poured into San Francisco and commercial and entertainment centers grew up in response.

The city's development was neither inevitable nor tidy, however, mainly because of the very speed with which it grew. Between 1848 and 1856 San Francisco went through "more years of bust than boom" because of a seasonal trade cycle and a scarcity-glut cycle, and

*Montgomery St., San Francisco, in 1852, painted by A.O. Dinsdale, B. Conrad, **San Francisco** (N.Y., 1959), p. 19.*

"the general uncertainty was so profound and tenacious that there was a widespread conviction that business in San Francisco was as much a game of chance as any played in the gaudy saloons on the Plaza".[10] The physical difficulties of a frontier town (no wharves, or warehouses, very bad streets, fire risks, etc.) compounded by a lack of accurate mercantile information and statistics on gold output, meant there was great fluctuation and uncertainty in the commercial sphere which Roger Lotchin has outlined in some detail. Fortunes were made and lost, goods were over-supplied or under-supplied, and speculation was rife — as Anthony Trollope observed twenty years later, "the trade of the place and the way in which money is won or lost are alike marvellous".[11]

When gold was discovered in January 1848 San Francisco was a village, governed by a military governor, and dependent on the hide and tallow trade for economic survival. Although, according to Lotchin, it "was enough of a city [by 1848] to attract the commerce induced by the discovery of gold", it is my contention that its smallness and lack of well-developed economic and political structures were largely responsible for the instability of the market in the following decade. Lotchin claims that San Francisco's economic role as "freight-handler" to California and the West Coast remained constant with the advent of the gold rush; though the products it handled changed, its trade network and economic function remained constant throughout the upheaval."[12] However, the problems of a small frontier town which had not yet developed a charter, a properly functioning town council, an elaborate communications system or a commercial network, and which was suddenly confronted with a massive influx of people demanding goods and services, must have resulted in the kind of boom-bust cycle that Lotchin outlines.

For the first seventy years of its existence, Yerba Buena, as San Francisco was then called, had grown in a rather leisurely way. It was first established by the Spanish as a mission and presidio in 1776, but the mission was never as large or as prosperous as the other California missions, and it was not till the 1830's that the economy of the Bay area began to pick up. After the missions were secularised in 1832, more and larger areas of California were taken over for ranching, and the port of Yerba Buena began to develop in response to the increasing numbers of ships entering the harbour. A brisk hide and tallow trade developed from the outlying ranches, and by 1835 the first houses were put up beside the cove.[13] This development before the gold rush is what Lotchin believes gave San Francisco the edge over its rivals when the development of California really began in 1849.[14] The impact of gold was to catapult San Francisco into the position of the foremost city on the West Coast within eight years, and to raise California to statehood within two years of the United States gaining sovereignity over the territory.

The immediate effect of gold on this pioneer settlement was to flood the town with immigrants and therefore to stretch the existing services beyond their capacity. The first requirement of all newcomers was of course accommodation, and "hence a rapid growth of very lightly and rudely built houses, half wood, half cloth all bringing enormous rents" occurred.[15] Needless to say these crude structures were extreme fire hazards, and consequently the first two years of the new city, from December, 1849 to June, 1851, saw no less than six fires (some of them deliberately set.)

Martyn Bowden, in his historical geography of San Francisco, has described the way the miners returning to the city in the fall of 1851

found a bewildering transformation. Three- and four-story brick buildings were common, down-

GREAT FIRE IN   SAN FRANCISCO

500 BUILDINGS BURNED

JUNE 14ᵗʰ 1850

Great fire in San Francisco, June 14, 1850. T. Watkins and R. Olmsted, **Mirror of the Dream** *(San Francisco, 1976).*

town streets had been paved, the main wharves had been greatly extended, and nine more jutting piers had been added. San Francisco had become a permanent...city. Within this period of intense activity on the part of the citizenry, one event was critical...that was the third San Francisco fire of June 14, 1850.[16]

It is hard to exaggerate the horror of fire in "this confused and hurriedly built town, crowded between the steep hills and the bay, with all its tents and its rude warehouses, and its flimsy gambling palaces set down at random".[17] It was a city too young to have an adequate water supply,[18] or a fully-organized fire company,[19] and it was not until after the holocausts of May and June 1851 that steps towards the protection of the city really made steady progress, and it was not until September, 1858, that a large-scale supply of water was finally introduced.[20]

This inadequacy in the water supply was a further problem for the city because it contributed to the poor health conditions of an over-populated and ill-housed citizenry. Lack of clean drinking water and proper sewage and drainage facilities, coupled with insufficient medical and hospital amenities served to make San Francisco a very unhealthy environment in the years immediately after the discovery of gold, and outbreaks of disease were frequent. *The Star and Californian* complained in 1848 that

> the demand for a public hospital at San Francisco is urgent. The unsheltered sick have been inhumanly neglected during the excitement created by the gold discoveries, and many have died who with proper attention... might have survived.[21]

Despite this early plea for more adequate hospital care, San Francisco relied very heavily on private, religious and ethnic "self-help" organizations to care for its sick long after it had become a "city without peer on the west coast."[22]

Not least of the new city's many problems was its search for law and order. Mary Williams, in her excellent study of the San Francisco Vigilance Committee, prefers to call this era a "Struggle for Organization" rather than a "Struggle for Order." She sees it more as a law-deficient society than a lawless one, and discusses in some detail the evolution and formulation of laws into the state constitution.[23]

Whatever the cause, however, the people of San Francisco at this time were very concerned about what they saw as an increasing crime rate. A regular police force had been formed in 1849, but its failure to control the alarming increase in crime led to the emergence of the Vigilance Committee in 1851 and its re-emergence in 1856. The story of this Committee has been well and frequently told.[24] Suffice to say here that the formation of such a vigilance committee, whether it be to control a mob or to lead one, was a direct consequence of the breakdown of the normal agencies of the law, and is further indication of the inadequacy of San Francisco's institutions to cope with its sudden and rapid growth in population.

Despite these many problems and hazards, life in San Francisco after the discovery of gold was, nevertheless, far from dull. When Mark Twain arrived there in 1864 he thought it was everything a man could want in a city, "the most cordial and sociable city in the Union... the livest, heartiest community on our continent."[25] Gambling was apparently the major form of recreation, but dancing, drinking, bull and bear fighting were also popular activities. Many of the goldseekers were unattached men far from home and families and, lacking the restraints normally imposed by a more stable society, they sought recreation and companionship in a frontier town gripped by gold-fever and insecurity. Consequently, observers like Daniel Woods for example, thought that pleasure-seeking must be the predominant occupation of the town. He wrote "intemperance next to gambling [must be] the most prevailing vice in California". He warned other young men to stay at home and not go to California

> unless [they have] firmness of principle enough to resist and forever hold at bay all the vices of the country, in whatever disguise they may present themselves and in however fascinating shapes they may appear.[26]

Perhaps the most striking effect of gold on the nature of San Francisco society was the influx of migrants from all over the world. The appeal of easy riches was international in impact, and immigrants from all corners of the globe flooded into the city until it was described as the "most cosmopolitan city on earth".[27] Roger Lotchin claims that heterogeneity was "a characteristic that the gold rush accentuated but did not inaugurate," that the first census of 1847 showed a marked variety of people with about one half the population American and that this was also true of the 1860 census.[28] However, the census of 1847 was dealing with a population of 850-1,000 people, that of 1860 with a population of closer to 100,000 people. This numerical increase in the different national groups must have contributed to a very large degree to the character of the city and its social life. When Bayard Taylor first arrived in 1848

> The streets were full of people, hurrying to and fro, and of as diverse and bizarre a character as the houses: Yankees of every possible variety, native Californians in sarapes and sombreros, Chileans, Sonorians, Kanakas from Hawaii, Chinese with long tails, Malays armed with their everlasting creeses, and others in whose embrowned and bearded visages it was impossible to recognize any especial nationality.[29]

In the familiar pattern of immigrants, these newcomers clustered together in their ethnic groups and made their own contributions to the larger society. The immigrant experience in any city is a subject in itself, but it is sufficient here simply to point out that the very existence of these groups, and their interaction with each

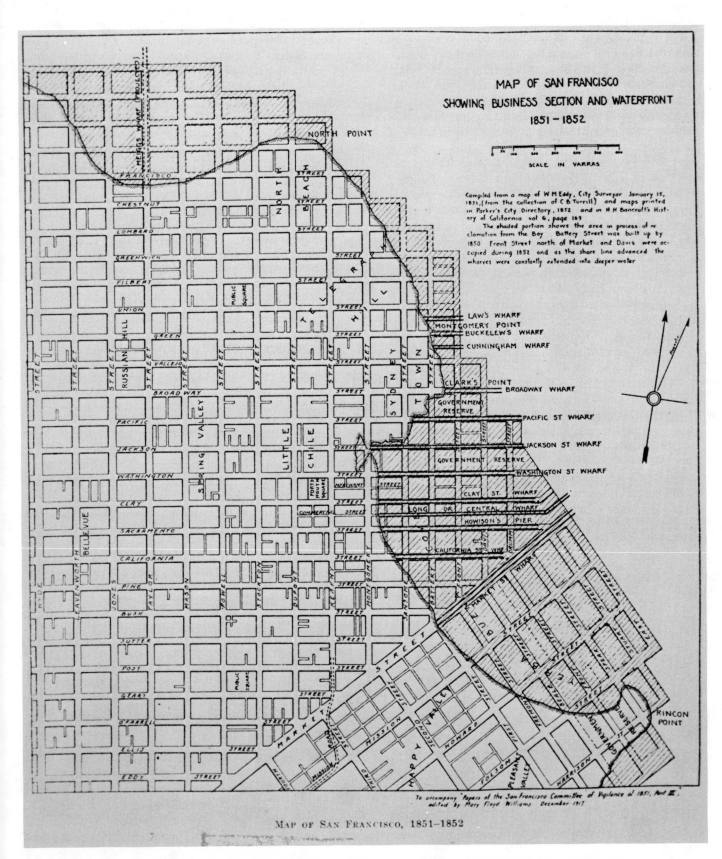

*Map of San Francisco 1851-52. M.F. Williams, **Papers of the San Francisco Committee of Vigilance of 1851** (U.C. Berkeley, 1919), p. xvii.*

other, enlivened San Francisco and contributed much to its individuality.

The impression one gleans from many writings on gold-rush San Francisco is that it was a hot-bed of vice and corruption. It was obviously rowdy, and seemingly uncontrolled, but it was more than that. Bernard Taper, in recreating the city that Mark Twain knew, describes "a literary movement of considerable force and originality that flourished in that boisterous...metropolis of the frontier." Living there at the same time as Twain were Henry George, Bret Harte, Ambrose Bierce, and other lesser lights, who out of the necessity of coping with the "raw lusty material of life in San Francisco and its even rawer, lustier hinterlands" developed a literary rebellion against "the proper Bostonian standards which ruled literature in the East."[30] The character of San Francisco as it had developed during the gold rush, and as it had continued afterwards, resulted in a uniquely American literary form, for it was here that Mark Twain decided on a career as an author, and it was here that he became a writer of national significance.

This literary verve was also in evidence in San Francisco's journalistic output. The first paper to begin regular issue was the *California Star* on January 9, 1847; the most famous of them all, the *Alta California*, began its career in January, 1849, just one year after the discovery of gold; and in the first eleven years of newspaper production, one hundred and thirty-two journals in all had commenced publication and had involved over one thousand people. Edward Kemble, who was associated with this journalistic production from its beginning, ascribes its abundance to "the sudden and great emergence which owing to her rapid growth have arisen in San Francisco's political and social life, requiring the instant establishment of organs of public communication."[31]

Perhaps the reason for such a flourishing media is simply San Francisco's pre-eminence in the political life of the state of California. Josiah Royce, in his excellent history of California, saw that San Francisco's significance lay not just in her position as a gateway to the gold fields or the Pacific, but in her role as the very centre of the state's mental life, and he believed San Francisco's survival to be largely indentical with the progress of the new state.

Upon the city by the Golden Gate all the permanent success of the good cause of lasting progress in California depended. Here the young State...was nourished. Here the ships and a great part of the immigrants came. Here was from the first the centre of the State's mental life, and to a great extent of its political life. Here good order must be preserved, if any permanent order was to be possible elsewhere. And so of course the progress of San Francisco was to be largely identical with the progress of the whole of the new State.[32]

So the effect of gold on San Francisco was to create a city out of the turmoil of disorder and disruption, and to create the thirty-first state in the Union out of the success of that city.

III

Nearly three years after gold was found on the American River, the first important discovery of gold in Victoria was made and the scene of the world gold rush changed location. The impact of gold on the city of Melbourne was profound. In many immediate respects — a population explosion, the overnight appearance of a tent city, the straining of the city's services for example — Melbourne's experience resembled that of San Francisco. And in the long term, in the ultimate trans-

Melbourne Hospital 1862. The foundation stone was laid in 1846, and the building was completed in 1856, **Victoria Illustrated** *(Melbourne, 1862).*

formation into a major metropolis, Melbourne's emergence paralleled that of the California city. However, in the meantime, in the nature of the city's response to this emergency, the Melbourne pattern varied to the extent that its previous development and character had been different.

Melbourne was founded in 1835 by squatter-pastoralists anxious to acquire more land. They were people "to whom town life was familiar" and the foundation of an urban environment was "a natural outcome of their cultural experience."[33] This cultural heritage was British and so Melbourne early adopted the characteristics of an English town, and in 1840 was described as "the largest, most highly civilized, most prosperous city in the world for the years of its existence." Not only was it reminiscent of England in the style of its buildings and houses, but also in its social life and institutions.

The site of the new town was on the Yarra River, that "tortuous, rapid little river with varied banks...which furnishe[d] the means of rowing to young men and water[ed] the Botanic Gardens."[35] This site had been determined by the fresh water supply above the Yarra Falls, though this was never a very satisfactory such source, and with the increased needs of a gold rush city in 1853, work was begun on a more satisfactory water supply, the Yan Yean water system.

Melbourne experienced a population boom from the very beginning of its settlement, and, although the provision of its services was always outstripped by the requirements of its citizens, in comparison to San Francisco it was much better able to cope with the vicissitudes of the gold rush.

As early as 1837 a grid-iron plan had been drawn up of very straight and wide streets which in winter were "of a porridge consistency" and which in summer "changed to deep ruts and choking dust", but municipal government was a reality by 1842, and so streets were slowly formed and surfaced and regular transport facilities were operating by the middle of that decade. The Melbourne and Hobson's Bay Railway, the first in Australia, opened in September 1854, just two years after the arrival of the first argonauts.[36]

The inadequacy of the sewage and drainage facilities meant that Melbourne had an even higher mortality rate than London, but unlike San Francisco, Melbourne had a public hospital to cope with its health problems eleven years after its foundation and five years before the onset of the gold rush. By 1839 permanent churches and resident ministers were an established feature and by 1845 there were at least thirty functioning schools (although of dubious quality according to Grant and Serle). The press was well-established in the early Forties, gas lighting in shops was introduced in 1849, and by the end of the decade the city's prosperity was resting on the secure basis of the pastoral industry. Modelled on English society, "balls, picnics, races and dinners were frequent and fashionable" and a flourishing landed gentry headed a fairly rigid class structure. Sport was early an important and popular activity in Melbourne. Mark Twain saying

> It has one specialty; this must not be jumbled in with...other things. It is the mitred metropolitan of the Horse-Racing Cult. Its raceground is the Mecca of Australasia.[38]

But particularly indicative of the nature of sport in Melbourne is this description of the first cricket match

> A Cricket Club was formed in Melbourne by the following gentlemen... and at a meeting held in the month of November, 1838,...the subscription was fixed at One Guinea. Two bats, balls, and stumps were purchased from Mr. Henry

First Presbyterian church in San Francisco, F. Soule et al, **Annals of San Francisco** *(N.Y., 1855).*

Collins St., Melbourne, in 1845. Unsigned painting in Mitchell Library, Sydney, Australia.

Davis, for which he received the sum of £2.3.0. The first match played was between the Club and the Military . . . We have not the particulars of the game before us, and can therefore, but briefly notice those who particularly distinguished themselves: after a duration of some hours it concluded by a triumph on the part of the civilians. Mr. Powlett's and Mr. Donald Gordon McArthur's bowling, and Mr. Robert Russell's batting attracted universal applause. On the whole the game was played with an esprit de corps, a judgement, and an activity that a first-rate club in England might not be ashamed to boast of.[39]

Throughout the decade of the 1840's Melbourne's growth was outward into suburbs, a very British "evidence of progession" and it was regarded as a matter of pride that "commodious and elegant mansions and villas" were being built from Melbourne's very beginnings.[40] This expansive residential development and fondness for wide streets was to cause much incon-venience to visitors and residents alike. Anthony Trollope in 1875 remarked that

> Melbourne is surrounded for miles by villa residences . . . it is impossible for a man not to be struck by the grandeur of the dimensions of the town . . . it seems strange that half a million of people should not be able to live together within reach of each other . . . It is the work of half a morning . . . to walk the length of some of the streets [and] when the hot winds are blowing in Melbourne . . . a very little walking is equal to a great deal of exercise.[41]

As late as 1893 Francis Adams described it as "a huge chessboard flung on to the earth,"[42] and Mark Twain in 1897 found it "spread over an immense area of ground . . . a stately city architecturally as well as in magnitude."[43]

When gold was discovered in 1851 Melbourne had been the administrative and commercial capital of a separate and self-governing colony for a year — after a decade of political agitation — so, unlike California, Victoria was not catapulted into statehood earlier than had been anticipated. Although the civil service was understaffed and inexperienced when the gold boom began, the very existence of the established structures of a constitutional government, a police force, and municipal authorities, provided a ready framework for the colony's, and the city's development.

When the news of the Victorian gold discoveries reached Europe a mass migration to the diggings via Melbourne began, just as it had to the California gold fields via San Francisco. But unlike San Francisco, Melbourne's newcomers were not of every national and racial group. The goldseekers rushing to the colonies were predominately from the British Isles, and so Melbourne did not develop as the cosmopolis San Francisco had. However, probably the most influential group of newcomers were the Americans. Although

they constituted only about 9% of the first 100,000 immigrants, they exerted an influence out of proportion to their actual numbers. The Victorian gold fields did not attract many diggers from California, but Australia was closer by sea to the east coast United States than California was, so it attracted those who perhaps may or may not have otherwise considered prospecting. The influence of Americans and American political ideas were important factors in the Australian revolution which developed out of the gold fields. This revolution was most dramatically expressed in the rebellion of the gold miners at the Eureka Stockade in December 1854 where the diggers demanded the abolition of the mining license and successfully called for greater public participation in the government of the state.[44]

Perhaps more important than the diggers, however, were the sea-going merchants who had traded successfully in California and knew what was saleable in a gold

Queen's Wharf, Yarra River, Melbourne, 1861. Charles Troedel, **Melbourne Album** *(Melb., 1863).*

rush. One such individual was George Francis Train, "a brash twenty-four year old with great ability and greater conceit," who arrived in Melbourne in 1853 with a large shipment of American goods on which he immediately realised two hundred per cent profit. Train made many contributions to the development of Melbourne, and these have been discussed in more detail elsewhere.[45] However, he was but one of many successful Americans — Freeman Cobb was another who provided badly needed services, and American entertainers such as Roe's American Circus, Edwin Booth and the New York Serenaders,— all were successfully received in gold-rush Melbourne. These enterprising Americans are an interesting contrast to the "Sydney Ducks" who caused such disturbance in gold-rush San Francisco and whose deportation by the Vigilance Committee likewise caused much hostility back in Australia.

IV

The effect on Melbourne society of the gold rush immigrants was profound. The influx of large numbers of people with different social and political ideas and not dependent on the land, coupled with the rise of a group of wealthy merchants, caused an overturning of the extant class structure. This was the most fundamental and far-reaching effect of the discovery of gold on Melbourne. Where before material wealth could not affect one's position in the social scale, now the town was no longer dependent on the landed gentry for prosperity, and their power and status declined. As a result, Melbourne became not simply another transposed English city but "the most American of Australian cities," with a new social order and a character of its own. As Mark Twain observed "the palaces of the rich in Melbourne are much like the palaces of the rich in America"[46] and Francis Adams remarked, "In Melbourne . . . much that is typically Australian is to be found."[47]

It was out of the gold rush that Australian democracy was born and "by 1870 it was clear that [new found] wealth and not position would set the tone of society."[48] Loud and long were the complaints of the displaced squattocracy; the colony "was ruined in the social point of view" for the upstarts were insufferably arrogant, and mostly drawn from the lowest ranks of society. As William à Beckett, the colony's Chief Justice and first knight, complained

> Nothing but harm ha[s] come from the discovery of gold; a moral and thoroughly British population, which was everyday expanding and strengthening, and giving promise of similitude in their institutions, manners, and tastes, to those of our glorious mother country [is] being destroyed and demoralized.[49]

Gold had indeed created a city, but it had not created a bustling, energetic, cosmopolitan metropolis out of a frontier outpost as it had in San Francisco. It had taken a well-established community in the English mould and created a new society.

> Although a curious mixture of the frontier and the old world, civilisation — bourgeois, 19th century [Australian] civilization — was triumphant.[50]

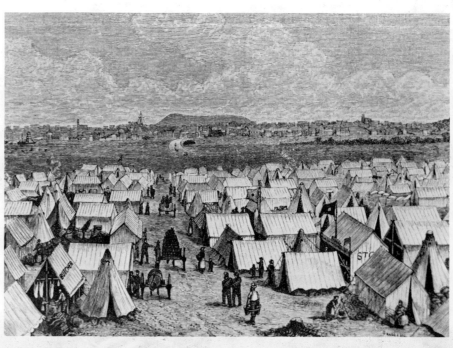

Canvas Town, South Melbourne, during the gold rush, A. Sutherland, Victoria and its Metropolis, vol. 1 (Melbourne, 1888), p. 329.

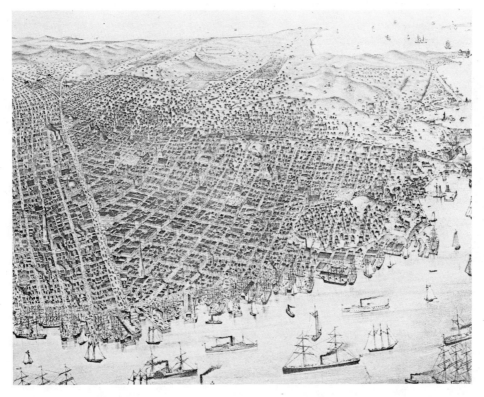

San Francisco in 1878. Reproduced from an original lithograph published by Currier and Ives in the Mariners Museum, Newport News, Virginia.

Melbourne in 1866.

Dianne Kirkby was born at Walgett, in the Australian outback, 400 miles northwest of Sydney. She has a B.A. from the University of New South Wales and took an M.A. in history at the University of California, Santa Barbara, during a year's visit to the United States in 1975-76. She is now employed as a professional researcher in Australian history at Sydney University.

Footnotes

1. Roger Lotchin, *San Francisco 1846-1856* (N.Y., 1974), p. 8 gives this population figure. The difficulty of a comparative study of this kind is in the nature of urban history in the U.S. and Australia — it would seem that population figures for Australian cities probably include the whole metropolitan area, those for American cities the city proper. For the purpose of this essay these population estimates are quite satisfactory.
2. James Grant and Geoffrey Serle, *The Melbourne Scene 1803-1956* (Melbourne, 1957), p.11
3. Grant and Serle, *Melbourne*, p.77; p.86
4. Lotchin, *San Francisco*, p.30
5. Ibid, p.45
6. Ibid, p. 82; Bernard Taper, Ed., *Mark Twain's San Francisco* (N.Y., 1963) gives San Francisco's population in 1864 as 115,000. Again, it's hard to know if either or both these figures include the suburbs.

Yerba Buena 1846-47, reproduced from an original lithograph in the Mariners Museum, Newport News, Virginia.

7. Lotchin, *San Francisco,* p.30
8. Ibid, p.vii
9. Bayard Taylor, *Eldorado or Adventures in the Path of Empire,* (N.Y., 1950), pp.153-4
10. Lotchin, *San Francisco,* p.55
11. Anthony Trollope, *North America* (N.Y., 1951). first pub. 1862.
12. Lotchin, *San Francisco,* pp.45-46
13. Oscar Lewis, *San Francisco: Mission to Metropolis* (Berkeley, 1966). p.8 et seq.
14. Lotchin, *San Francisco,* pp.8-10
15. Josiah Royce, *California* (Boston, 1886)
16. Martyn Bowden, *The Dynamics of City Growth: an Historical Geography of the San Francisco Central District, 1850-1931* (Unpub Ph.D. thesis, U.C. Berkeley, 1967)
17. Royce, *California,* p.380
18. Lotchin, *San Francisco,* pp.181-3
19. Lotchin, *San Francisco,* pp.176-8
20. Ibid, p. 183.
21. Quoted in Lotchin, p.188
22. Ibid, pp. 183-8
23. Mary Williams, *History of the San Francisco Committee of Vigilance of 1851* (Berkeley, 1921)
24. Ibid. See also George Stewart, *Committee of Vigilance: Revolution in San Francisco 1851* (Boston, 1964) although this is more a popular account than a scholarly one.
25. Mark Twain, *Roughing It* (N.Y., 1871) 2 vols., p.161

26. Daniel Woods, *Sixteen Months at the Gold Diggings* quoted in Milo Quaife, *Pictures of Gold Rush California* (Chicago, 1949), pp.291-3
27. *Alta California,* quoted in Lotchin, *San Francisco,* p.106
28. Lotchin, *San Francisco,* p. 103
29. Bayard Taylor, *Eldorado,* p.43
30. Bernard Taper, *Mark Twain's San Francisco,* p.ix
31. Edward Kemble, *A History of California Newspapers 1846-1858,* edited by Helen Bretnor (1962)
32. Josiah Royce, *California,* p.377
33. K. Fairbairn, *Melbourne: An Urban Profile* (Sydney, 1973)
34. Rolf Boldrewood, *Old Melbourne Memories,* edited by C.E.Sayers (Melbourne, 1969), first published Melbourne 1884.
35. Anthony Tollope, *Australia and New Zealand* (St. Lucia, Qld., 1967), first published 1873.
36. Grant and Serle, *Melbourne,* p.8 et seq. for these details.
37. Boldrewood, *Melbourne Memories,* p.4
38. Mark Twain, *Following the Equator* (1897), p.162
39. Grant and Serle, *Melbourne,* pp. 31-2
40. Asa Briggs, *Victorian Cities* (London, 1963), p.88

41. Trollope, *Australia,* p.376; p.384
42. Francis Adams, *The Australians, A Social Sketch* (London 1893), p.24
43. Mark Twain, *Following the Equator,* p.162
44. The story of the Eureka Rebellion is told in some detail in Geoffrey Serle, *The Golden Age: A History of the Colony of Victoria 1851-1861* (Melbourne, 1963). The interaction between Americans and Australians is a fascinating study and well-covered in Jay Monaghan, *Australians and the Gold Rush: California and Down Under 1849-1854* (Berkeley, 1966); also E. Daniel and Annette Potts, *Young America and Australian Gold: Americans and the Gold Rush of the 1850's* (St. Lucia, Qld., 1974)
45. See Monaghan, *Australians and the Gold Rush;* and E. Daniel and Annette Potts, *A Yankee Merchant in Goldrush Australia: The Letters of George Francis Train 1853-55* with an introductory sketch of his life (Melbourne, 1970)
46. Mark Twain, *Following the Equator,* p.169
47. Francis Adams, *The Australians,* p.28
48. Grant and Serle, *Melbourne,* p.86
49. Ibid, p.31
50. Ibid, p.86

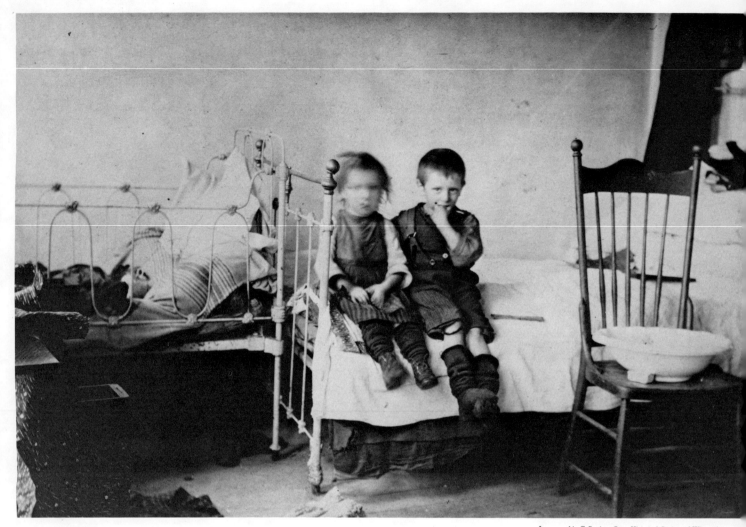

Children in a slum bedroom typical of the conditions into which newborn babes found themselves thrust in St. Cyril's Parish in the 14th Ward, City of Milwaukee, 1909.

Make Milwaukee Safe For Babies: The Child Welfare Commission and the Development of Urban Health Centers 1911-1912

By Patricia Mooney Melvin

From the mid-nineteen sixties, when the nation rediscovered" the neighborhood as the crucible for the "new democracy," interest has focused upon the notion of community organization for health care. But the present fascination with the neighborhood health center is not new; its roots lie back in the second decade of the twentieth century. During those years health and social reformers envisioned a new institution, the neighborhood health center, as the hope for the future. An organization grouping under one roof all the public and private health and welfare activities of a specifically defined area, the urban health center was believed to

*Detail from the **Wright Directory** map, Milwaukee, 1911, showing the 14th Ward straddling the railroad tracks.*

promise fuller service as well as the potentiality for social change.

The city of Milwaukee during the period when Wisconsin represented the leading progressive state, hosted the pioneering experiment in neighborhood health care. Under the direction of Wilbur C. Phillips and with the backing of Milwaukee's newly elected socialist administration, the baby health care center in St. Cyril's Parish signified a general acceptance of the assumption that "educational" programs based in the neighborhood could advance the living conditions of the poor and raise the welfare of the entire citizenry. In this "center for social betterment"[1] socio-health workers labored during 1911 and 1912 to create machinery to involve all neighborhood residents in the active pursuit of health care in order to conserve one of the nation's most valuable resources, the citizen.[2]

This emphasis upon the neighborhood as a health unit grew out of a move toward viewing American society, and in particular, the city in a new way. During the late nineteenth century the United States experienced extraordinary urban growth, geographic specialization of land use, and a general sorting of people on the basis of race, occupation, ethnicity and income. In their search to impose order upon this rapidly changing urban environment those interested in urban affairs began to think in terms of interdependence. Adopting the organic analogy popular in descriptions of society, these students of the city thought of it as an organism, an interdependent system of complementary parts. The "cells" of this new city were the neighborhoods, seen as the local units of citizen participation and identification. While each neighborhood exhibited certain differences, proponents of the organic view stressed the existence of a symbiotic relationship between the local units and the city as a whole. Insisting that the well-being of the whole depended upon the health of the parts, numerous groups, among them social reformers, public health activitists and settlement workers, attempted to organize neighborhoods to meet local needs in the hope of creating a sound city.[3]

This recognition of interdependence manifested itself not only in the definition of urban structure but also in the nature of the attack on urban problems. This was particularly true in the field of public health. Throughout the nineteenth century those interested in that branch of public health work which focused upon the conservation of infant life sought to eliminate infantile diarrhea, the most deadly and common complaint associated with dirty milk, by cleaning up the physical environment in which milk was produced. From the late 1840's, when Robert Hartley of the New York Association for Improving the Condition of the Poor, began a protracted fight for clean milk, infant mortality crusaders concentrated upon sanitary engineering to clean up the physical conditions under which milk was produced and to distribute clean milk to needy urban residents. But despite these efforts to purify the milk environment and to distribute clean milk to increasingly larger numbers of the population, high rates of infant mortality persisted. Gradually, by the end of the century, some public health workers began to look beyond the more narrow definition of the environment and started to concentrate upon the people within that environment as well.[4]

This shift in focus from purely physical environmental conditions to the human aspects of the infant mortality question occurred as infant welfare crusaders decided that infant mortality was not only a medical problem but also a social problem, the twin products of poverty and ignorance. Once they realized that infant mortality resulted from more than "dirty milk," these public health workers transferred their emphasis from "milk to motherhood."[5] Central to this change in orientation was an inchoate move toward viewing the human as an organism, a unitary and integrated structure that operated in a complementary manner with the total environment to form a larger whole. Exclusive emphasis on only one part, that is, on either physical environmental conditions or on human biological conditions, failed to produce a sound organism. By building upon these notions, child welfare workers not only took important steps to combat infant mortality, but also eventually recognized and advertised the importance of mobilizing the entire community in the pursuit of health and social welfare.[6]

When tied to the notion of neighborhood, this new environmentalism resulted in a new institutional form, the urban health center. During the formative period of health center activity, from 1910 to 1915, child welfare workers attempted to relate health services for infants to a definite population unit. Realizing that different areas of a city needed particular services and that the city, from a single office, failed to determine adequately the varying neighborhood needs, these public health workers designed programs that attacked health problems from the standpoint of the community. The health center proponents believed that all health and welfare services within the district that touched on infant welfare should cooperate, coordinating their services to avoid duplication of information and activities. By mobilizing local sentiment for the work of the center, child welfare workers hoped to instill in the local residents an appreciation of preventive health care and to encourage local participation in the health center's activities. In such a way, the health center would "do things for everybody and do them together within a given district."[7] It represented an attempt to view the child and the city as a whole, not just in particular parts.

The neighborhood health center first took organized form in Milwaukee under the direction of Wilbur C. Phillips. As Secretary of the New York Milk Committee (NYMC) from 1907 to 1911, Phillips, a leader in the shift from milk to motherhood, helped to mobilize community resources for the NYMC's campaign against infant mortality. Under his direction the

NYMC attempted to save infant lives through the establishment of infant milk depots which offered maternal instruction in the principles of infant hygiene and by devising the best methods with which to secure a clean and inexpensive milk supply. In his work with the depots Phillips found that programs focusing both on the physical environment, that is on clean milk, and on the child contributed to a dimunition of the infant death rate and elevated infant health and welfare. He became increasingly interested in the interplay among the educational, social and medical aspects of child welfare that he saw operating in the NYMC's depots. By 1911 he wanted to go farther than the NYMC in this area. Rather than continue the Committee's practice of caring only for those babies whose mothers sought help or were brought accidentally to the attention of the depots' workers, Phillips wanted to reach all mothers and all infants in the neighborhoods served by each depot. On the basis of his New York experience he believed that if the area served by each depot was limited, it would be possible to reach all mothers and babies. If able to establish a close and continuing relationship with the mothers, Phillips believed, the depot would grow into a social center and, as he told members of the Child Conference for Research and Development in 1909, would "radiate the influences of education and social betterment" and improve the whole environment of the child. If duplicated in each neighborhood across the city such a program would improve the conditions of life for all. Anxious to implement his ideas about child welfare organization, in the spring of 1911 Phillips left the NYMC and went to Milwaukee where he believed the new Socialist administration would be favorably inclined to support any program that looked toward social betterment.[8]

Emil Seidel, Milwaukee's Socialist mayor, approved of Phillips's plan and, after some politiking, the Common Council, Milwaukee's governing body, voted to establish a Child Welfare Commission. Supported by both municipal and private funds, the Commission was charged with the responsibility of investigating all conditions relating to infant mortality and child welfare in Milwaukee and of advising city officials on the most practical, economic and efficient methods of dealing with infant mortality. As Secretary of the Commission Phillips encouraged his fellow Commission members to

Milwaukee County Historical Society

Emil Seidel, Socialist Mayor of Milwaukee.

Milwaukee County Historical Society

Gerald Bading, Health Commissioner, who ran for Mayor, defeated Seidel, and abolished the Child Welfare Commission.

Wilbur C. Phillips, leader of the New York Milk Commission, who came to Milwaukee to head the Child Welfare Commission.

establish a child welfare station in order to ascertain the difficulties involved in extending expert medical and nursing care to all babies under one year old before devising a city-wide plan for infant health and welfare.[9]

The Child Welfare Commission (CWC) selected St. Cyril's Parish, located in the Fourteenth Ward on Milwaukee's South Side, for the demonstration of infant health services. South Side, the poorest and most ethnically diverse area of the city, had grown rapidly with the expansion of industrial establishments into the Menomonee Valley. During the 1870's and 1880's large numbers of unskilled Poles, Germans and Irish settled in this region. The new wards soon had the highest population density in the city. Not surprisingly this section led the city in the number of infant births and deaths each year. And of the new wards, the Fourteenth, an area of 870 acres and 32,542 people, led the entire South Side. Due to insufficient funds, the district covered in the demonstration was restricted to that part of the Fourteenth Ward corresponding to the parish boundaries of St. Cyril's Church. The infant population of this area, according to a preliminary census taken by the CWC, stood at approximately 360.[10]

After the selection of St. Cyril's Parish for the demonstration district, Phillips and the CWC began setting up the neighborhood organization. Because the physicians occupied a central place in the fight against infant mortality, Phillips focused on them first. Rather than follow the usual practice of soliciting the aid of volunteer physicians who could afford to give a few hours "to charity," Phillips decided to draw upon the community doctors instead. He felt that an important part of the success of the station depended upon securing the confidence, understanding and help of the local practitioners. Phillips had found in the NYMC work that when a station's staff drew mainly from outside the area served, the local doctors resented the "interlopers." These neighborhood physicians feared the close contact between the mothers and the "foreign" doctors, and believed that when illness struck the mothers might seek the private services of the station's doctors. So, Phillips convinced the CWC to turn the baby station over to the local doctors, to pay them for their preventive services, and, to insure sound pediatrics, to provide a local eminent pediatrician to supervise them in their work. The twenty-two doctors who practiced in St. Cyril's Parish met together and selected seven of

their colleagues to staff the station. Doctors F. S. Wasiolewski, Irene Tomkiewicz, K. Wagner, Alfred Schulz, D. J. Dronzniekewicz, John Rock and H. Gramling agreed to work at the baby station and their duties included holding weekly clinics for the mothers during which they would weigh and examine the babies and would give the mothers formal instruction in the principles of child care.[11]

After organizing the doctors, Phillips and the CWC concentrated upon the selection of a nursing staff to assist the physicians at the station and to follow up the station's work in the infants' homes. The nurses were to be in charge of establishing and sustaining contact between the station and the mothers. Their duties entailed visiting all babies each week and providing home instruction in the principles of infant hygiene. On the advice of various members of the medical community the Commission selected Misses Jessie Bernoski of the Maternity Hospital, Mina B. Zimmerman, a Visiting Nurse Association worker in the Fourteenth Ward and Helen Hogan, a specialist in infant feeding problems. Under the supervision of Mrs. Price Davis, a former supervisor of the Visiting Nurse Association, each

Street scene in Milwaukee, 1909.

nurse surveyed a section of the baby district. Armed with cards of introduction from the local parish priest, Father Szukalski, the nurses canvassed the area to discover their charges. In the week before the opening of the station the nurses acquainted themselves with the mothers of all the children under one year of age, explained the station to them and began home instruction.[12]

The week before it opened, the newspapers publicized the station. Numerous articles encouraged the mothers to register at the baby center for instruction and to come under the care of the physicians. On the Sunday preceding the opening of the station, the Commission distributed handbills explaining the work and urging the mothers to take advantage of the preventive care and education offered to them. Finally, early Monday morning, July 24, 1911, the newly painted child welfare station opened its doors at 990 Eighth Avenue to the mothers and babies of St. Cyril's Parish.[13]

But despite a general curiousity about the station, only a handful of mothers actually brought their infants in for the medical examinations. Despite the hundred per cent visitation by the nurses, they realized that they had not won the level of esteem, confidence and friendship necessary to encourage the mothers' participation. They found that certain difficulties hindered the effectiveness of their role as Liason between the mothers and the station. First, they encountered a language difficulty. Only one of the nurses spoke Polish. The others had to rely on German, which most of the residents understood to some degree, or on an interpreter. This, of course, hampered communication between the station and the mothers. Secondly, the nurses found that the mothers felt the nurses were "blowing their own horns" by proclaiming the value of their services. The women in the Parish had not requested the station; most did not realize the value of the instruction. Thenurses discovered that it was much easier to interest the mothers in coming to the child welfare station if they were urged by a person not attached directly to the health center, a "disinterested advocate."[14]

As a result of the nurses' problems, a new group joined the doctors and nurses in the baby station organization. In order to create a corps of disinterested advocates to promote the station and to encourage the mothers to attend, Father Szukalski helped the CWC select eight of the most popular and influential women in his parish. Once convinced of the value of the work, they served as the "selling agency" for the station. They informally contacted a majority of the parish mothers and sponsored regular meetings in the basement hall of the parochial school. Only part of each meeting was instructive, the remainder of the sessions consisted of entertainment by different groups of residents. In these congenial settings the families got to know the station's staff and to hear about their work. By stirring up interest and by securing good will for the station, this "Committee of Eight" helped the atten-

dance grow.[15]

To supplement the station's activities the Child Welfare Commission sponsored a number of activities to investigate conditions and to disseminate information concerning child welfare in Milwaukee. The major investigatory project consisted of a comprehensive survey of all conditions affecting child life in Milwaukee. The survey included a statistical study of infant mortality, an examination of the work of all individuals and institutions caring for babies, and a study of the problem of securing a clean and safe milk supply for Milwaukee's infant population at a low cost. The educational activities included lectures on infant care, exhibits, and a daily child welfare column in the local newspapers which supplied information on infant and child health care. Both the survey and the educational activities were designed to emphasize that child welfare meant the whole child, that it was important to consider a multiplicity of factors in the solution of health problems. These activities reflected Phillips's acceptance of the new environmentalism.

During the remainder of 1911 the baby station in St. Cyril's Parish absorbed the work of numerous child oriented public and private agencies active in the area. Each organization sent agents into the nieghborhood, asked residents similar questions, duplicated many actions and frequently antagonized residents with continuous demands on their time. Such a situation was inefficient, both in terms of the time and the money spent in the effort to secure information. For instance, in St. Cyril's Parish, the registration of births, the education and control of local midwives, the prevention of infant blindness, the placing out of babies and foster home supervision involved the Health Department and many local social service agencies. As the baby station established itself in the district, Phillips and the station personnel found that they were able to perform more completely, inexpensively and efficiently with one group of workers the tasks performed by the various organizations. The station was growing into a one stop center for infant welfare for the residents of St. Cryil's Parish.[16]

In January 1912 the Child Welfare Commission submitted a report of six months work to the Common Council. It noted that as a result of the constant and watchful supervision by the station's staff and the maternal instruction, the death rate for the months of September, October, November and December in 1911 was 4.4 per cent as compared with 12.5 per cent for the corresponding period in 1910. Only seven babies died during the test period. The Commission believed that the decline in the death rate indicated a positive step toward the promotion of infant welfare and on the basis of these results advocated the expansion of the program to other neighborhoods of the city. To cover this expansion, the Commission requested a larger appropriation and also full municipal status as a part of the Health Department.[17]

But, unfortunately for the Commission, a change in municipal administration dashed these hopes. In the 1910 election the Socialists had won a plurality of votes which enabled them to exercise a fair degree of control over the Common Council. Traditional socialist support had been combined with a voter reaction against the traditional parties whose leaders were tainted by a number of Grand Jury indictments. However, in 1912, the voters, satisfied that good government had been preserved by turning the rascals out, were ready to return to the chastised parties. These parties, caught up in a wave of non-partisanism and determined not to lose again to the Socialists, entered into a coalition. Together, Milwaukee Democrats and Republicans backed former Health Commissioner Dr. Gerald Bading for Mayor.

Bading, a firm believer in streamlined government and budget cutting opposed any party that viewed city government as expansive or activist. He viewed government as a necessary evil, whose purpose was regulation rather than an instrument of public service. During his campaign he chided the Socialists for going beyond regulation and promised, if elected, "to sweep away socialist programs" that cost money and that resulted in an "unnecessary" expansion of government. Evidently Milwaukee voters agreed with him, decided they had their fill of reform, and swept Bading into office. On April 2, 1912 Bading defeated incumbent mayor Emil Seidel by 43,179 votes to 30,273.[18]

Bading's election proved significant for the fate of the Child Welfare Commission. As Health Commissioner Bading supported only sanitary engineering; he did not back programs designed to promote activities for good health. During his tenure of office the Health Department concentrated upon cleaning up the physical environment to eliminate disease in Milwaukee. To combat infant mortality he supported only those programs designed to secure a clean milk supply. As an old environmentalist *par excellence* he believed that community health depended only on medical causes. Not sympathetic to the interdependence of the world around him, Bading, like many other health officers, failed to recognize how a social specialist could aid the medical specialist in the solution of health problems. Clearly, then, Bading did not appreciate the purpose of the Child Welfare Commission's project. Once in office he took up the question of the CWC's future and labored to secure its dissolution.[19]

Iconographic Collection, State Historical Society of Wisconsin

Turn of the Century Milwaukee showing the sort of houses in which the Child Welfare Commission found its mothers and which its nurses visited.

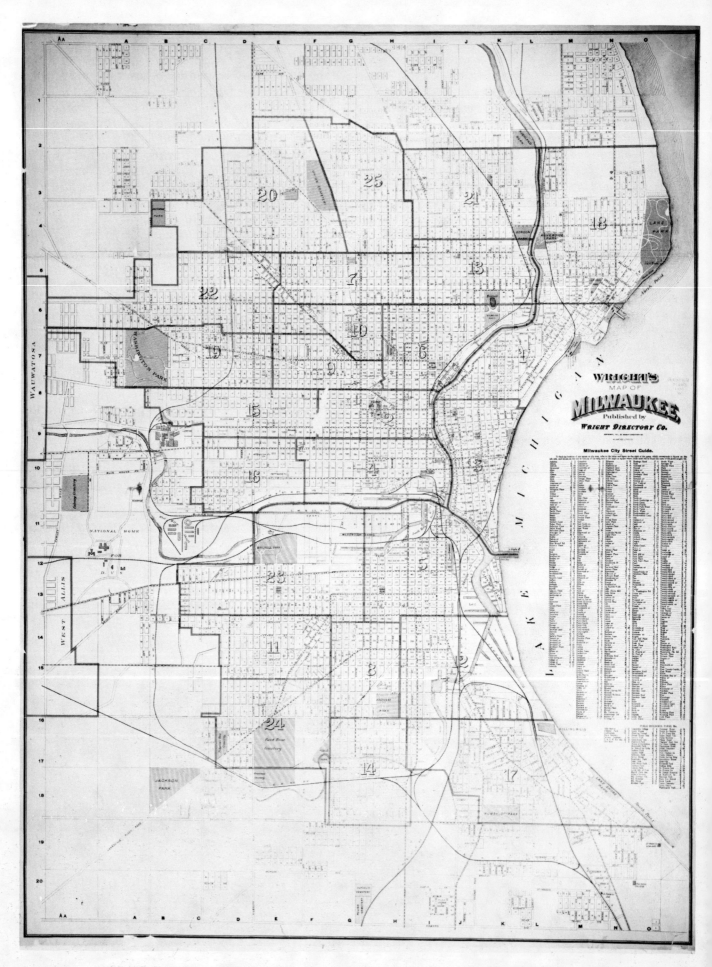

*General map of the City of Milwaukee in 1911 from the **Wright Directory**. The 14th Ward is bottom center.*

In his inaugural address to the Common Council Bading stated that he wanted the Health Department to assume the child welfare work. He also outlined his version of a child welfare program. He wanted a drastic reduction of the scope and orientation of the work. To be headed by a physician, child welfare work under the aegis of the Health Department would attempt to regulate the purity of the milk supply, oversee periodic dispensation of clean milk to needy areas of the city and attempt to provide rudimentary care only for those sick infants who happened to come to the attention of the Health Department. When Bading's supporters proposed the act providing for this type of work, the supporters of the Child Welfare Commission launched, what turned out to be, a last ditch effort to save the Commission's program.[20]

The ensuing debate centered around the question of the relationship between medical and social specialists. Supporters of the CWC insisted that good child welfare work depended upon securing the most competent man available for the work, whether a doctor or not. In fact, they suggested that perhaps the Health Department had "enough medical men" and could use an "organizer" instead as the child welfare director. The supporters believed in the necessity of an attack on the entire complex of the infant health and welfare problem and felt that such work demanded the leadership of a "sociologist," or social expert, able to collect and analyze data on infant mortality and to educate the public about its role in the prevention of disease and the promotion of good health.[21] But the Bading supporters on the Council stood firm and voted against what they considered the "mysterious abracadabra" of the sociologist.[22] On June 17th, 1912 the Common Council delivered the death blow to the Child Welfare Commission. The passage of the act relieved Phillips of his duties with the Commission and created a Division of Child Welfare, under the direction of a physician, in the Health Department. Dr. E. T. Lobedan, a Bading supporter, took over the administration of child welfare work in Milwaukee. Phillips left Milwaukee, returned to New York, and began to think through and to sharpen his plan of neighborhood organization for health.[23]

While not successful in all respects, Phillips, during his year with the Child Welfare Commission demonstrated that geographical localization and administrative coordination, complemented by the social organization of a neighborhood produced efficient and practically one hundred per cent health care and interest. It was the earliest attempt to fashion a plan of action suited to the needs of a particular community. For many health workers the CWC demonstration provided a base from which to develop other health centers in their own areas. By 1915 child welfare workers had opened neighborhood health centers in Philadelphia, New York City, Cleveland, Buffalo and Boston, all designed to coordinate functions, shape administration in accordance with local needs and to foster community spirit.[24]

But the early twentieth century world of the first neighborhood health centers, with its belief both in the necessity and the possibility of social reconstruction, passed as America entered the decades of the twenties and thirties. Social crusaders ceased to concentrate upon the interplay of environment and citizen and began to focus more on individual adjustment. Like others, many public health workers opted for service rather than reform, concentrating more on means rather than ends. Their backers sought less to provide "centers of social betterment" than primarily medical facilities for those unable to patronize other establishments. No longer positively oriented they failed to serve as rallying points for neighborhood residents; they were no longer synonymous, as Phillips hoped they might be, with social programs. As America entered the latter half of the nineteen sixties social activists once again emphasized neighborhood planning and participation, calling the neighborhoods the crucibles for social change. And, as part of this new movement, community organizers and health workers once again envisioned a strong system of neighborhood health care and organization.

Patricia Mooney Melvin is Curator of Labor History at the Ohio Historical Society. She holds her M.A. from the University of Cincinnati and is a doctoral candidate at that institution. Ms. Melvin's interests include early twentieth century urban history, the history of American public health, labor history and the history of women. This present paper is a part of her dissertation, "The Social Unit Organization: A Case Study in Neighborhood and community in America."

This article was originally a paper presented at the Missouri Valley History Conference, March 11, 1977.

REFERENCES

1. Wilbur C. Phillips, "The Achievements and Future Possibilities of the New York Milk Committee," *Proceedings of the Child Conference for Research and Development* 1 (Worcester, Mass., 1909), pp. 191-192.

2. For a good discussion of Wisconsin's prominence in the progressive reform movement see David P. Thelen, *The New Citizenship: Origins of Progressivism in Wisconsin, 1885-1900* (Columbia: University of Missouri Press, 1972). The best studies of reform in Milwaukee and its relationship to municipal socialism during the first two decades of the twentieth century are Frederick I. Olson, "Milwaukee's First Socialist Administration, 1910-1912: A Political Evaluation," *Mid-America* 43 (July 1961): 197-207 and Sally M. Miller, "Milwaukee: Of Ethnicity and Labor," in *Socialism and the Cities*, ed. Bruce Stave (Port Washington, New York: Kennikat Press, 1975), pp. 41-71. Charles R. Van Hise, *The Conservation of Natural Resources in the United States* (New York: Macmillan Co., 1910), p. 379; Wilbur C. Phillips, "The Trend of Medico-Social Effort in Child Welfare Work," *American Journal of Public Health* 2 (November 1912): 876-882.

3. See Jean B. Quandt, *From the Small Town to the Great Community: The Social Thought of Progressive Intellectuals* (New Jersey: Rutgers University Press, 1970); Henry C. Adams, ed., *Philanthropy and Social Progress* (New York: Thomas Y. Crowell and Co., 1893); Robert A. Woods, "The Neighborhood in Social Reconstruction," *American Journal of Sociology* 19 (March 1914): 577-591; Robert A. Woods, "The City and its Local Community Life," in the *Neighbor and Nation Building*, ed. Robert A. Woods (Boston: Houghton-Mifflin, 1923; reprint ed., New York: Arno Press, 1970), pp. 191-196. For a discussion of urban definition see Zane L. Miller, "Scarcity, Abundance, and American Urban History," *Journal of Urban History* (Forthcoming, February 1977).

4. R. L. Duffus and L. Emmett Holt Jr., *L. Emmett Holt: Pioneer of a Children's Century* (New York: D. Appleton-Century Co., 1940), p. 166; George Rosen, *A History of Public Health* (New York: MD Publications, 1958), pp. 238-239; Phillips Van Ingen and Paul Emmons Taylor, "Infant Mortality and Milk Stations," (New York: New York Milk Committee, 1912), p. 24; Infantile diarrhea, aso called cholera infantum, "summer complaint," "bowel complaint" and dysentery, represented the most serious of all gastro-intestinal diseases. It was spread through bowel excreta under conditions of inadequate sanitary facilities or through water or milk contamination. Judith W. Leavitt, "Public Health in Milwaukee 1865-1910," (Ph.D. Dissertation, University of Chicago, 1975), p. 28.

5. John Spargo, *The Common Sense of the Milk Question* (New York: Macmillan Co., 1908), p. 144; Michael M. Davis and Andrew R. Warner, *Dispensaries: Their Management and Development* (New York: Macmillan Co., 1918), p. 304.

6. For a good discussion of the notion of the human as organism see Dom Cavallo, "Social Reform and the Movement to Organize Children's Play During the Progressive Era," *History of Childhood Quarterly* 3 (Spring 1976): 509-522. The notion of the child as organism was an integral part of the child study movement of the late nineteenth century. The proponents of this movement, led by G. Stanley Hall, believed that the child developed sequentially, that all systems, muscular, nervous and so forth, were interdependent and that the child was the microcosm of the adult. If any aspect of the "natural" development of the child and the environment (physical, moral, biological) was not functioning properly, the result would be a "defective" individual. This organic mode of thought influenced such things as the beliefs concerning the structure of education and the organization of play. Bernard Wishy, in *The Child and the Republic: The Dawn of Modern American Child Nurture* (Philadelphia: University of Pennsylvania Press, 1968), a study of child-bearing literature and children's books, reveals the existence of the notion of organism during the late nineteenth century. Unfortunately, in what could have been an excellent attitudinal study, Wishy fails to explain adequately the changes in the perception of nurture over time or that he even understands the implications of the changes.

7. "The Historical Development," *American Journal of Public Health* 11 (March 1921): 212; C.-E. A. Winslow, "The Health Center Movement," *Modern Medicine* 1 (August 1919): 327; Davis and Warner, *Dispensaries*, pp. 318-319; *The Reminiscences of Dr. Haven Emerson*, Oral History Project, Columbia University, p. 33; "What is a Health Center?" *American Journal of Public Health* 1 (August 1920): 677; Michael M. Davis, *Clinics, Hospitals and Health Centers* (New York: Harper and Bros., 1927), p. 357.

8. Ernest C. Meyer, *Infant Mortality in New York City: A Study of the Results Accomplished by Infant Saving Agencies 1885-1920* (New York: Rockefeller Foundation, 1921), p. 82; Wilbur C. Phillips, *Adventuring for Democracy* (New York: Social Unit Press, 1940), pp. 24-60; New York Milk Committee, "Infant's Milk Depots and Their Relation to Infant Mortality," (New York: New York Milk Committee, (1908), pp. 10-64; Helen Worthington Rogers, "All Hands 'Round for the Baby," *The Survey*, March 5, 1910, p. 876; Wilbur C. Phillips and Elsie C. Phillips, "A Plan for Social Organization or the Unit Method of Gradually Building Up a Complete System for Studying and Meeting Social Needs," unpublished ms., (1912-1914), p. 188; Michael M. Davis, "The Health Center Idea: A New Development in Public Health Work," *Public Health Nurse Quarterly* 8 (January 1916): 24-25.

9. *Milwaukee Free Press*, May 19, 1911, p. 4; Milwaukee, Wisconsin, *Proceedings of the Common Council of the City of Milwaukee for the Year Ending April 11, 1912*, File #272, May 8, 1911, pp. 77-78.

10. Roger David Simon, "The Expansion of an Industrial City: Milwaukee 1880-1910," (Ph.D. Dissertation, University of Wisconsin, 1971), pp. 216, 220; "Statement of Infant Mortality Rate in the Fourteenth Ward, Showing Why the Child Welfare Commission had Selected This District for the Establishment of Baby Welfare Centers," (1911), pp. 1-12, Wilbur C. Phillips Papers, University of Minnesota, Minneapolis, Minn.; U.S. Department of Commerce, Bureau of the Census, *Thirteenth Census of the United States, 1910: Population*, vol. 3, p. 1101; Phillips, *Adventuring*, p. 67.

11. List of the Physicians in the Baby District, n.d., Wilbur C. Phillips Papers, University of Minnesota, Minneapolis, Minn.; National Social Unit Organization, *A Statement of the Practical Experience on Which the Unit Plan is Based*, Bulletin 2-A (Cincinnati: National Social Unit Organization, 1918), pp. 16-18; Phillips and Phillips, "Plan for Organization," pp. 94-99.

12. *Milwaukee Journal*, July 21, 1911, p. 3; *Milwaukee Sentinel*, July 24, 1911, p. 5; *Milwaukee Free Press*, July 25, 1911, p. 5.

13. Phillips, *Adventuring*, pp. 72-72; *Milwaukee Sentinel*, July 24, 1911, p. 5; *Milwaukee Free Press*, July 19, 1911, p. 1; (Baby Station), (1911), Wilbur C. Phillips Papers, University of Minnesota, Minneapolis, Minn.

14. Phillips, *Adventuring*, pp. 72-73; National Social Unit Organization, *Statement of Practical Experience*, pp. 5-7; Phillips and Phillips, "Plan for Social Organization," p. 99.

15. Phillips, *Adventuring*, p. 73; National Social Unit Organization, *Statement of Practical Experience*, pp. 7-14.

16. National Social Unit Organization, *Statement of Practical Experience*, pp. 22, 28-29; Phillips, *Adventuring*, pp. 74, 83.

17. *Milwaukee Sentinel*, July 24, 1911, p. 5; *Milwaukee Leader*, May 20, 1912, p. 4; Milwaukee, Wisconsin, *Proceedings of the City of Milwaukee for the Year Ending April 11, 1912*, File #1743, January 29, 1912, p. 1181; National Social Unit Organization, *Statement of Practical Experience*, pp. 22-29.

18. Olson, "Milwaukee's First Socialist Administration," 197-198; Miller, "Milwaukee," pp. 48-50, 54; Bayrd Still, *Milwaukee: The History of a City* (Madison: State Historical Society of Wisconsin, 1948), p. 519; Leavitt, "Public Health in Milwaukee," p. 355; Phillips, "Trend Child Welfare," 880.

19. John Duffy, *A History of Public Health in New York 1866-1966* (New York: Russell Sage Foundation, 1974), p. 634; Leavitt, "Public Health in Milwaukee," p. 355; Phillips, "Trend in Child Welfare," 880.

20. *Milwaukee Free Press*, April 14, 1912, p. 5.

21. *Milwaukee Free Press*, June 5, 1912, p. 6; *Milwaukee Free Press*, June 9, 1912, pp. 1, 12.

22. *Milwaukee Sentinel*, June 8, 1912, p. 6.

23. *Milwaukee Sentinel*, June 25, 1912, p. 1; Milwaukee, Wisconsin, *Proceedings of the Common Council for the City of Milwaukee for the Year Ending April 14, 1912*, File #2262, June 17, 1912, p. 270; *Thirty-six Annual Report to the Commissioner of Health of Milwaukee for the Year 1912*, pp. 11, 13, 87, 89.

24. Davis, "Health Center Idea," 27-30; Davis and Warner, *Dispensaries*, pp. 321-323; George Rosen, "The First Neighborhood Health Center Movement: Its Rise and Its Fall," in *From Medical Police to Social Medicine: Essays on the History of Health Care*, ed. George Rosen (New York: Science History Publications, 1974), pp. 304-327; Duffy, *History of Public Health*, pp. 268-269.

DENVER
Queen of the Rocky Mountain Empire

Fred Yonce

"Men make cities. Given the leadership of aggressive and far-sighted men and a tolerably favorable site for a city, transportation will come, business will come, population will come." There is perhaps no better illustration of Glenn C. Quiett's explanation of the rise of cities than Denver. The confluence of Cherry Creek and the South Platte River was no inevitable site for the metropolis of the Rockies, or even for a major city. It was, however, the site of the first, though minor, gold discoveries and attendant settlements, and from the beginning aggressive, far-sighted, and, yes, acquisitive men parlayed the town's head start into permanent primacy. Though briefly challenged from time to time by mining and railroad boom towns, Denver has continuously held sway as the most populous city of the region, its political and economic center, its port of entry and focus of activity and decision-making.

For its first two years the infant town boomed as the supply and service center for the mining districts, then languished in the 1860s, beset by adversities — mining depression, Civil War and Indian hostilities, fire and flood, isolation. But Denverites persevered. The city was rebuilt, rail connections were brought in, and the metallurgical problems of refining Colorado's ores were solved. Denver became the territorial and later state capital and the market and supply center for a new boom based on gold and silver, railroads, stock raising, and agriculture.

Denver's population grew to 35,000 in the 1870s and to more than 100,000 in the '80s. The wealth from the silver mines transformed the city. Business blocks, magnificent hotels and theaters, pretentious gilded mansions, and a massive state capitol were erected. Banks, businesses, and factories multiplied, as did utilities and amenities, and new subdivisions sprang up around the town. The silver crash and depression retarded growth in the early '90s, but Cripple Creek gold and expanding tourism and agriculture soon took up the slack.

Early in the 20th century, Denver achieved home rule and under dynamic Mayor Speer built a civic center and auditorium, established parks and boulevards, and made numerous improvements. Denver grew steadily in the first four decades of the century, a great residential and tourist town, the commercial and financial center of the region.

World War II inaugurated a new era of burgeoning growth and metropolitanization. The war brought large federal military and civilian installations and related defense industries, particularly ordnance. Thousands of servicemen returned as permanent residents, and postwar Denver became a center for research, defense, and aerospace industries. Tourism has boomed, especially skiing, and with the energy crunch of the '70s, Denver has become a mecca for energy companies, as the metropolis of a vast region of undeveloped oil, coal, uranium, oil shale, solar and geothermal energy.

The dramatic changes in the face of Denver are represented in the photographs that follow, selected from 275,000 in the Western History Department of the Denver Public Library, long recognized as one of the outstanding collections of Western Americana in the country. The library grew up with Denver, assembling comprehensive research materials on the city and the region and ultimately, in 1935, organizing the Western History Department around this nucleus. Such a major Western collection was, and still is, unique in a public library.

While emphasizing the Rocky Mountain region, the Department's collection reflects all phases of development of the trans-Mississippi West. In addition to photographs, it includes some 50,000 cataloged books and pamphlets, 3,000 maps, hundreds of Western journals and newspapers, and large holdings of manuscripts, business records, scrapbooks, prints and original art. Among a number of notable special collections are publications of Western railroads, reports and maps of Colorado mines, trade catalogs, autographed books and articles illustrated by Frederic Remington, records and memorabilia of Buffalo Bill's Wild West shows, frontier theater programs, land grant materials, territorial imprints, and extensive clipping files.

The Department is proud of its reputation for service. It assists hundreds of patrons by phone and mail each month in addition to those personally visiting the library. Staff regularly index and clip Denver newspapers, Western journals, and other materials, and our 3,000,000-entry General Index has proved an invaluable reference tool.

The Department has over the years published more than a dozen reference guides and original narratives, and in 1976 it produced *Nothing Is Long Ago: A Documentary History of Colorado 1776/1976*, a catalog of its outstanding Centennial/Bicentennial exhibit. The volume features 120 major documents, maps, art works, and photographs, most from the Department's own collections and many beautifully illustrated, with each set in historical perspective, the annotations together comprising a capsulized history of Colorado.

Eleanor M. Gehres is head of the Western History Department, which is located in the

Central Denver Public Library at 1357 Broadway, Denver, Colorado 80203, telephone (303) 573-5152.

Photographs selected by A.D. Mastrogiuseppe and Fred Yonce.

Contemporary views by Thomas Pyle.

Text by Fred Yonce.

Photos courtesy of Denver Public Library, Western History Department.

The "Queen City of the Plains" owes its regal status to its proximity to the mountains. Though at times a barrier to Denver's development, the Rocky Mountains have also been the source of her lure and wealth. They have made tourism Denver's third-greatest economic asset. The city's Overland Park was the best known of the Western auto camps in the 1920s. After World War II, skiers who had trained with the famed 10th Mountain Division in Colorado helped establish numerous ski resorts in the old mining towns west of Denver.

Stapleton International Airport has replaced Union Station as the hub of intercity passenger transportation. Like the railroads, the transcontinental air routes at first bypassed Denver for the low passes to the north and south of Colorado, but Denver met the challenge by building an irresistibly attractive airport that has become the 7th busiest in the nation and must soon be dramatically expanded or replaced.

Despite a general scarcity of water, Denver has periodically had too much of it. In 1864 a disastrous flood roared down Cherry Creek, sweeping away buildings constructed in the stream's "dry" bed by those who ignored Indian stories of "big water". In 1965 a second great "hundred-year flood" wreaked havoc along the South Platte. Today such floods are hopefully history with the recent completion of Cherry Creek and Chatfield dams upstream. The Platte's course through Denver is rapidly being converted into a 10-mile-long riverfront park, complete with kayak run.

The look of downtown Denver has been transformed since World War II. Great skyscrapers now cut off the northwest view of the mountains from the State Capitol. Some twenty giants are now in construction or planning, many financed by Canadian investors.

Denver's main street, 16th, has changed considerably since 1900, but the distinctive Daniels and Fisher Tower remains. The adjoining department store has been razed in the massive lower downtown urban renewal project, but the city is determined to save and renovate the old tower, patterned after the campanille of St. Mark's Cathedral in Venice. The street will change even more dramatically in the next three years with its conversion to a tree-lined, bus-and-pedestrian-only mall.

Denver has so many federal offices and facilities, such as the Denver Mint, that it has long been called "the second national capital." Now it is fast becoming a second energy capital after Houston. Its strategic location at the edge of the Rocky Mountain mineral empire has attracted hundreds of oil and energy companies who have occupied the new office skyscrapers like the Anaconda Building.

This could be a suburban scene in any city. With its rapid growth, Denver now has much the same look, problems, and challenges as other big urban conglomerates. But Denver has also become conscious of preserving what has made it distinctive — its past. A row of middle-class Victorian era homes were saved and restored as Ninth Street Historic Park on the new downtown three-college campus of the Auraria Higher Education Center.

Index